Business Valuation

Marco Fazzini

Business Valuation

Theory and Practice

Marco Fazzini
European University of Rome
Rome, Italy

ISBN 978-3-030-07786-0   ISBN 978-3-319-89494-2   (eBook)
https://doi.org/10.1007/978-3-319-89494-2

© The Editor(s) (if applicable) and The Author(s) 2018
Softcover re-print of the Hardcover 1st edition 2018
This work is subject to copyright. All rights are solely and exclusively licensed by the Publisher, whether the whole or part of the material is concerned, specifically the rights of translation, reprinting, reuse of illustrations, recitation, broadcasting, reproduction on microfilms or in any other physical way, and transmission or information storage and retrieval, electronic adaptation, computer software, or by similar or dissimilar methodology now known or hereafter developed.
The use of general descriptive names, registered names, trademarks, service marks, etc. in this publication does not imply, even in the absence of a specific statement, that such names are exempt from the relevant protective laws and regulations and therefore free for general use.
The publisher, the authors, and the editors are safe to assume that the advice and information in this book are believed to be true and accurate at the date of publication. Neither the publisher nor the authors or the editors give a warranty, express or implied, with respect to the material contained herein or for any errors or omissions that may have been made. The publisher remains neutral with regard to jurisdictional claims in published maps and institutional affiliations.

Cover image © blackred/Getty Images
Cover design by Ran Shauli

Printed on acid-free paper

This Palgrave Macmillan imprint is published by the registered company Springer International Publishing AG part of Springer Nature.
The registered company address is: Gewerbestrasse 11, 6330 Cham, Switzerland

*To Cesare and Giacomo,
may they appreciate the value of what really matters in life*

Preface

If you are leafing through this book you might wonder whether a new textbook on business valuation is really necessary, as so many books have been published on this subject in recent years. In my opinion there is still something to say; let me try to explain why.

First, many textbooks address business valuation as if the valuation method were all that mattered.

In fact, most business valuation textbooks are specifically focused on calculation methods. Unquestionably, these play a very important role, as they are the formal part of the entire process. The risk, however, is to place too much emphasis on the quantitative dimension, without adequately considering the context in which the valuation is made.

The method chosen is the result of a broader analysis through which the characteristics of the firm are investigated. It is the method that must adapt to reality not the other way around.

The purpose of this textbook is to offer a guideline for the application of an integrated approach, thereby avoiding "copy and paste" valuations, based on prepackaged parameters and the uncritical use of models. Specifically, an Integrated Valuation Approach (IVA) should be adopted that encompasses, within any specific method, a wide range of elements reflecting the characteristics and specificities of the firm to be valued.

Secondly, many textbooks do not adequately consider the role of valuation standards. In both the literature and professional practice, business valuation is now circumscribed to some specific models, although many variations can be found in their practical application. Valuation standards allow for an alignment of both the methods and their application, providing a common basis for valuers. This book is based on the International Valuation Standards

(IVS) issued by the International Valuation Standards Council. These standards significantly help the valuation work, both generally (scope of the work, investigation and compliance, reporting, basis of value, valuation approaches and methods) and specifically (business interests, intangibles, plant and equipment, real property, development properties, financial instruments), and provide useful indications.

To write this book I had to take time away from my family; thus, I am grateful to my wife Laura and my children for their patience and to whom I dedicate this book.

Rome, Italy   Marco Fazzini, PhD

Contents

1 Value, Valuation, and Valuer ... 1

2 Integrated Valuation Approach (IVA) ... 23

3 Financial Statement Analysis ... 39

4 Income-Based Method ... 77

5 Market-Based Method ... 123

6 The Cost Approach ... 175

7 Intangible Assets Valuation ... 183

8 Premiums and Discounts in Business Valuation ... 209

Index ... 219

List of Figures

Fig. 1.1	Range of plausible values	5
Fig. 1.2	General requirements of a valuation report	14
Fig. 2.1	Investments and financial sources	34
Fig. 3.1	Functional reformulation of the balance sheet	43
Fig. 3.2	Relationship between assets and liabilities	43
Fig. 3.3	Reclassification example	44
Fig. 3.4	Net assets	45
Fig. 3.5	Working capital	45
Fig. 3.6	Business assets	45
Fig. 3.7	Non-current net debt	46
Fig. 3.8	Current net debt	46
Fig. 3.9	Net debt	46
Fig. 3.10	Financial statement at a glance	46
Fig. 3.11	The income statement	47
Fig. 3.12	Reclassified income statement	48
Fig. 3.13	Gross margin distribution	48
Fig. 3.14	Cash flow statement	49
Fig. 3.15	Example of financial statement	55
Fig. 3.16	Business assets	56
Fig. 3.17	Turnover of individual assets	58
Fig. 3.18	Mismatch between profit and cash flow	58
Fig. 3.19	Balance between investments and financial sources	66
Fig. 3.20	A part of current assets is covered by long-term sources	67
Fig. 3.21	A part of non-current assets is covered by current debt	67
Fig. 4.1	Asset-side and equity-side valuation	81
Fig. 4.2	The logic of discounting	83
Fig. 4.3	Comparison between the returns of different government bonds	87

Fig. 4.4	CAPM at a glance	102
Fig. 4.5	Cash flows and EBITs trend	115
Fig. 5.1	Asset-side and equity-side approaches	129
Fig. 5.2	EV/EBITDA % change over one year	132
Fig. 5.3	EV/FCF and EV/Sales regression	141
Fig. 8.1	Basics of value. (Source: NACVA, Valuation Discount and Premiums, 2012)	210
Fig. 8.2	Control premium and discount for lack of control	212

List of Tables

Table 1.1	Facebook financial key figures and market value (2013–2016)	3
Table 2.1	Amazon.com statement of operations (in $ millions)	35
Table 3.1	Cost of sales	64
Table 3.2	Operating working capital turnover	64
Table 3.3	Dividend payout ratio and sustainable growth rate	71
Table 3.4	Effect of a decrease in revenues	74
Table 4.1	US Treasuries yields (first semester 2017)	88
Table 4.2	Euro Area Yield Curve (November 2017)	90
Table 4.3	Beta by industry in the US, Europe, and Japan	92
Table 4.4	Peer group beta	95
Table 4.5	Business unit key data	96
Table 4.6	Business unit's levered betas	96
Table 4.7	ERP by country	100
Table 4.8	Sensitivity analysis on CAPM	103
Table 4.9	Sensitivity analysis on total value	103
Table 4.10	Rating definitions	106
Table 4.11	Example of expected cash flows series	111
Table 4.12	Cash flows versus EBIT	114
Table 4.13	Value of the firm without growth rate	116
Table 4.14	Value of the firm with growth rate	116
Table 4.15	Value of the firm using an EBITDA multiple	118
Table 4.16	Cash flow statement	119
Table 4.17	Asset-side valuation	119
Table 4.18	Equity-side valuation	120
Table 4.19	Expected earnings	121
Table 4.20	Expected dividend per share	121
Table 4.21	Value per share	121
Table 5.1	Key statistics of food and beverage industry	131

Table 5.2	Comparison between two peer groups	138
Table 5.3	Peer group's standard deviation	139
Table 5.4	Standard deviation of EV/EBITDA	139
Table 5.5	Correlation between multiples and EBITDA margin	140
Table 5.6	Application of the EV/Sales	142
Table 5.7	Application of the EV/EBITDA	144
Table 5.8	Application of the EV/EBIT	145
Table 5.9	EV/EBITDA and EV/EBIT in automotive industry (Q1 2016, Source: Capital IQ)	147
Table 5.10	The peer group	150
Table 5.11	Evolution of the EV/EBITDA multiple	154
Table 5.12	Evolution of the EV/EBIT multiple	156
Table 5.13	YoY percentage change of the EV/EBITDA multiple	158
Table 5.14	YoY percentage change of the EV/EBIT multiple	160
Table 5.15	Multiples standard deviation (2005–2015)	162
Table 5.16	Application of P/E ratio	165
Table 5.17	Application of P/E ratio	166
Table 5.18	Beverage companies multiples ($ mil)	171
Table 5.19	Multiples statistics	171
Table 5.20	Distribution in quartiles	171
Table 5.21	Multiples statistics without outliers	173
Table 5.22	Distribution in quartiles without outliers	173
Table 5.23	Target company's income statement	173
Table 5.24	Enterprise value of the target company	173
Table 5.25	Stress test matrix	174
Table 6.1	Book value of the firm	176
Table 6.2	Adjustment to book value	176
Table 7.1	Investments in intangible assets (% officially measured value added)	184
Table 7.2	Factors considered in the adjustment of the royalty rate	192
Table 7.3	Comparable transactions royalty rate	193
Table 7.4	Value of the patent	194
Table 7.5	With and Without scenarios	197
Table 7.6	Value of the brand by comparing the "With" and "Without" DCF	197
Table 7.7	Value of the brand by comparing the value of the firm in the "With" and "Without" scenarios	197
Table 7.8	Revenue and expenses related to the contributory assets	199
Table 7.9	Contributory assets charges (fixed assets and working capital)	200
Table 7.10	Contributory assets charges (fixed assets and working capital)	200
Table 7.11	Greenfield method	201
Table 7.12	Average salary per person	205

Table 7.13	Statistics on recruitment cost and on unproductive training period	205
Table 7.14	Value of the workforce calculation	206
Table 7.15	Replacement cost of software	207
Table 7.16	Replacement cost new	207
Table 7.17	Functional obsolescence	208
Table 7.18	Economic obsolescence	208
Table 7.19	Value of software	208
Table 8.1	Control premium and controlling interest	215

1

Value, Valuation, and Valuer

1.1 What Does Making a Valuation Mean?

In life we continuously make valuations. When we go shopping, for example, we make sure that the proposed price reflects quality; when we book a room, we make sure that the rate is in line with the hotel features and the services it offers; when we choose a school for our kids, we assess the quality of the programs and the teachers' standing; when we buy a house, we make sure that the value is in line with that of other houses in the neighborhood.

In short, valuations are part of our daily experience; generally, they consist of two components: an objective one, which regards the intrinsic value, and a subjective one, linked to the valuer's perception of the object to be valued. Separating these two components is difficult, as our choice is never entirely based on either the subjective or the objective component, but on a mix of both. For example, when buying a house, we do not choose the house with the best price per square foot, regardless of its characteristics; nor do we solely rely on our aesthetic perceptions, neglecting the price. Not surprisingly, we make choices based on a trade-off between objective circumstances (price) and subjective perceptions (location, finishes, interior design, etc.).

This mechanism is easy to find in contemporary art auctions. Given an objective value, based on previous auctions, expert judgment, quality of the work, and so on, the results may differ significantly, reaching amounts that have little to do with the characteristics of the work or with the prices attained in previous auctions.

Business valuations work in the same way. There is an objective component of value, based on valuations methods, and a subjective one, based on the valuer's experience and ability to capture reality.

This means that two equally knowledgeable persons, with similar sensitivity, will hardly get the same result, although they start from the same assumptions and quantitative inputs. To make a comparison, think of two chefs who are given the same ingredients to prepare a certain dish. The result may appear similar, but the different combination of timing, cooking processes, doses, creativity, experience, and dish presentation will lead to different outcomes.

In this book, we will deal with the objective component, which is how we determine the value of a business based on generally accepted valuation methods.

What does it mean to value a business? We can respond that valuation is the act of estimating or setting the potential value of a business by considering both internal and external variables.

The internal variables look at the results a firm has achieved in the past; for example, the debt-to-equity ratio, EBITDA (earnings before interest, tax, depreciation, and amortization), revenues, and cash flow provide us with an understanding of what characterizes the business and constitute a basis for determining its value. The external variables look at the environment in which the company conducts its business and include, for example, market features, the company's competitive positioning, distribution channels, or consumers' tastes. In short, it is necessary to develop a comprehensive opinion that encompasses in one single model both the theoretical business value and the value that considers the environment where that business develops and performs its activity.

This is why the method presented in this volume is called integrated valuation approach (IVA). According to this approach, the evaluation process does not end with the application of a model, but requires considering the business as a whole.

1.2 The Business Valuation

Valuing a business is a complex exercise for various reasons.

First of all, the *characteristics of the business change quickly*. Over time, changes may occur that affect the value of the business, for example, a reduction in profit, higher investments, new debts, different revenues. Value, therefore, is neither constant nor immutable, but must refer to a specific date and situation. A valuer is like a photographer who has to take a picture of a moving object. To obtain a clear image he or she needs the right camera and the right setup and must have enough experience for this type of shot. Likewise, valuers must be able both to choose the model that better interprets the value and to apply it correctly.

Secondly, *the value of a firm can be seen from different perspectives.* As we will see further on, we can use methods that are based on expected cash flows (income methods, see Chap. 4), market values (market methods, see Chap. 5), and reproduction/replacement cost (cost method, see Chap. 6). Each of them considers some specific aspects of the firm and can lead to partially different results. As mentioned in IVS 105 (International Valuation Standard 105) "the goal in selecting valuation approaches and methods for an asset is to find the most appropriate method under particular circumstances. No one method is suitable in every possible situation." Valuers must therefore apply their experience and judgment to identify the most suitable approach; it means that value depends not only on business characteristics but also on the model applied.

Furthermore, *not all assets can be measured.* The value drivers of a firm are often based on elements that can only be quantified through the output they produce. For example, the value of Facebook is linked to assets such as the number of users, competitive positioning compared to other social networks, the ability to innovate, and integration with other platforms such as Instagram and WhatsApp. Evaluating Facebook based on financial figures only could be an oversimplification.

As shown in Table 1.1, the market value of Facebook rose by 109.80% from 2013 to 2014, from $66.4 billion to $139.3 billion. Assuming there is no constant relationship between market value and financial data (otherwise we would now have the "safe" investment formula), none of the key figures have changed in the same way as market value. Expectations about the company's value were evidently higher than the results achieved. Market value increased more than proportionally compared to key financial figures also from 2014 to 2015.

Table 1.1 Facebook financial key figures and market value (2013–2016)

Consolidated data ($/Mil)	2013	YoY growth (%)	2014	YoY growth (%)	2015	YoY growth (%)	2016
Revenues	$7872	58.36	$12,466	43.82	$17,928	54.16	$27,638
Income from operations	$2804	78.10	$4994	24.65	$6225	99.63	$12,427
Free cash flow	$3458	58.91	$5495	41.89	$7797	48.99	$11,617
Market value	$66,420	109.80	$139,350	56.39	$217,930	39.19	$303,330

It was only from 2015 to 2016 that the increase in market value was lower, probably due to investors' perception of a stronger alignment between key financial figures and market value.

Hence, financial results do not perfectly reflect the value of a firm and, although they are the basis on which business valuation is built, there are other aspects that cannot be measured reliably.

Finally, there is a *difference between price and value*: in an ideal world they should coincide, but in practice they may differ, and the gap can be significant.

Price is the amount requested to purchase an asset. It is an empirical quantity that is influenced by supply and demand. Value, on the other hand, is the result of an estimate and may reflect a potential price in a transaction between two independent parties.

Here are some examples to help you better understand this price/value gap.

A cotton T-shirt made by an haute couture company, with a modest intrinsic value of a few dollars, is put on the market at a price of tens or hundreds of dollars. In this case, price is higher than the value of the good.

Here is another example: in a crisis situation, people may have to sell out some of their property (e.g. jewelry, buildings, art collections) for amounts lower than their intrinsic value. In this case, price is lower than value.

We face the same problem when valuing a company. How much is 2% of a small firm's equity worth when another shareholder owns the other 98%? In theory, that stake is worth 2% of the total value of the company; in practice, the price may be impossible to define or close to zero, as there would be no buyer due to lack of marketability. Indeed, who would want to spend money to buy a minority interest that (a) is difficult to sell and (b) has absolutely no influence on the majority shareholder? In this case, again, price and value may have no correlation at all.

If we generalize the concept, value reflects a potentiality; price, on the other hand, reflects the here and now. The misalignment between value and price is sometimes significant, but no amount is "truer than another". They can both be justified, depending on the characteristics of the good to be traded and the circumstances. Moreover, as Oscar Wilde once said, "nowadays people know the price of everything and the value of nothing".

1.3 What Is Value?

"Value" is not a concept that can be easily enclosed in a universally valid definition; there is no unique measure for it, not even from a quantitative standpoint, since, depending on the instruments used, the data taken as reference,

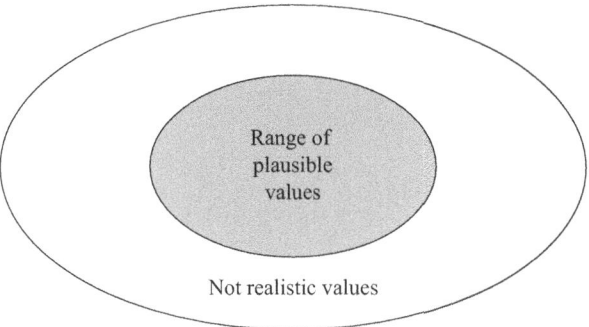

Fig. 1.1 Range of plausible values

and the interpretation proposed, we may obtain different results, all of them equally plausible and consistent.

Correctly applying a formula is not enough to reach the reasonable certainty that the result is *the value* of the entity, since it is highly unlikely that an equation can capture the complex set of conditions surrounding a firm.

A value is much more likely to be defined, in quantitative terms, through a range of plausible values, the breadth of which depends on methodological accuracy and the ability of the model to interpret the business specificities (Fig. 1.1).

Value, therefore, is neither an absolute nor a unique concept. There is, actually, more than one configuration of value, depending on the purpose of the assignment and the characteristics of the business. This is precisely why referring to *bases of value* is more appropriate, as suggested by the IVSs.

According to IVS 104, "bases of value (sometimes called standards of value) describe the fundamental premises on which the reported values will be based". The standard adds that "it is critical that the basis (or bases) of value be appropriate to the terms and purpose of the valuation assignment, as a basis of value may influence or dictate a valuer's selection of methods, inputs and assumptions, and the ultimate opinion of value".

1.3.1 Common Elements of the Bases of Value

As described in IVS 104, while there are different bases of value used in valuations, most have certain common elements:

1. an assumed transaction;
2. an assumed date of the transaction; and
3. the assumed parties to the transaction.

1.3.1.1 Assumed Transaction

According to IVS 104, depending on the basis of value, the assumed transaction could take different forms:

(a) a hypothetical transaction;
(b) an actual transaction;
(c) a purchase (or entry) transaction;
(d) a sale (or exit) transaction; and/or
(e) a transaction in a particular or hypothetical market with specified characteristics.

A transaction is hypothetical when the other party has not yet been identified or the time is not ripe to initiate a transaction. For example, a valuer could be appointed by the shareholders to evaluate a company in the event of a potential sale, in order to identify a range of plausible values to be used as reference for the deal.

A transaction is actual if both the asset to be valued and the parties are known, there being, however, no specific constraints regarding the type of transaction.

A purchase transaction or a sale transaction imposes greater constraints on valuers, as they may be required to consider the value of potential synergies or potential valuation discounts or premiums.

Finally, a transaction in a particular or hypothetical market with specified characteristics requires that the valuer examines and is familiar with some specific aspects. For example, in a transaction involving financial assets in a Middle Eastern country, a valuer should be familiar with the fundamentals of Islamic finance and be able to distinguish between legal (*halal*), non-risky (*gharār*), and non-speculative (*maysīr*) investments.

1.3.1.2 Assumed Date of the Transaction

The assumed date of a transaction influences what information and data a valuer has to consider in a valuation. Value is indeed a matter of timing and the assumed date is a relevant variable, especially in a dynamic context characterized by frequent changes.

1.3.1.3 Assumed Parties to the Transaction

Identifying the parties also plays an essential role in the valuation process, since, as noted in IVS 104, "most bases of value reflect assumptions concerning the parties to a transaction and provide a certain level of description of the parties". IVS 104 underlines that "in respect to these parties, they could include one or more actual or assumed characteristics, such as: hypothetical, known, or specific parties, members of an identified/described group of potential parties; whether the parties are subject to particular conditions or motivations at the assumed date (e.g. duress), and/ or: an assumed knowledge level".

1.3.2 Bases of Value

IVS defines to following bases of value:

1. market value;
2. market rent;
3. equitable value;
4. investment value/worth;
5. synergistic value;
6. liquidation value.

According to IVS 104, *market value* is the "estimated amount for which an asset or liability should exchange on the valuation date between a willing buyer and a willing seller in an arm's length transaction, after proper marketing and where the parties had each acted knowledgeably, prudently and without compulsion".

Market value, in accordance with the IVS conceptual framework, is "the most probable price reasonably obtainable in the market on the valuation date". In other words, it is the best price reasonably obtainable by the seller and the most advantageous price reasonably obtainable by the buyer. The market value of an asset reflects its highest and best use, that is, the use of an asset that maximizes its potential and that is possible, legally permissible, and financially feasible.

According to IVS 104, *market rent* "is the estimated amount for which an interest in real property should be leased on the valuation date between a willing lessor and a willing lessee" at the same conditions of the market value.

According to IVS 104, *equitable value* is "the estimated price for the transfer of an asset or liability between identified knowledgeable and willing parties that reflects the respective interests of those parties". The value in this case reflects the respective advantages or disadvantages that each part will gain from the transaction. This value is different from market value, which excludes any advantage that is not accessible to all the parties.

According to IVS 104, *investment value* is "the value of an asset to a particular owner or prospective owner for individual investment or operational objectives". The value of an investment is linked both to the characteristics of the asset being valued and to those of the buyer and the seller. It may consider specific synergies or whether there are any advantages for a specific party.

According to IVS 104, *synergistic value* is "the result of a combination of two or more assets or interests where the combined value is more than the sum of the separate values". In this book we mainly look at stand-alone valuations, that is, those that are independent of potential synergies. Synergistic value is often associated with the evaluations made by a potential buyer who estimates not only the value of the asset but also the contribution that an asset may bring to the other assets already held. It is therefore an internal evaluation that can only be appreciated by those who can determine the benefit from combining several assets together.

According to IVS 104, *liquidation value* is "the amount that would be realised when an asset or group of assets are sold on a piecemeal basis". A business can be liquidated as a natural or forced process. A business would be "naturally" liquidated when it reaches the end of its life cycle and this condition is accepted by its shareholders. Forced liquidation occurs when the seller is forced to sell, which places the seller in a weak position with an obvious adverse impact on value.

1.3.3 Objective and Subjective Component of Value

Given these definitions, we can conclude that there are two dimensions of value: an objective dimension, which reflects the value of the asset per se, that is, the intrinsic value that is assigned to an asset in an efficient market, and a subjective dimension, linked to the characteristics of the parties to the transaction, each of whom seeks to maximize their own benefits.

In general, each valuation contains both an objective and a subjective element. A valuer should stick to the objective dimension as closely as possible, by making use of the generally accepted methods. Inevitably, however, the subjective element that is linked to our own perception and experience also plays a role in the valuation process; such element, however, should be nothing but a background noise that does not affect the stand-alone perspective.

The more the valuer can count on a complete set of information, the less is the risk associated with the subjective variable.

When asked to make a valuation based on limited information, valuers will tend to fill the information gap using their own experience and making analogies with similar cases they may have dealt with in the past. A valuer should therefore point out any lack of information, especially if it can influence the choice of the valuation method and the processing of data.

1.4 Valuation Methods at a Glance

Various business valuation methods have been developed over the years. Each of these reflects a very precise logic and no one method is better than another in absolute terms. Rather, there are methods that, in certain circumstances, are more appropriate than others in interpreting the value of a business.

According to valuation standards, the various methods can be grouped in three main areas: cost-based approach, income-based approach, and market-based approach.

If we compare them based on the assumption that evaluating a company is not so different from evaluating a used car, we can better understand the logic of these approaches: there is no single metric to establish a fair value, but multiple perspectives that we need to consider.

When you go to a dealer, you will first check the car and see if there are any scratches or dents on the bodywork, check the tire wear, the brake and engine operation, and any optional features such as air conditioning, safety devices, sunroof, and so on. In short, you will examine the car "as is", adjusting the price accordingly.

Not unlike a car, a firm can have its "scratches on the bodywork", which can reduce its book value, such as receivables that are difficult to recover, obsolete equipment, contingent liabilities, and so on; at the same time, there may be enhancing elements, such as trademarks and goodwill that give the firm a competitive advantage, although they are not necessarily recorded in the financial statement.

As for a car, it is possible to estimate the *value of a firm "as is"*, based on a reasoned examination of its assets and liabilities. To do this, we must examine the items in the financial statements and check whether their book value reflects their fair value; in case of discrepancies, if the book value is lower than the fair value, we should make an upward adjustment, and, vice versa, if the book value is higher than the fair value, a downward adjustment. The valuation method in question is known as *cost-based method.*

Going back to the car example, we cannot simply look at its current condition; we must also consider expectations on its future use: purchasing a five-year-old car with 200,000 miles is quite different from purchasing a car of similar age, but with 20,000 miles. In the first case, the car certainly has a shorter residual life and we will likely face higher maintenance costs; in the second case, the car is relatively new and will presumably require less expensive maintenance. The expected benefit, that is, what is expected from the vehicle taking into account its intrinsic characteristics, is therefore anything but secondary. If we apply this reasoning to businesses, we can determine the *value of a business based on future expectations*, that is, based on the results it could potentially achieve. This valuation method in question is known as *income-based method*.

Finally, we can determine the value of the car by comparing the price proposed by the dealer with the values found in magazines and specialized websites, to make sure that the requested price falls within a range of plausible amounts, taking into account the characteristics of the car such as age, wear and tear, optional features, and so on. A company can likewise be *evaluated based on a comparison with comparable entities*. This valuation method in question is known as *market-based method*.

When we buy a used car, many valuation methods should be applied. Looking at the conditions of the car does not exclude an estimate of its future use nor a comparison with the prices published on specialized websites and magazines. Indeed, it is precisely through several approaches that we can assess if the price of a car is fair.

When valuing a business, on the other hand, we must choose a specific method. In fact, depending on the method, the results may be very different from one another. How is it possible? First, a business is more complex than a car, which is obvious. Second, the approaches refer to different parameters:

- the cost-based method looks at the present and evaluates a business "as is";
- the income-based method looks at the future and evaluates a business based on "what it will do";
- the market-based method is based on the value of similar companies or transactions involving comparable companies; in practice, it evaluates a business based on "what others do".

When using more methods, the results obtained may be similar, but this is not a foregone conclusion. Each method is based on different logics and parameters and the value of the same business may differ due to the different perspective inherent in each method.

Sometimes a combination of a main method and a control method can be used, to base the valuation on an increased number of variables. If the two methods correctly interpret the value of the business, the result can be similar; otherwise the values may differ significantly.

1.5 Types of Valuation

There are different types of valuation according to the purpose of the assignment. Specifically, the following types can be identified:

1. third-party valuation;
2. in-house valuation;
3. valuation opinion;
4. fairness opinion;
5. calculation engagement;
6. valuation review.

A *valuation performed for a third party* is a document containing an opinion on the value of a business that is obtained through an independent and complex valuation process. In this case, valuers rely on the information gathered and on their personal experience, in order to carry out a comprehensive valuation, in accordance with the purpose of the assignment. If the valuation is commissioned by a seller, it is a sell-side valuation; if it is commissioned by a buyer, it is a buy-side valuation.

The purpose of the work can partially influence the choice of method and the final assessed value. For example, in a sell-side valuation, the valuer may have access to internal documents, such as a business plan, which may point toward a DCF (discounted cash flow) method. On the other hand, a buy-side valuer could tend to use multiple methods, given the absence of internal information.

There may be various reasons for making an *in-house valuation*, such as assessing whether selling the business, in whole or in part, is a good deal, or to test a subsidiary company for impairment. The technicalities used are the same as those of the valuation performed for a third party and internal information may obviously be used.

The *valuation opinion*, also called expert opinion or expert report, consists in an assessment process limited to some aspects or based on unverified inputs provided by the client. It may concern, for example, determining a discount rate to be applied to the cash flows provided by the client and not reviewed; updating some parameters of a previous valuation; determining value based on a limited information base; and so on. This group includes equity research carried out by external analysts.

A *fairness opinion* consists in verifying the reliability of a valuation process carried out by another party, given the inputs used, the method applied, and the conclusions reached. The aim of this opinion is to assess how reasonable a third-party valuation or a valuation opinion is.

A *calculation engagement* is not a real valuation, but a check of specific inputs used by another party. For example, this opinion may concern the development of a peer group to be used in the multiples method, or the analysis of the coefficients contained in the weighted average cost of capital (WACC) formula.

Finally, the *valuation review* consists of a critical analysis of the work carried out by another valuer, to verify its correctness or to update it. Sometimes a valuation review involves a second opinion by an expert valuer, to verify the results; in other cases, it is a review carried out months or years after the valuation was made, with the aim of verifying whether the data or conclusions are still valid or whether they need an updating.

1.6 Who Is the Valuer

According to the International Valuation Standards Council (IVSC), a valuer is "an individual, group of individuals or a firm who possesses the necessary qualifications, ability and experience to execute a valuation in an objective, unbiased and competent manner".

As mentioned, a valuation arises from a reasoned opinion based on estimates and is never the mere application of a mathematical calculation. Therefore, an expert should not just be able to "apply the formulas", but also satisfy a broader set of requirements, including:

1. respect for professional ethics;
2. independence;
3. objectivity in researching and selecting information;
4. expertise and diligence in carrying out the assignment.

The *respect for professional ethics* involves complying with a series of requirements, such as those contained in the "Code of Ethical Principles for Professional Valuers" issued by the IVSC.

According to the IVSC, a professional valuer is expected to comply with the following ethical principles:

(a) integrity: to be straightforward and honest in professional and business relationships.
(b) objectivity: not to allow conflict of interest, or undue influence or bias to override professional or business judgment.

(c) competence: to maintain the professional knowledge and skill required to ensure that a client or employer receives a service that is based on current developments in practice, legislation, and valuation techniques.
(d) confidentiality: to respect the confidentiality of information acquired as a result of professional and business relationships and not to disclose such information to third parties without proper and specific authority, nor to use information for the personal advantage of the professional valuer or third parties.
(e) professional behavior: to act diligently and to produce work in a timely manner in accordance with applicable legal requirements, and technical and professional standards.

A valuer must ensure *independence* with regard to the type of engagement. According to the IVS, "the process of valuation requires the valuer to make impartial judgements as to the reliability of factual data and assumptions. For a valuation to be credible, it is important that those judgements are made in an environment that promotes transparency and minimises the influence of any subjective factors on the process."

For example, if a valuer is appointed by a court to solve a dispute, he or she must act impartially with respect to the parties involved. Conversely, in valuations performed for a specific party, certain aspects that support the interests of the client may be emphasized, while respecting the objectivity and diligence requirements.

Valuers must clearly disclose that they are not independent when acting in the interest of a party. Any direct or indirect conflicts of interest must be reported, specifying the reasons why the valuer considers that they are not an impediment to the performance of the assignment.

Sometimes, conflicts of interest are not apparent at the time of the engagement, but may occur later. Valuers must therefore verify their independence for the entire duration of their mandate.

Valuers must ensure *objectivity in researching and selecting information.* In carrying out the assignment, an expert can gather information from the company, from third parties, from research bodies, or from databases. The source from which the information was taken must always be mentioned and facts must be distinguished from personal opinions. For example, when applying the multiples method, a valuer has some discretion in the selection of the peer group; discretion, however, is not arbitrary judgment, but must be guided by a consistent methodology that leads to a selection of comparables based on truly homogeneous data.

Expertise and diligence in carrying out the assignment refer to the ability to identify the most appropriate valuation method in relation to the purpose of the assignment and to apply it correctly, in compliance with valuation standards. According to the IVS, "if a valuer does not possess all of the necessary technical skills, experience and knowledge to perform a valuation, it is acceptable for the valuer to seek assistance from specialists in certain aspects of the overall assignment, providing this is disclosed in the scope of work".

For example, valuing a company engaged in the renewable energy sector or in waste treatment requires knowledge of national and local laws regulating these matters. If they are not knowledgeable on these matters, valuers can be assisted by an expert in the sector.

1.7 The Valuation Report

Each valuation is different, and the valuation process can be influenced by various factors, including the purpose of the work, the completeness of data, the complexity of the assets to be evaluated, any variables that are difficult to interpret, and so on.

In general, the valuation report must provide all the information necessary for a third party to understand how the valuation process took place. According to IVS 103, "it is essential that the valuation report communicates the information necessary for proper understanding of the valuation or valuation review".

For this reason, the valuation report must satisfy some general requirements (Fig. 1.2). Such requirements may be explicitly included in a report or incorporated into a report through reference to other documents (engagement letters, scope of work documents, internal policies and procedures, etc.).

Identity of the Valuer If the valuer is an individual or a small company, a brief description of the valuer's experience in business valuations should be provided. This is not necessary for advisory firms whose standing is well known. Any limitations in the performance of the assignment or partial

(1) Identity of the valuer	(8) Nature and sources of information
(2) Identity of the client (if any)	(9) Business and environmental analysis
(3) Asset(s) being valued	(10) Special assumptions
(4) Purpose of valuation	(11) Applied method (or methods)
(5) Valuation currency	(12) Type of report
(6) Valuation date	(13) Restriction on use of the report
(7) Valuer's work extent limitation thereon	(14) Compliance to standards

Fig. 1.2 General requirements of a valuation report

conflicts of interest must be disclosed. Likewise, valuers must state if they sought the assistance of other parties in the performance of some parts of the assignment.

Identity of the Client (if Any) The form and content of the report must respond to the client's needs. For example, in an in-house valuation, a very detailed disclaimer is probably redundant, since this work involves limited professional responsibilities. Valuers should also specify if the valuation is going to be used by third parties in addition to the main customer; for example, a valuation could be requested by a company, which must then share it with other companies in a group or joint venture.

Asset(s) Being Valued The asset being valued must be well identified. It can be an asset; a liability; a group of assets and liabilities; an ownership interest in any of the above; a right to use any of the above; an asset that is utilized in conjunction with other assets. When valuing a company, it is necessary to specify whether the valuation regards all or just part of the shares; in the latter case, it is mandatory to specify whether it is a controlling interest or a minority interest and whether any valuation discounts or premiums are applied.

Purpose of Valuation The purpose of the valuation influences both the basis of value and the choice of the valuation method. Different purposes can lead to different valuations of the same entity.

Valuation Currency If the valuation concerns a company based in the country where the business report is required, the currency is obviously not an issue. However, if the valuation concerns companies operating in different countries, the foreign currency must be converted into the local currency and the reference exchange rate must be specified.

Valuation Date The assumed date of transaction is usually different from that of the valuation report and may also refer to remote periods. For example, a valuation ordered by a court could refer to events that occurred in the past, in order to ascertain if managers acted appropriately. In this case, the data and information which was available to a valuer at that date should be used.

The Nature and the Extent of the Valuer's Work and Any Limitation Thereon Valuers must consider that there can be information asymmetries and that, therefore, the information they possess may be incomplete or distorted. Valuers must report any circumstances that may affect the value of the firm and whether they can reduce the significance of their conclusions.

The Nature and Sources of Information Upon Which the Value Relies Information is the key to valuations. Valuers must always specify the information base they have used and any limitations found.

The information must be objective and complete and valuers must analyze it with professional skepticism. This involves performing an in-depth analysis based on a meticulous scrutiny of the information collected, to verify if the information is reliable and adequate for the purposes of the valuation. This analysis should cover both past and prospective information.

Valuers should not accept assignments: (a) if the remuneration is not consistent with the cost to be incurred to ensure the quality of the information; (b) if the required timing is not consistent with the information to be gathered.

The data used can be:

(a) generated internally by the company, such as accounting data, information on commercial and investment policies, and so on. According to IVS 102, "significant inputs provided to the valuer, require assessment, investigation, and/or corroboration. In cases where credibility or reliability of information supplied cannot be supported, such information should not be used";
(b) from open sources, such as web statistics, analyst reports, and so on;
(c) from high-quality databases;
(d) from other experts involved in the valuation of specific assets or liabilities. When valuers use data from other experts as input for their own valuation, they must check them with professional skepticism and report any limitations. If they are unable to assess the adequacy of this information, they must report this circumstance.

Valuers should always specify the source and describe how the data were processed; they should also clearly state if they consider that some of the data is unreliable or cannot be adequately verified.

Finally, IVS 102 establishes that "investigations made during the course of a valuation assignment must be appropriate to the purpose of the valuation assignment and the basis(es) of value" and that "sufficient evidence shall be assembled by means such as inspection, inquiry, computation and analysis to ensure that the valuation is properly supported".

Business and Environmental Analysis The choice of the valuation method depends on the characteristics of the business and the surrounding environment. The selection of comparables in the multiples method, for example, can only be made if the valuer has an accurate knowledge of the business to be valued. Similarly, assessing the adequacy of the expected cash flows requires that the financial statements of prior years be analyzed, in order to capture how profit, EBITDA, EBIT (earnings before interest and taxes), debt, and so on, developed over the years.

In some cases, past results may not be relevant. For example, if a change in the business model, governance, or strategies has taken place, the information on prior years may become less relevant.

Identify any Significant Assumptions and/or Special Assumptions All information that can be relevant to explain the valuation process to a third party must be included in the valuation report. In some cases, assumptions must be made to simplify some variables that could not otherwise be used in valuation models. In this respect, the following assumptions can be identified:

(a) hypothetical assumptions: they refer to hypothetical events that are not certain to occur, but that are consistent with the valuation purpose. For example, the valuer must check the consistency of the expected cash flows under the DCF method: such cash flows must be consistent with the business characteristics, competitive positioning, financial structure, past performance, and so on;
(b) special assumptions: these are assumptions on circumstances that differ from those verifiable at the time of valuation. For example, the opening of a new business unit can affect the expected cash flows. As these cash flows affect the valuation result, the valuer must verify whether this special assumption is consistent with the characteristics of the business;
(c) key assumptions: these are assumptions that have a significant impact on the result. For example, when valuing utilities (such as electric, gas, and water firms), a key assumption is that the specific regulatory framework for the sector will not change;
(d) sensitive assumptions: they refer to assumptions that are highly likely to change over time and which may influence the final valuation result.

Method or Methods Applied Valuers must specify which method they considered appropriate from among those available, describing the calculation process. If more than one method can be used, the valuer must specify which one should be considered as the main method and which is (are) the control method(s), stating the reasons. Valuers are also required to justify their decision to exclude other valuation methods that could theoretically be fit for the assignment.

Type of Report Being Prepared The type of report, hence the way the results are communicated, depends on the type of assessment. For example, a third-party valuation requires that details be provided which are not usually required in an in-house valuation, which is prepared by the internal staff for an internal audience and requires less formalities. Generally, reports may range from comprehensive narrative reports to brief summary reports.

Restriction on Use, Distribution, and Publication of the Report Disclosure of the report depends on the type and purpose of the valuation. If the report is intended for a public company as part of a market deal, the report could be examined by many parties and limiting its distribution would be difficult. If the report concerns an in-house valuation designed to decide on the purchase of a company, it can be less formal. In general, it is appropriate to provide a disclaimer that limits the distribution of the report to parties not involved in the deal.

Compliance to Standards There are currently various valuation standards that can be applied and valuers must specify which standard has been used as a reference. For example, in this book, the IVS guidelines have been adopted, although other standards are also taken into consideration.

1.8 Compliance with Valuation Standards

The need to enclose practice within a systemic and shared framework led some organizations to identify the best practices and to formalize them in standards of conduct. Their binding effect is on a different level compared to accounting standards, such as the IFRS (International Financial Reporting Standard), which in some European countries have been implemented as law.

The contribution provided by valuation standards is more that of moral suasion, their intent being to define a reference guideline.

To date, several organizations have attempted to define some sort of company valuation standards. In some cases, they are true standard setters, such as the IVSC, and in other cases they are professional associations, such as the American Institute of Certified Public Accountants (AICPA), which have felt the need to issue some guidelines for their members and for all those who share their approach.

In general, a "voluntary" approach has prevailed until now, which has prompted various entities to make their own contribution to the definition of business valuation rules and principles, although without any real endorsement, unlike the International Accounting Standard Board (IASB) in the formulation of the accounting standards. However, the current fragmented scenario of standard setters is likely to gradually evolve toward a rationalization; as the IVSC is commanding increasing recognition, other bodies may be led to converge toward a set of shared principles, at least as regards the general approach.

What is currently limiting this kind of path is that not all the organizations were established with the main purpose of contributing to business valuation; some of them have their origin in similar areas, such as that of real estate appraisals, and subsequently extended their expertise to other areas. The difficulty in drawing clear boundaries is clearly shown by IVSC-accredited members, who include real estate appraisers, chartered accountants, and other professionals.

This is not surprising, considering that business valuation often requires the involvement of different skills, each of which contributes to defining the overall value.

If we are to avoid making it an uncritical application of methods, business valuation must reflect a collective effort, where different parties work together to reach a reasonable and consistent result. Thus, the inherent eclecticism of some standard setters should be viewed favorably, as it enables them to establish rules that have a broader scope and are not confined to a single analytical perspective.

To date there are dozens of organizations that, in various capacities, devote their attention to these issues; just think of IVSC, which has over 70 members, although from different fields, grouped into professional associations/orders, institutions, universities. Here, we only focused on those that have most contributed to the definition of business valuation standards:

1. IVSC;
2. National Association of Certified Valuators and Analysts (NACVA);
3. Canadian Institute of Chartered Business Valuators (CICBV);
4. American Society of Appraisers (ASA);
5. The Appraisal Foundation;
6. AICPA;
7. The European Group of Valuer's Associations (TEGoVA);

These bodies are not in competition; they rather share the objective of working together in the definition of high-quality standards, with specific attention to their respective operating fields; IVSC's members include the CICBV, the AICPA, and the ASA; the Appraisal Foundation also contributes as sponsor.

An overview of the main standard setters is provided below.

1.8.1 International Valuation Standards Council

The IVSC is an independent and not-for-profit organization established in the 1960s whose stakeholders, as noted above, include other standard setters. The standards currently in use were updated in 2017.

In recent years, the IVSC has launched an ongoing and in-depth review of the standards, seeking proposals for improvement from its members and adapting some topics to the current guidelines.

Overall, the scope of these changes is quite broad and also contributes to improving harmonization between valuation standards and between these and the IFRSs.

The standards comprise two groups:

- the general standards focus on the Scope of the work (IVS 101), Investigation and compliance (IVS 102), Reporting (IVS 103), Bases of Value (IVS 104), Valuation approaches and methods (IVS 105);
- the asset standards focus on the valuation of specific assets (business interests, intangibles, plant and equipment, real property, development properties, financial instruments).

1.8.2 National Association of Certified Valuators and Analysts

The NACVA was established in the 1990s with the aim of establishing business valuation standards and certifying the professional qualifications of its members, by offering a range of training courses. In general terms, the NACVA aims to provide a set of rules of conduct, without however claiming the status of "general accepted standard" (GAP) setter. Though schematic and concise, these standards nevertheless constitute a good benchmark and are widely used especially in North America.

The current "Professional Standards" entered were applied in June 2017 and have the peculiarity of paying little attention to the methods while focusing more on ethical issues, the analysis prior to the valuation process, and the valuation report.

In general, they have a strongly operational approach which is perhaps more suited to a guideline for professionals than to a standard aimed at setting general principles and rules.

1.8.3 Canadian Institute of Chartered Business Valuators (CICBV)

The CICBV was founded in the early 1970s and sets business valuation standards both nationally and internationally. Like the NACVA, the principles are addressed to its members, but the scope of application is more extensive. The standards currently in use were largely updated in 2014.

The CICBV distinguishes between the "Code of Ethics" and the "Practice Standards". These standards essentially focus on describing the content of the valuation report, but do not go into the merits of the methods.

1.8.4 American Society of Appraisers (ASA)

The ASA is an international association that provides guidelines not only in terms of business valuation, but also in the field of jewelry, plant and machinery, real estate, and so on. It is therefore a multidisciplinary entity with a very wide range of action. Again, the ethical issues are assessed separately from the valuation standards.

The "Principles of Appraisal Practice and Code of Ethics" do not specifically concern the valuation of companies, but are general principles of conduct applicable to any valuation procedure.

The "Business Valuation Standards" were enacted in 1992 and revised several times; they were most recently updated in 2008. Their approach is rather concise and, especially in relation to the methods, is more a reasoned summary than a standard.

To complete the picture there are the "Statements on SBV" that deal with specific subjects, such as public companies and transactions; the "Advisory opinions" that focus on the applicability of the standards in some contexts; the "Procedural guidelines", to be used in special cases, for example, when a valuer is appointed as an independent expert during a trial.

1.8.5 The Appraisal Foundation

The Appraisal Foundation is a not-for-profit private educational organization, responsible for the operation of the Appraisal Practice Board (APB), the Appraisal Qualification Board (AQB), and the Appraisal Standard Board (ASB); the ASB is the standard setter of the "Uniform Standards of Professional Appraisal Practice" that regulate valuation in various areas, including business valuations.

In their most recent 2016–2017 updated version, they comprise ten standards, including two for "business appraisal". In addition, there are ten "Statements of Appraisal Standards", which provide an in-depth analysis on specific issues, such as the DCF method.

The "USPAP Frequently Asked Questions" are also worth mentioning; they consist of about 300 detailed questions and answers designed to explain some common operational issues.

1.8.6 American Institute of Certified Public Accountants (AICPA)

Technically, the AICPA is not a standard setter, but one of the most important professional associations. To provide its own contribution, it published a "Statement on Standards for Valuation Services" entitled "Valuation of a Business, Business Ownership Interest, Security, or Intangible Asset".

1.8.7 The European Group of Valuer's Associations (TEGoVA)

TEGoVA, an organization established at the end of the 1990s, has over 60 member associations and organizations from about 30 countries, which, for various reasons, are engaged in the valuation field.

In 2016 the seventh edition of the "European Valuation Standards" was published. It is a guideline that covers different areas where an estimation process is required: from financial reporting, to financing, insurance, and environmental impact. Despite some interesting ideas, the attempt of bringing together subjects that are too far apart makes this standard unsuitable for business valuers.

2

Integrated Valuation Approach (IVA)

2.1 The Traditional Valuation Approach

Most business valuation textbooks are focused on calculation methods. Unquestionably, these play a very important role, as they are the formal part of the entire process. The risk, however, is to place too much emphasis on the quantitative dimension, without adequately considering the context in which the valuation is made.

For example, market-based valuation methods are sometimes based on a peer group of comparable companies or transactions that have qualitatively little or no resemblance with the target company, the only thing they have in common being the industry in which they operate. Thus, if the peer group is based on an uncritical selection of companies, you may end up comparing a start-up of the clothing sector with established brands such as Gucci, Prada, or Ferragamo, whose reference market, business model, organizational structure, and brand potential are completely different from those of the target company.

It is as if you were evaluating the performance of a Smart using a Ferrari, a Porsche, or a Lamborghini as a benchmark. They all have a steering, four wheels, and an engine in common. But the similarities end there: performances, road holding, usability are completely different.

Similarly, in a business valuation all the variables that affect value should be critically examined. In other words, an integrated valuation approach (IVA) should be adopted that encompasses, within any specific method, a wide range of elements reflecting the characteristics and specificities of the firm to be valued.

Otherwise, the valuation process runs the risk of becoming the mere application of a formula.

Determining the value of a business is a complex exercise that involves not just the application of a model but, above all, the choice of parameters that make that model suitable to represent value. While technicality is important, an integrated analysis of the firm is indispensable.

This approach is often disregarded in business valuation textbooks, which focus on methods and do not pay sufficient attention to the methodological assumptions and input selection.

Evaluating means translating into quantitative terms a set of qualitative elements based on certain strategic choices. Thus, value is the numerically expressed result of a decision-making process, part of which has been completed while the other part is still in the making.

An overview of the main methods clearly shows that factoring in historical and prospective circumstances is an essential part of the entire valuation process.

This is true for all models without exclusion and regardless of whether they are based on expected cash flows or on market multiples.

In the first case, the expected flows must be consistent with past performance, while taking into account the business outlook, in addition to being in accordance with the macroeconomic scenario, industry performance, and strategic focus. In the second case, the most suitable variables for a peer group selection must be defined, with respect both to the current situation and to how the business is likely to evolve.

The combined analysis of both historical and prospective view is, therefore, an essential step for a consistent and reliable business valuation.

Thus, valuing a business is not a mere formula-application exercise, but a broader process that requires:

1. an integrated assessment of the internal and external variables of a firm;
2. the ability to place them within a coherent system;
3. the sensitivity to identify the model that best fits such system.

The purpose of this textbook is to offer a guideline for the application of an integrated approach, thereby avoiding "copy and paste" valuations, based on prepackaged parameters and the uncritical use of models.

2.2 Integrated Valuation Approach (IVA)

The analytical process that leads to the definition of an IVA is outlined in the following pages. It is based on three steps:

1. context analysis;
2. analysis of previous financial statements;
3. identification of the valuation method.

Context analysis consists in a thorough examination of the competitive scenario where the target entity operates. This in-depth analysis helps gain an understanding of the set of complex elements that influence the firm and is a necessary preliminary step in the overall valuation process.

The analysis of historical results is essential not only in terms of numerical results but also with regard to how such results were obtained and summarized. Notably, attention must be paid both to the financial and to the non-financial information generated by the reporting system.

Finally, context analysis and the analysis of previous financial statements support the identification of the most appropriate business valuation approach.

2.3 Context Analysis

Context analysis requires an examination of the company's internal and external elements.

The internal elements are:

1. company history, shareholders, and governance;
2. organizational structure;
3. products and services;
4. competitive advantages.

The external elements are:

1. industry;
2. industry trends;
3. characteristics of demand;
4. characteristics of supply;
5. competitors.

2.3.1 Internal Elements Analysis

The first step involves gaining an understanding of the *company history* and identifying its *main stakeholders*.

Thus, the main events that have marked the evolution of the company over time must be examined. In this respect, it is important to identify the circumstances through which the firm has acquired the competitive advantages that most influence its value. In valuing a firm, its history and the events that helped shape it cannot be disregarded.

Information about its shareholders can also be relevant. For example, valuing a company with few shareholders requires different logics and instruments compared to the valuation of a listed company. In valuing a family business, on the other hand, special attention must be paid to the relationships in place between family members. Furthermore, the identification of controlling interests and, therefore, the quantification of premiums and discounts are affected by the shareholders' agreements in place.

Finally, information on the company's *governance* should be obtained to verify whether the company board members and key officers (CEO, CFO, CoO, etc.) meet the requirements and have the necessary skills to ensure that business plan targets are achieved or that performance levels are such as to justify the use of certain market multiples.

Secondly, information should be obtained on the *organizational structure* and whether it is suitable for the achievement of targets. This aspect is crucial when valuing a start-up, whose organizational structure is often still in the making. Furthermore, where the development of new businesses is planned, the staff must have adequate experience or sufficient resources must have been allocated to hire new staff.

In assessing distressed companies, the possibility that some of the staff could be laid off should be considered, as this may negatively affect the achievement of business plan targets.

In general, it is important to consider that human resources are one of the most significant value drivers in all contexts, both in labor-intensive scenarios and when the ability to innovate underpins the firm's competitive advantage.

Thirdly, one has to gain a perfect understanding of the *business*. All too often a "copy and paste" approach is used in business valuations, disregarding the characteristics of the products and services offered and the business model. For example, the value prospects of an entity that manufactures products likely to become obsolete in a short time are totally different from those of an entity that constantly invests in R&D. Valuers are not required to perform a full-fledged market analysis, nor to build a competitive position matrix, but they should have a clear perception of industry attributes and of how the target company fits within it.

In this regard information should be obtained on:

(a) brand loyalty, by analyzing sales volumes and order intakes;
(b) the trend of prices and profit;
(c) the bargaining power, notably by analyzing the costs incurred to ensure that products are placed in the market;
(d) brand extension, that is, the brand's ability to transfer its strategic potential to a wider range of products.

For example, when valuing a company engaged in the food sector and with a local market, we may wonder whether using the multiples of global multinational firms like Kraft, Heinz, Nestlé, or Kellogg makes sense, unless we make some adjustments to account for the elements mentioned above.

In general, before embarking on a business valuation, we have to understand its specificities and the key *competitive advantages* that positively influence its value. With regard to these competitive advantages, we must further explore:

(a) what they are;
(b) how they can change over time;
(c) their impact on the value of the firm.

Competitive advantages are to be found in many areas other than just the product or the brand. They can be an efficient operational structure; lower cost than that of competitors; differentiation in terms of quality; effective economies of scale or scope; ability to develop integration processes; logistics; the ability to relate to the market; widespread presence; adequate pricing policies; or the ability to support promotional campaigns. Valuers must develop the sensitivity to understand how all these elements affect the value of a firm.

2.3.2 External Elements Analysis

An important aspect of the valuation process consists in correctly identifying the *industry* in which the company operates, as this allows for the results to be seen in context and in relation with the trends of that industry.

Accurately drawing the boundaries of an industry is a less obvious step than it may at first appear, as certain businesses cut across several industries, which make them difficult to circumscribe to any single or specific area.

For example, Apple may at first be qualified as a computer manufacturer (Mac). However, it is also active in other businesses, including music players (i-Pod), smartphones (iPhone), tablets (i-Pad), watches (i-Watch), operating systems (iOS), and software. These are complementary, but partially different areas in terms of target market, product life cycle, technological content, and so on. Even competitors differ from one business to the other.

The Mac should be compared with companies such as HP, Dell, Acer, Asus, Lenovo, and so on, although the product is not directly comparable; music players with Sony, Panasonic, Philips, and so on; smartphones with Samsung, HTMC, Huawei, and so on; finally, tablets with Samsung, Huawei, Asus, and so on.

As none of the businesses is significantly more relevant than the others, identifying the reference industry is not straightforward; choosing just one of them may lead to oversimplification.

Furthermore, each of the aforementioned competitors, in turn, has operations in other industries. For example, Samsung manufactures air conditioning systems, washing machines, televisions; Phillips manufactures video equipment, electric razors, baby products, household appliances, light bulbs, household products.

What lesson can we draw? We can draw the conclusion that to unequivocally identify the industry a firm is engaged in is not an easy task, as industry boundaries are less clearly defined than in the past.

However, correctly identifying the industry a company falls into is crucial for a correct valuation. For example, in the multiples method each industry has its own average benchmarks; choosing to place a firm in one industry rather than another can significantly affect the result.

In addition, the characteristics of an industry change over time. For this reason, valuers must consider the following aspects: the industry trend (both at the macroeconomic and at the local level); the characteristics of the demand; the characteristics of the supply; the analysis of the main competitors.

Industry trend has to do with the elements that most influenced the business developments; this helps understand whether certain aspects are attributable to the target company only, or if they involve the entire sector.

In a globalized economy, industry trends are certainly not constrained within national boundaries; consequently, trends that take on certain traits at the national level may appear different outside the national borders, thus broadening the scope of investigation. For example, the textile sector, which has been in the doldrums for years in Europe, grew more than 3% per year globally, and the same is true in the engineering, furniture, and building industries.

The breadth of the reference sector is therefore anything but secondary when it comes to choosing a valuation method. In the DCF method, for example, the financial outlook must be consistent with the specificities of the industry and the sales channels. Similarly, in the multiples method, the peer group of comparables should be based on the same markets the target company is engaged in. For example, if a company's operations are mainly in Europe, we have to look for companies that are mainly active in Europe; if multinationals are included in the peer group of comparables, the relevance of the outcome may be affected.

Obviously, valuers are not required to become market analysis experts, but they must be able to draw the necessary elements for an understanding of the trends from specialized databases and from easily accessible open source documentation, such as research by specialized observatories and market memorandums.

The characteristics of the *demand* are linked to many factors, such as the geographical area, lifestyle, consumption trends, average per capita revenues, expectations, interest rates, price regime, evolving social and economic environment, and so on. The question is neither abstract nor immutable, but has well-defined connotations and changes over time, depending on the industry distinctive elements.

In recent years we saw how technological changes influenced business models and business strategies. Especially when using the DCF method, we must ensure that the expected cash flows reflect potential market and demand changes, notably when the cash flow projection horizon is long (four/five years).

The characteristics of the *supply* can be explored by analyzing the market positioning of the target company's products and/or services compared to those of competitors. As demand changes, supply must adjust accordingly, providing suitable answers. For example, if a company in a highly technological sector does not make adequate investments in R&D, the products and services it offers will likely weaken compared to those of its competitors.

It is not necessary for valuers to be experts in the business the target company is engaged in, but they must assess whether a firm is able to positively respond to changes and can adjust its products and services to potential market developments.

As we have previously stated, the identification of *competitors* depends on the correct identification of the reference industry. If the reference industry has been correctly identified, valuers will have a peer group of similar companies to be used as benchmark, in order to capture similarities and differences. In practice, in the multiples method the selection of comparables is made using databases that can select the peer group based on dimensional parameters of the target company.

2.4 Analysis of Past Results

The value of a firm is linked to future expectations, regardless of the method used. A firm is worth something only if there is reasonable certainty that its value is consistent, that is, is based on sufficiently solid assumptions. If, under ordinary circumstances, the value of a company "vanishes" within a short period, then its value was likely not consistent but was rather a "bubble". If we look back to the last 20 years, we find various examples of overvalued "bubbles".

One way to make sure a value is consistent is to examine the past trend of the target company. Let's take two companies, A and B. In company A, revenues and cash flows grew steadily over the years, investment in R&D was adequate, debt was kept under control, and dividends were in line with results. In company B, revenues and cash flows were volatile, investment in R&D was occasional, the debt-to-equity ratio fluctuated, and high dividends were consistently distributed to the shareholders. At the assumed date, however, both companies have similar parameters and a similar value is obtained from application of the valuation methods.

The question is, are these companies worth the same? Probably not, as their value rests on different bases: more solid those of company A; more volatile those of company B.

For comparison, let's take two golfers: player A has a handicap of 0 and player B a handicap of 10. During a tournament, both players get a par at all 18 holes, closing the tournament with the same number of hits. Can we say that those players play at the same level? Probably not, as between a 10-handicapper and a 0-handicapper there is a certain difference; the fact that player B played well (or was lucky) in that specific tournament does not mean he or she will be able to repeat the performance consistently.

Likewise, understanding the company's track record is important in business valuation and it is the valuer's task to make sure that past and future results are consistent.

For this reason, an analysis of the results achieved by the target company in the two/three years prior to the assumed valuation date is a necessary preliminary step of the valuation process.

Specifically, what is the valuer's task? Valuers are not auditors; ascertaining the truthfulness of past data is not their task, much less so ascertaining the truthfulness of future data contained in business plans. Rather, valuers are required to analyze the target company's figures to make sure the valuation is based on reliable metrics. In other words, a valuer should not take the figures provided by the company at face value, but should put them under scrutiny to make sure they provide an adequate basis for determining that company's value.

Valuers must approach the company's data with professional skepticism (see Chap. 1) and propose changes if they consider those data as not representative of the company's value.

For example, in the DCF method, the valuer must ascertain that the expected results are consistent with past results. This is not always the case. Some values may indeed be in contrast or, at least, not entirely in line with past data and with the current situation. For example, an anomalous increase in revenues compared to the historical growth trend that is not supported by adequate investments is probably incompatible with reality; likewise, if a medium-term business plan assumes an increase in cash flows based on the entry into new markets without, however, being supported by marketing and logistic investment, commercial agreements, and infrastructure (or these are expected to be incurred in a way that is inconsistent with financial resources), that plan is probably not very reliable.

We must not forget that figures are representative of facts. If figures are not consistent, facts are also inconsistent. Many business valuation books devote large sections to how a business plan is technically implemented. As a matter of fact, drawing up the business plan is not the valuers' task; taking on this responsibility is beyond the scope of their assignment and might lead to a company valuation that is biased by valuers' expectations. Valuers should rather verify that the assumptions underlying the plan are consistent, taking into account both the company's past performance and the current situation.

Valuers are required to perform a financial statement analysis for the most recent two/three years, as a way to gain a better understanding of the company's performance and verify the consistency of its business plan. Performing a financial statement analysis is a must, regardless of the valuation method used, as it enables valuers to acquire greater familiarity with the company and make a more informed choice of the valuation method.

Chapter 3 provides a guideline for carrying out a preliminary financial statement analysis in preparation of the business valuation.

2.5 Choosing the Valuation Approach

The choice of valuation approach depends on several circumstances, such as:

1. the characteristics of the company and the industry;
2. the documentation available;
3. the purposes of the valuation.

Even before applying a method, business valuation is about choosing a method. Valuers do not merely apply a formula, they must apply judgment and interpret the situation where they are called to provide their experience. Choosing a valuation method rather than another can lead to different results, although the methods have been properly applied.

Each approach tends to focus on certain aspects of a company. For example, the DCF method emphasizes a company's ability to achieve a certain level of free cash flows. On the other hand, a multiple based on EBITDA focuses on the ability to achieve a certain level of operating profit. If there is a temporal misalignment between operating profit and free cash flows, the value of the business may differ. The valuer must be aware that no one approach is superior to the others, but that there are circumstances in which one approach provides a more reliable result than another.

For this reason, the valuer must be familiar with the *characteristics of the business and the industry*, as the choice of valuation method is strictly linked to the surrounding circumstances. Thus, the analysis described in the previous paragraphs is a necessary step for identifying the method that best represents the specific surrounding environment.

The *available documentation* is a second aspect that guides the choice of valuation method. A company may have only a limited amount of information, and be unable to provide any further information. For example, a small company without a business plan cannot be valued using a DCF method, or there may not be sufficiently reliable market values to evaluate a company in a business niche. For example, there could be no companies truly comparable with a firm engaged in the biotechnology industry offering highly specialized services for the multiples method to be consistently applied.

Finally, the valuation could concern companies operating in different countries where there is no obligation to prepare any accounting documents; in this case the valuer must base the analysis on whatever material is delivered, specifying the inherent limitations.

The *purpose of the valuation* also affects the choice of method. For example, the valuation for an initial public offering (IPO) is based on different logics compared to the valuation of a minority interest in a private held company.

Technical savvy is not the only skill required from a valuer, as the ability to systemize information and context variables in order to identify the most appropriate method is equally important. The valuer's objective is not to find the "correct" value irrespective of the characteristics of the company and the industry, but the "more consistent" one.

2.6 Is a Business Worth Something Only If It Creates Value?

Over the last 30 years, the concept of value has been the subject of much debate in the literature and in practice. For a long time, creating value has been viewed as the main purpose of a company. Today the emphasis on a "value-centric" approach has been greatly reduced, partly the result of the post-2007 crisis that somehow reshaped the concept of value.

Despite wide debate on the subject, a formula capable of summarizing the creation of value has never been found. A possible answer to the question "when is value created?" is the following: a company creates value when the return on invested capital (IC) is greater than the cost incurred to acquire it. In other words, a company creates value when the spread between ROI and WACC is positive:

$$ROI - WACC > 0$$

where:

ROI: (Return on Investment) is calculated as the ratio of EBIT to business assets (see Sect. 3.7.1.2);

WACC: is the weighted average cost of capital (see Sect. 4.6).

Let's see why this statement is true from a logical and quantitative standpoint.

To carry out its business, a firm must make certain investments which make up its business assets. According to the most basic reasoning, if a firm needs business assets amounting to $100, it must have financial sources of $100, consisting of equity and debt (Fig. 2.1).

Business assets must generate an adequate return; this return (ROI) varies according to how the business assets are "used". This depends on various elements, such as the business model, management skills, industry characteristics, market positioning, and other variables.

An adequate ROI is essential to remunerate both the shareholders (cost of equity) and the lenders (cost of debt).

If the ROI is higher than the WACC (cost of equity + cost of debt), the company is carrying out its business profitably and therefore it creates value:

$$\text{Value Creation} = ROI - WACC$$

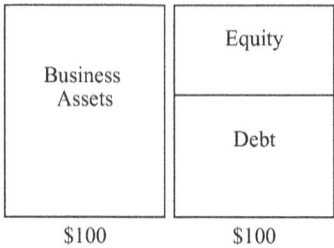

Fig. 2.1 Investments and financial sources

This is a profit-based interpretation of value creation. Like all simplifications, it is not perfect and probably fails to represent the complex system of variables that influence the firm. Nevertheless, it is a good approximation and contains some interesting implications.

In practice if:

(a) (ROI − WACC) > 0 the company creates value, as the ROI is greater than the cost incurred to obtain it;
(b) conversely, if (ROI − WACC) < 0, the enterprise is destroying value;
(c) if (ROI − WACC) = 0 the firm is in a state of apparent equilibrium although, based on the entropic principle, it is closer to value destruction than to value creation.

This formula is a different representation of economic value added (EVA™). If we consider that:

- business assets can also be defined as invested capital (IC);
- after-tax ROI is equal to (Nopat/IC), where Nopat (net operating profit after taxes) = EBIT × (1−% tax):

the value creation formula can be developed as follows:

$$\begin{aligned}
\text{Value Creation} &= \text{ROI} - \text{WACC} = \\
&= (\text{IC} \times \text{ROI}) - (\text{IC} \times \text{WACC}) \\
&= \left(\text{IC} \times \frac{\text{Nopat}}{\text{IC}}\right) - (\text{IC} \times \text{WACC}) = \\
&= \text{Nopat} - (\text{IC} \times \text{WACC}) = \text{EVA}^{\text{TM}}
\end{aligned}$$

Is it correct to affirm that a firm creates value when ROI is greater than WACC? It is correct as long as:

(a) the spread is analyzed in a medium-long-term perspective. In the short term, ROI may be lower than cost—this is typical of start-ups or during a corporate turnaround; companies that have launched significant investment plans, the positive effects of which still have to materialize, may also find themselves in this situation;
(b) we are aware that both the ROI and WACC metrics are influenced by various factors. ROI is influenced by the accounting standards, notably as regards revenue recognition, depreciation and amortization policies, accruals treatment, and so on; the WACC is influenced by the capital asset pricing model (CAPM) inputs, such as the risk-free rate, the beta coefficient, and the risk premium.

2.6.1 Actual Value and Potential Value

There are many examples of companies that, while not apparently creating value for a long period, have a potentially high value. Amazon.com is a prime example. Amazon.com started in 1994 as an online bookstore and later diversified to sell DVDs, CDs, videogames, and so on. Amazon's initial business plan was unusual; it did not expect to make a profit for four to five years. This "slow" growth caused stockholders to complain that the company was not reaching profitability fast enough to justify their investment or even survive in the long term. The company finally turned its first profit in the fourth quarter of 2001. More recently, Amazon.com has seen very positive years alternating with years of losses, as can be seen in Table 2.1:

In 2012 and 2014, Amazon recorded a loss. Is this circumstance sufficient to assume a loss in value, without considering that this result may be caused by investments that will produce positive results in subsequent years? The answer is no, as value creation is measured in the long run only.

Table 2.1 Amazon.com statement of operations (in $ millions)

Statement of operations	2012	2013	2014	2015	2016
Net sales	$61,093	$74,452	$88,988	$107,006	$135,987
Operating income	$676	$745	$178	$2233	$4186
Net income (loss)	($39)	$274	($241)	$596	$2371
Basic earnings per share	($0.09)	$0.60	($0.52)	$1.28	$5.01

This example tells us that the value of a firm is not a temporary circumstance and that the path to value creation is not necessarily smooth nor without any steps backward. The valuer must be able to discern what is just a temporary situation and consider how the results will affect value in the long term.

Intangible assets, such as the customer portfolio, patents, research-oriented approach, know-how, and so on, play a decisive role in the formation of a firm's competitive advantage, and therefore its value. Traditional valuation methods (DCF and multiples) are often unable to measure the contribution of intangible assets, especially if their positive effects have not yet fully materialized in terms of EBITDA, EBIT, or cash flow. Valuers mainly rely on financial information, which is influenced by accounting standards that place limits on the recognition of intangible assets.

Furthermore, valuers tend to conservatively consider only the data that can reliably be assessed at the valuation date; the effects of an intangible asset, that are uncertain or remote, might be disregarded in the valuation process. Moreover, valuations that strongly focused on the value of intangibles resulted in unreasonable overestimations in recent years, as was the case with the speculative bubble of the new economy.

Nevertheless, measuring the creation of value based on current and demonstrable circumstances only is wrong. Sometimes, value is linked to projects and prospects that may not be reflected in short-term figures, but which are fundamental value drivers in the long run. In the case of Amazon.com, if the company had been valued in the 1990s based on accounting results only, the outcome would have shown a company with a bleak future and relying on a utopian business model of modest value.

2.7 Can Valuation Be Standardized?

The advantage of shared valuation methods is that of having defined globally accepted guidelines. Value creation can be measured using the same metrics, making the comparison between operators a smoother process.

Like all human events, valuation approaches follow the latest trend.

In the 1990s and early 2000s, the most commonly used method was the DCF method. The statement "cash is king" formulated in a well-known business valuation textbook perfectly describes this tendency. Excessive confidence in expectations has sometimes led to an overestimation of firms, especially when over 70% of the value depends on a theoretical measure such as the terminal value. Moreover, the International Financial Reporting Standard

(IFRS) defined the DCF method as a second-tier method compared to the market-based approach.

As a result, operators, especially investment banks and analysts, shifted their focus to the multiples method, which has become the most widespread approach after the start of the financial crisis. This method has some limitations too, as its ability to correctly interpret the value of a firm depends on how consistently the peer group of comparables firms has been built. In some cases, simply including or excluding a few companies in the peer group may lead to different values.

There is no method where you can just go on automatic pilot and get a consistent result. A method works and provides a correct interpretation of value if the pilot, that is, the valuer, can drive it properly. In some cases, the DCF method is the most suitable, while in others using the multiples method is preferable; what makes the difference is the human factor, that is, the ability to read the situation and identify the most suitable method, considering the surrounding circumstances.

Unfortunately, as already mentioned, "copy and paste" approaches are not unusual, with valuation methods and inputs used in a standard way, without considering the peculiarities of the company being assessed.

Valuation methods are very useful as they free the entire process from the valuer's subjectivity. On the other hand, they should not be used as an alibi or as rigid instruments circumscribed to the mere application of a formula.

An integrated valuation approach can be a satisfactory solution when it combines the formal consistency of methods and formulas with the valuer's perception.

3

Financial Statement Analysis

3.1 Introduction

An integrated valuation approach requires that a financial statement analysis be carried out for prior years in order to:

1. understand the target company's track record;
2. make sure the projected outlook is consistent with past results;
3. identify the most appropriate valuation method.

A financial statement analysis is necessary to understand the performance of a company and gain greater insight on:

- the relationship between investments and financial sources;
- the company's ability to meet its obligations;
- the ability to generate positive cash flows;
- the propensity to remunerate investments;
- the attitude to efficiently operate.

3.2 How to Set Up the Financial Statement Analysis

The financial statement analysis comprises two steps: a technical step and an interpretation step.

The *technical step* consists of acquiring information and organizing it according to a consistent logic. The financial statement analysis must have a "bespoke" approach, in the sense that it must fit the characteristics of the company, just like a "tailor-made suit". Therefore, the analysis must be carried out taking into account the surrounding environment and the target company's specific situation.

The technical step is made up of two substeps:

1. reclassification of the financial statements;
2. selection of the most suitable ratios.

The first substep consists in reclassifying the financial statement items according to a different logic. Companies often use different terminologies and formats to present their financial results. Consequently, comparing performance across different companies, and sometimes within the same company over time, may prove difficult. Through accurate reclassification a single template may be used for the balance sheet, income statement, and cash flow statement.

The reclassification is not merely an uncritical reorganization of financial statement items. Other aspects must be considered, such as:

(a) the accounting standards adopted: although countries are gradually shifting toward the IFRS, in many of them several accounting standards coexist, which impose different rules and criteria to present information. In Europe, for example, the IFRSs are mandatory only for listed companies, banks, and financial companies; they may also be applied by other companies on an optional basis (but not everywhere).
(b) accounting changes in accounting estimates: over time, a company may change the way it treats financial statement items;
(c) quality of disclosures: in addition to the mandatory minimum information required by the accounting standards, each company can provide the information it deems most relevant. An accurate disclosure allows for better understanding and, therefore, more accurate classification of financial statement items;
(d) segment information: companies engaged in several businesses are required to provide information for each of them. If an enterprise does not have an efficient segment reporting, the financial statement reclassification may lead to inconsistencies;
(e) non-financial information: sometimes non-financial information provides useful elements to better understand financial information; an integrated reporting approach considerably extends the set of information a valuer can draw from when applying an integrated valuation approach.

The second substep consists in *selecting the ratios* that are most appropriate for the purpose of showing:

(a) the company's ability to meet its obligations;
(b) the balance between investments and financial sources;
(c) profitability.

Valuers must select the ratios that best fit the purposes of their assignment.

Once the technical step is completed, the *interpretation step* follows, which is considered as the most complex part of the whole analysis process. Based on the information provided by the combined analysis of all ratios, the valuer must draw a summary assessment on the company's "state of health".

The quotation marks are not by coincidence, as a valuer must formulate a diagnosis on the company's condition, just like a doctor.

Just like a doctor is required to interpret the symptoms, a valuer must develop the ability to grasp what is behind the figures and establish logical relationships between the various elements available. In other words, valuers must sharpen their acumen to combine apparently unrelated financial and non-financial information into a coherent whole. Data should not be read as isolated pieces, but in relation to the sector of the target company.

3.3 Comparing Values

The financial statement analysis provides a consistent framework for a firm's results. For greater completeness these results must be seen in relation:

1. to the performance of the ratios over time (time-series comparison);
2. to the values of comparable companies (cross-sectional comparison).

In general, analyzing just one year is not sufficient for an effective financial statement analysis; for a complete picture, the *performance of the company over time* must be analyzed.

For example, how can we interpret a firm's 5% profitability figure? This figure alone is of little use: it must be seen as part of a historical series in order to grasp how it changes over time. If in the last three years profitability was 2%, 3%, and 4%, a value of 5% reflects an improvement; conversely, if the historical evolution was 15%, 12%, 10%, then a 5% figure shows a drastic worsening.

A time-series comparison enables for the results to be put in perspective. In general, the number of years taken as a reference for the analysis must be consistent with the length of the business cycles: three years is usually an acceptable period for acquiring meaningful information.

In addition, a *comparison with comparable companies* in terms of geographical area, business, size, governance, and so on must be performed. In other words, when analyzing a 5% profitability figure we cannot disregard the characteristics of that firm's specific industry. In the food sector, for example, this percentage is remarkable, while in the construction sector, it is rather modest.

Thus, a financial statement ratio cannot be read as the scale of a thermometer, where a 40-degree temperature (104 Fahrenheit) is considered "high" by whoever measures it. Values must be put in context. This requires comparing the results of comparable companies in order to better understand the peculiarities of each sector.

3.4 Reclassified Balance Sheet

The balance sheet can be reclassified according to a functional approach which requires making a distinction between (Fig. 3.1) operating assets and liabilities; financial assets and liabilities.

Assets are reclassified as follows:

- *operating non-current assets*: they include long-term investments, such as intangible assets (brands, leasehold rights, goodwill, etc.) and tangible assets (building and land, equipment, tools, fixtures and fittings, long-term receivables, etc.);
- *operating current assets*: they include trade receivables, inventories, held for sale assets;
- *financial non-current assets*: they include long-term financial investments, derivatives, and so on;
- *financial current assets*: they include short-term financial assets, such as cash and marketable securities.

Liabilities are reclassified as follows:

- *operating non-current liabilities*: they include long-term trade payables, provisions for pensions, deferred tax liabilities, and so on;
- *operating current liabilities*: they include short-term trade payables, accrued expenses, social security and payroll taxes, current provisions, and so on;

Financial Statement Analysis 43

ASSETS	LIABILITIES
Operating non-current assets	Equity
	Operating non-current liabilities
Operating current assets	Operating current liabilities
	Financial non-current liabilities
Financial non-current assets	
Financial current assets	Financial current liabilities

Fig. 3.1 Functional reformulation of the balance sheet

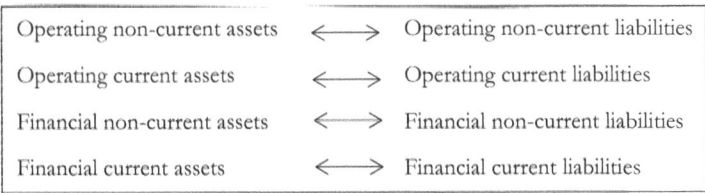

Fig. 3.2 Relationship between assets and liabilities

- *financial non-current liabilities*: they include long-term loans, finance lease obligations, convertible debentures, and so on;
- *financial current liabilities*: they include short-term loans, overdrafts, and so on.

As shown in Fig. 3.2, assets and liabilities share certain aspects in terms of nature (operating and financial items) and time horizon (current and non-current).

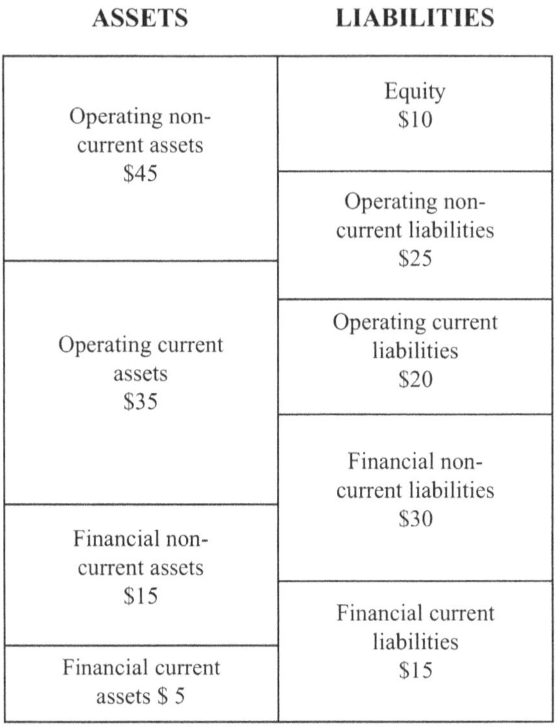

ASSETS	LIABILITIES
Operating non-current assets $45	Equity $10
	Operating non-current liabilities $25
Operating current assets $35	Operating current liabilities $20
	Financial non-current liabilities $30
Financial non-current assets $15	
	Financial current liabilities $15
Financial current assets $ 5	

Fig. 3.3 Reclassification example

If we group items by nature and time horizon, the balance sheet can be reclassified as shown in Fig. 3.3.

3.4.1 Business Assets

Business assets are equal to the difference between operating assets and operating liabilities. Specifically:

1. Operating Non-current Assets − Operating Non-current Liabilities = Net Assets (Fig. 3.4).
2. Operating Current Assets − Operating Current Liabilities = Working Capital (Fig. 3.5).
3. Net Assets + Working Capital = Business Assets (Fig. 3.6).

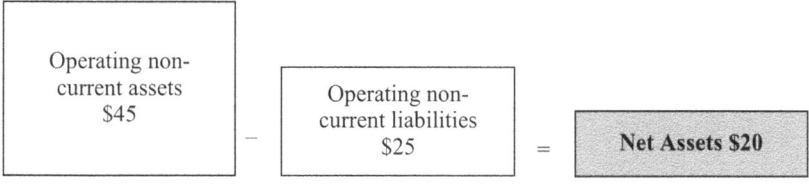

Fig. 3.4 Net assets

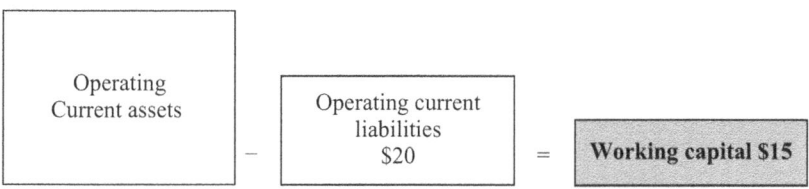

Fig. 3.5 Working capital

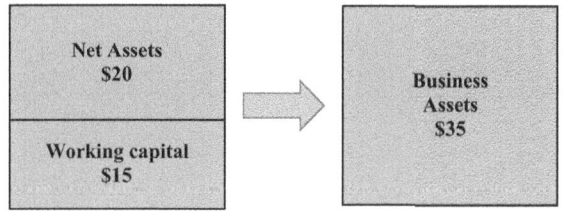

Fig. 3.6 Business assets

3.4.2 Net Debt

Net debt is the difference between financial assets and financial liabilities.

If financial assets are greater than financial liabilities, net debt has a positive balance; in the opposite case, the balance is negative. Net debt may also be broken down into current and non-current items.

1. Financial Non-current Assets − Financial Non-current Liabilities = Non-current Net Debt (Fig. 3.7).
2. Financial Current Assets − Financial Current Liabilities = Current Net Debt (Fig. 3.8).
3. Non-current Net Debt + Current Net Debt = Net Debt (Fig. 3.9).

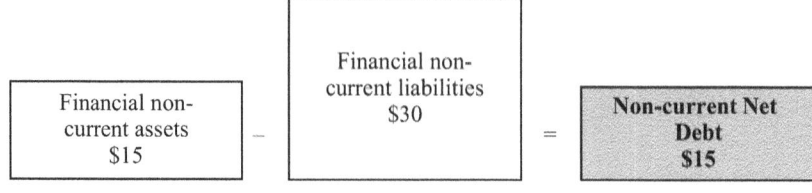

Fig. 3.7 Non-current net debt

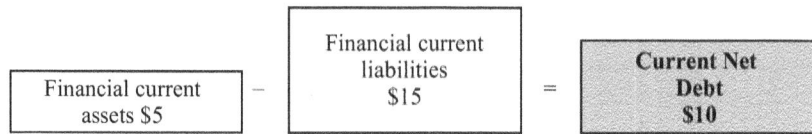

Fig. 3.8 Current net debt

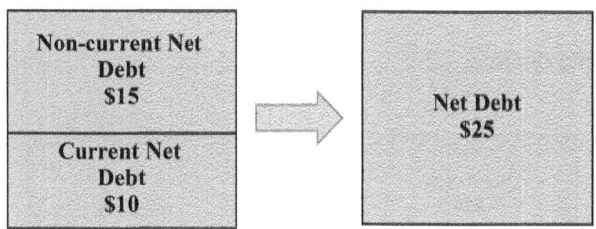

Fig. 3.9 Net debt

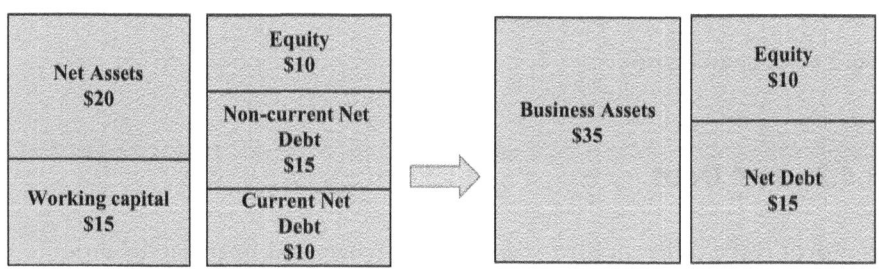

Fig. 3.10 Financial statement at a glance

By reclassifying the balance sheet, we can identify (Fig. 3.10):

- the amount of business assets, consisting of net assets and working capital;
- the breakdown of financial sources, consisting of equity + debt (both non-current and current);
- the relationship between business assets (investments) and financial sources.

Based on the above example, we observe that:

- Net assets are greater than working capital and are equal to 57% (= 20/35) of total investments;
- Non-current financing sources (equity and non-current net debt) are equal to 72% (= 25/35) of total investments;
- 28% (= 10/35) of investments is financed with equity and 72% with debt;

3.5 Reclassified Income Statement

The income statement reclassification (Fig. 3.11) is somewhat less complex than the balance sheet reclassification.

The income statement reclassification consists of adding some intermediate margins in the operating section. The analytical diagram is shown in Fig. 3.12. The costs a company incurs to carry out its activities are kept separate:

- operating costs (raw materials, services, leasing, etc.);
- labor cost;
- amortization and depreciation.

Gross margin is equal to the difference between sales and operating expenses. It measures the company's ability to remunerate both the factors of production and the stakeholders (Fig. 3.13). Gross margin must:

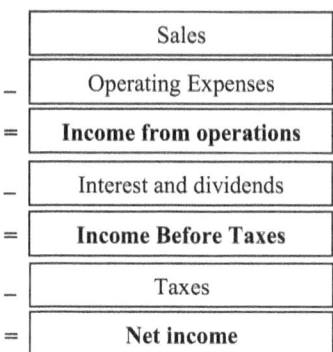

Fig. 3.11 The income statement

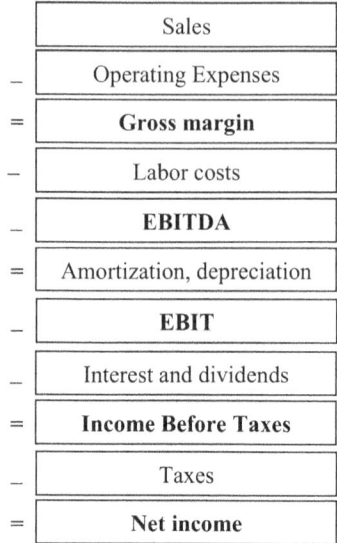

Fig. 3.12 Reclassified income statement

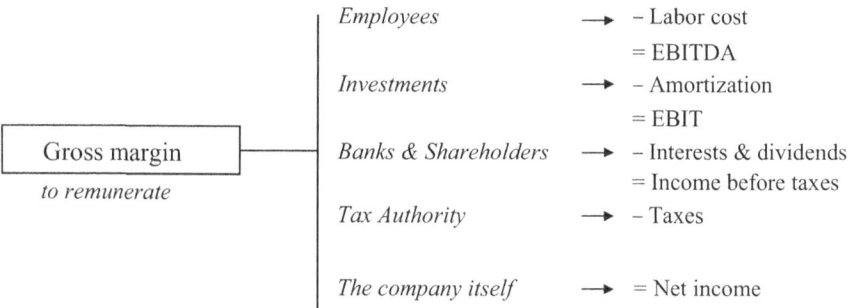

Fig. 3.13 Gross margin distribution

- remunerate those who provide their work (labor cost);
- recover the capital expenditures made to purchase assets (depreciation/amortization);
- remunerate the lenders (interest expenses);
- remunerate the shareholders (dividends);
- fulfill obligations toward the tax authority (taxes);
- remunerate the company (net income).

EBITDA (earnings before interest, taxes, depreciation, and amortization) and *EBIT* (earnings before interest, taxes) correspond to the gross and net operating profit, respectively.

3.6 The Cash Flow Statement

The cash flow statement is the link between the balance sheet and the income statement and provides a different and further analytical perspective. Cash flows are a more neutral measure of performance than profit since:

1. they are not influenced by either accounting standards or accounting policies;
2. they objectively measure the performance of a company.

A perhaps overused expression reminds us that "cash is a fact, profit is an opinion".

Profit may be a "questionable" measure in the sense that it reflects both the accounting standards and the accounting policies which, although they are designed to provide a true and fair view, influence the amount of profit.

On the other hand, cash flow is a neutral metric, as it measures the liquidity created or absorbed as a result of inflows and outflows. Figure 3.14 shows the cash flow statement.

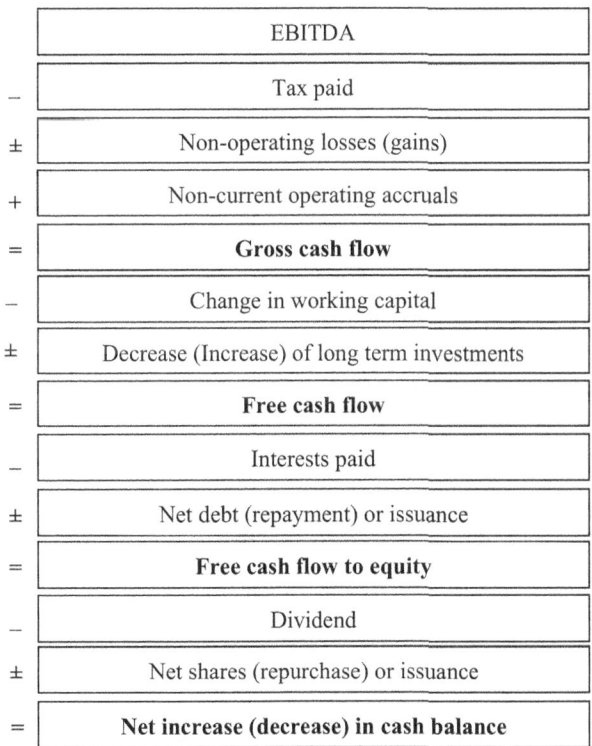

Fig. 3.14 Cash flow statement

3.7 Ratio Analysis

The value of the firm is determined by its ability to achieve a profit and operate under efficient financial conditions. Both these elements are influenced by the ability to:

1. operate efficiently (profitability);
2. repay debts (liquidity management);
3. maintain a balanced financial structure (financial strategy);
4. adequately remunerate the shareholders (dividend policies).

Based on the reclassified financial statement, the ratio analysis should provide the valuer with useful information regarding the four aspects mentioned above.

Numerous ratios have been identified in the literature and through professional practice. The most relevant ratios are examined in the following pages.

3.7.1 Profitability

Profitability measures the firm's aptitude to produce a profit that is sufficient to cover costs and remunerate investments. There is no right profitability level in absolute terms. Indeed, profitability must be seen in relation to various elements, such as:

1. operating risk;
2. financial structure;
3. amount and quality of the capital employed;
4. business life cycle;
5. general operating performance;
6. time horizon.

First, *return must be consistent with the risk* incurred to undertake a specific project. In general, the greater the risk, the higher the return should be, although there is no constant relationship linking the two variables. The risk appetite is linked to elements that are difficult to measure, such as strategy, market positioning, characteristics of the industry, leadership style, and so on.

Second, return must take into account the firm's *financial structure* as profit must enable the repayment of debt and the remuneration of equity; in other words, profit must satisfy both lenders and shareholders. For lenders, the remuneration is based on a contract that establishes the duration and the interest rate of the loan. For shareholders, the remuneration must be proportional to the risk assumed and the return offered by alternative investments.

The *amount* and *quality of the capital employed* must also be considered. Profit must adequately remunerate investments. The higher the investments, the greater the return must be; a profit of $10 can be considered remarkable if obtained with an investment of $100, but modest if obtained with an investment of $1000. Furthermore, profitability must also be examined in terms of quality. Assets that give the firm a competitive advantage (such as trademarks, patents, goodwill, etc.) must be more profitable compared to assets that do not have similar characteristics.

Furthermore, the level of profitability is closely linked to the *business life cycle*. A business in the development stage, with growth prospects, tends to achieve a higher profitability than mature and consolidated businesses; a valuer should always compare the characteristics of the target company with industry comparables.

The *general economic trend* can also influence the company's results. For example, a crisis in the industry adversely affects the profitability of all companies in that industry; a favorable cycle also benefits the laggards.

Finally, the *time horizon* should be considered. Depending on the business, there may be a significant mismatch between the time the investment is made and the time it generates a return. For example, for pharmaceutical companies, investments in R&D take a long time before satisfactory profits can be achieved; in this case, return cannot be assessed in the short term, but only by considering an appropriate time horizon.

The main profitability ratios are the following:

- ROE (return on equity);
- ROA (return on assets);
- ROI (return on investment);
- EBITDA/EBIT margin;
- Turnover.

3.7.1.1 Return on Equity (ROE)

ROE is the ratio of net income to shareholder's equity:

$$ROE = \frac{Net\ Income}{Shareholder's\ Equity}$$

ROE measures the remuneration of shareholders. For example, if a company achieves a net income of $10 with shareholder's equity of $100, the ROE is 10% (= $10/$100); this is a theoretical return, as the shareholders do not actually receive $10. In practice, only a portion of the net income is paid out as dividend; usually companies retain some of the earnings to be reinvested in their core business, to create growth opportunities, or to pay debt. Generally, the more dividends are distributed, the less earnings are retained.

Sometimes it is useful comparing ROE with retention ratio, which is the portion of earnings kept in the business as retained earnings:

$$\text{Retention Ratio} = 1 - \text{Dividend Payout Ratio}$$

For example, if the dividend payout ratio = 0.45 (i.e. 45% of net income is distributed to the shareholders), the retention ratio = 0.55 (i.e. 55% of the net income is retained by the company).

ROE reflects the adequacy of net income compared to equity, taking into account the risk assumed by the shareholders: a generic market risk and a specific risk that depends on the characteristics of the company and the industry. A priori defining what an appropriate return should be is not possible, since it varies according to the industry and the risk appetite; however, it is reasonable to state that an appropriate return must be at least greater than the cost of capital, which is conventionally measured by the CAPM, capital asset pricing model (see Sect. 4.4):

$$\text{ROE} - \text{CAPM} > 0$$

If ROE is lower than CAPM, it means the company cannot remunerate risk; in the long run this negatively affects the creation of value.

In the short term, ROE may be lower than the CAPM, for example, in a start-up or turnaround stage; if this circumstance persists over time and the valuer has good reasons to believe this trend cannot be reversed, the valuer must take this into account in the valuation process.

Since each sector has an average ROE that depends on the characteristics of the business, the valuer must compare the target company's ROE with that of a homogeneous peer group.

3.7.1.2 ROI (Return on Investments) and ROA (Return on Assets)

ROE measures profitability for the shareholders. ROI, on the other hand, measures the firm's profitability, that is, the adequacy of operating profit with respect to the capital employed. The adequacy of ROI changes according to the industry; each company has assets proportionate to its operating needs, size, business, financial structure, and so on. For example, the level of EBIT required to remunerate the assets of a manufacturing company is different from that required to remunerate the assets of a service company.

ROI is calculated as the ratio of EBIT to the amount of business assets, as considered in Sect. 3.4:

$$ROI = \frac{EBIT}{Business\ Assets}$$

ROA is a ratio similar to ROI, but it has net income in the numerator and total assets in the denominator:

$$ROA = \frac{Net\ Income}{Total\ Assets}$$

Both ratios enable us to assess the adequacy of income (operating income for ROI and net income for ROA) with respect to investments, taking into account the risk assumed.

Although for both ratios, an adequate level of remuneration cannot a priori be established, it is reasonable to state that it must at least be higher than both the cost of equity and the cost of debt, which are conventionally measured by the weighted average cost of capital (WACC, see Sect. 4.6):

$$ROI(ROA) - WACC > 0$$

A ROI (or ROA) lower than the WACC means that the company cannot remunerate risk.

Valuers will certainly benefit from comparing the ROI and ROA of the target company with the ROI and ROA of a peer group.

3.7.1.3 Differences Between ROE, ROA, and ROI

The above profitability ratios provide complementary information and differ in terms of "perspective": the ROE's perspective is *equity side*, that is, its purpose is to calculate the remuneration of *equity*; ROI and ROA, on the other hand, have an *asset-side* perspective, and their purpose is to calculate the remuneration of investments.

Let us consider, for example, the financial statements shown in Fig. 3.15.

The ROE provides an answer to the following question: to what extent has shareholder's equity been remunerated? By comparing net income ($12) to equity ($100) you get an ROE of 12.00% ($12/$100). As mentioned, this is a potential return, given that the company does not fully distribute its net income.

On the other hand, ROI and ROA reply to a different question: how much is the ROI, which is financed in part by equity and in part by debt?

If the objective is to measure total profitability, the ROA should be used, calculated as the ratio of net income ($12) to total assets ($700) and amounting to 1.71% ($12/$700).

If, on the other hand, we want to identify operating profitability, the ROI is used, which is calculated as the ratio of EBIT ($30) to the value of business assets ($200), calculated as shown in Fig. 3.16. The ROI is 15.00% ($30/$200).

Finally, if we want to reply to the question "what is the company's profitability?", there are three possible answers:

- shareholder's profitability (ROE) was 12.00%;
- operating profitability (ROI) was 15.00%;
- total profitability (ROA) was 1.71%.

No one profitability is "truer" than another; as they all provide a representation of one single reality through different perspectives. The valuer's task is to put together a puzzle made up of many pieces; each of them provides a contribution to obtain a clear picture.

3.7.1.4 EBITDA/EBIT Margin

EBITDA margin and EBIT margin are measures of a company's operating profitability as a percentage of its total sales:

ASSETS	LIABILITIES
Operating non-current assets $200	Equity $100
	Operating non-current liabilities $150
Operating l current assets $300	Operating current liabilities $150
	Financial non-current liabilities $200
Financial non-current assets $150	
	Financial current liabilities $100
Financial current assets $ 50	
$700	**$700**

Income statement	
Sales	$120
− Operating expenses	($75)
= **EBITDA**	**$45**
− Amortization	($15)
= **EBIT**	**$30**
− Interest expenses	($10)
= **Income Before Taxes**	**$20**
− Taxes	($8)
= **Net Income**	**$12**

Fig. 3.15 Example of financial statement

$$\text{EBITDA Margin} = \frac{\text{EBITDA}}{\text{Sales}}$$

$$\text{EBIT Margin} = \frac{\text{EBIT}}{\text{Sales}}$$

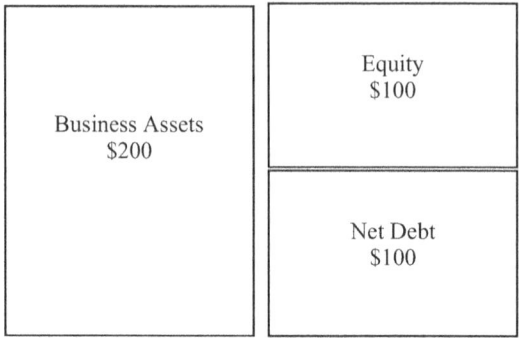

Fig. 3.16 Business assets

In the income statement of Fig. 3.15, the EBITDA margin is 37.50% ($45/$120) and the EBIT margin is 25.00% ($30/$120).

This information can be read in two ways. Taking the EBIT margin as a benchmark, for each $100 of sales the company generates $25 of operating income, which is used to pay for interest expenses, dividends, and taxes, as well as to finance the business. In a complementary perspective, every $100 of sales the company incurs $75 of operating costs.

Identifying a suitable value for the EBITDA margin and the EBIT margin is difficult, as return depends on both internal efficiency and external market conditions. The first affects the ability to operate in an economically advantageous way, by containing costs and generating adequate revenues; the latter affects sales prices, purchase costs (of materials, goods, and services), commercial costs, and so on. Thus, both ratios are influenced by both the business model and the characteristics of the industry.

The EBITDA margin and the EBIT margin have a different degree of reliability.

As it only considers operating costs, the EBITDA margin is not influenced by accounting policies. The EBIT margin also considers amortization and depreciation costs. These costs are more dependent on accounting policies and affect EBIT, especially in investment-intensive companies.

Therefore, the EBITDA margin provides a more neutral result and allows for better comparability with a peer group, as it does not consider the influence of investments, which may differ, including between companies in the same industry.

For valuers, the EBITDA/EBIT margin is perhaps the most representative ratio, as it provides an indication of both the efficiency and the profitability of a company over time.

In the DCF method, for example, by comparing the historical EBITDA/EBIT margins with those contained in the business plan, the valuer may face potentially anomalous situations. For example, an unjustified improvement in efficiency measured by an increase in EBITDA margin could be a sign of poor reliability of the plan, if no specific actions are planned to justify the improvement.

An analysis of the historical EBITDA/EBIT margins is equally essential in the multiples method, given that, from an asset-side perspective, the value of the firm is directly calculated based on these performance measures.

3.7.1.5 Turnover Ratio

Each company requires a certain level of investments based on the business model, the characteristics of the industry, and the size of the company. In the long term, sales must be consistent with the assets; if this is not the case, either the management is unable to properly use the assets, or the assets are excessive compared to operating needs.

Turnover tells us how many dollars of sales have been made for each dollar invested in assets. Turnover is equal to the ratio of sales to total assets:

$$\text{Turnover} = \frac{\text{Sales}}{\text{Total Assets}}$$

The higher the turnover, the more efficient the use of assets. For example, two companies, A and B, have the same level of investments (total assets = $100); company A achieved sales of $400 and company B of $550. Company A's turnover is 4.0 ($400/$100); company B's turnover is 5.5 ($550/$100): this means that, for various reasons (greater efficiency, more consistent strategies, more skillful management, etc.), company B has been able to use its investments in a better way than company A.

Sometimes it is useful to calculate the turnover of individual assets (Fig. 3.17).

3.7.2 Liquidity Management

Liquidity analysis shows a company's ability to cope with current liabilities through current assets (inventory, receivables, cash, etc.).

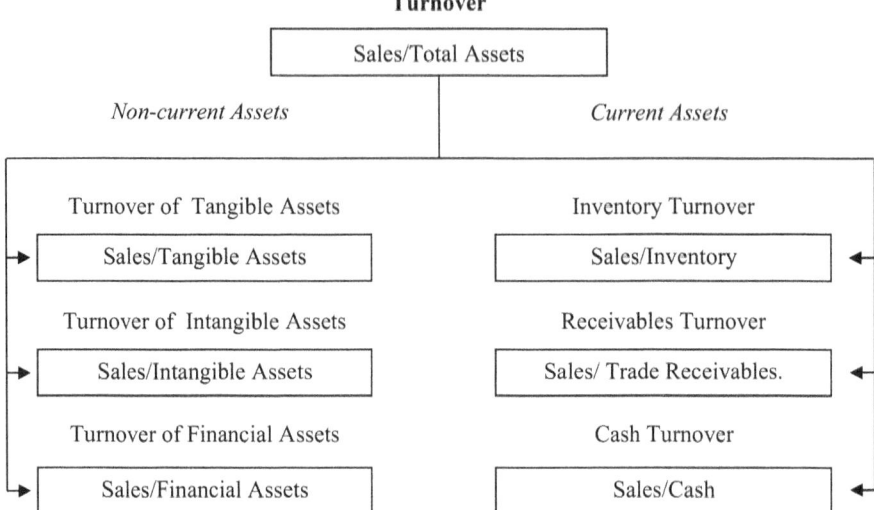

Fig. 3.17 Turnover of individual assets

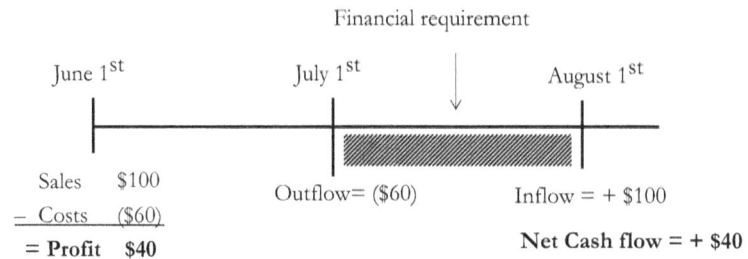

Fig. 3.18 Mismatch between profit and cash flow

While profitability analysis helps gain a better understanding of costs and revenues, liquidity analysis helps understand inflows and outflows better. In the long run, revenues and inflows, as well as costs and outflows, tend to reconcile. In the short term, however, there may be a mismatch between revenues and inflows and between costs and outflows. This concept can be explained with an example (Fig. 3.18).

On June 1st a company:

- buys a product for $60; the payment will be made on the 1st of July;
- sells the same product for $100; the price will be collected on the 1st of August.

From an economic standpoint the transaction generates a profit on the 1st of June (sales $100 − costs $60 = profit $40). However, this is a potential value, since, at that time, the company did not pay nor collect anything.

On the 1st of July, the company has an outflow of $60. Assuming that the company does not own cash, it is forced to borrow.

It is only on the 1st of August, when the $100 inflow takes place, that the company can repay the loan and "actually" make its profit.

The example shows the effect of just one transaction. In practice, the management of a business involves a succession of transactions, so that the balance must be assessed as a whole, based on how those transactions interact within the business cycle.

This example helps us understand that there is a natural mismatch between revenues/costs and inflows/outflows. The larger the temporal gap, the less significant the profit, which refers to a result that has been earned but not actually realized.

Thus, liquidity analysis provides us with a better understanding of the short-term financial trend. The most useful ratios are the following:

- ratios that measure short-term liquidity;
- ratios that measure operating working capital turnover.

3.7.2.1 Short-Term Liquidity Ratios

Short-term liquidity ratios measure a company's ability to pay debt and its margin of safety. Current liabilities are analyzed in relation to current assets in order to evaluate the overall liquidity. Although solvency is not directly correlated to liquidity, liquidity ratios present a preliminary expectation regarding the solvency of a company.

Specifically, there are three ratios that increasingly measure the company's margin of safety:

$$\text{Current Ratio} = \frac{\text{Current Assets}}{\text{Current Liabilities}}$$

$$\text{Quick Ratio} = \frac{\text{Cash and Marketable Securities} + \text{Net Trade Receivables}}{\text{Current Liabilities}}$$

$$\text{Cash Ratio} = \frac{\text{Cash and Marketable Securities}}{\text{Current Liabilities}}$$

If the ratio is equal to or greater than 1, a company is potentially able to pay its current liabilities. Conversely, a ratio that is less than 1 means that current liabilities are higher than current assets; in this case, a company does not have sufficient current assets to meet its short-term obligations. In case of need, the company could sell its non-current assets, but this is more easily said than done; in this situation, the regular conduct of the business could be undermined.

In general, short-term liquidity ratios may be assessed by comparing the target company's results with those of a peer group.

Let us now examine each ratio in detail.

The *current ratio* shows whether a company is able to meet its current liabilities by using all its current assets: cash and marketable securities, trade receivables, inventory. The propensity of being turned into cash is obviously different across these asset classes.

Cash and marketable securities are liquid by nature.

Trade receivables may have contractual deadlines or deadlines arising from the specific characteristics of the sector in which they operate. Their marketability may not be immediate, especially in sectors where collection times are on average long or, otherwise, do not allow for the immediate repayment of a debt. In some cases, the company can collect receivables ahead of the original deadline by entering into commercial agreements (e.g. by offering customers better conditions for future supplies or by paying for transport costs), or by obtaining advances from a bank or a factor company.

Selling the inventory is potentially more complex.

First, not all inventories can be sold in the same way. Some may be partially obsolete, or their usefulness may be limited to the company that owns them. This is the case, for example, of spare parts for machines that are no longer on the market: they are essential for the proper functioning of production, but they have a very low market value and it is not easy to sell them. In other cases, although the goods can be sold in theory, the sale might be complex due to their intrinsic characteristics. For example, a company that makes food products may face difficulties in reselling raw materials such as flour, oil, and sugar, as their quality is linked to a consumption deadline and optimal maintenance conditions, which can only be partially proved.

Secondly, although the inventories are entirely marketable, a sale could undermine the company's efficiency, as the smooth running of the business requires maintaining a minimum level of stock. Inventories partially qualify as current assets because their turnover is relatively rapid (also based on the specific industry) and partially as non-current assets, as a minimum amount of stock is necessary to run the business. Therefore, selling the inventory can be more complex than liquidating a trade receivable or marketable securities, as the impact on the firm's efficiency is greater.

The *quick ratio* only considers cash, marketable securities, and receivables. This ratio provides more reliable information on the actual ability to pay current liabilities. By excluding the value of the inventory, this ratio focuses on that part of current assets that can be more easily sold in a short time.

More easily, however, does not mean immediately. For example, the early collection of trade receivables with respect to their contractual maturity may be complex, as the counterparty may not be willing to accept. In addition, the early collection almost always involves transaction costs, due to the commissions charged by the factor or the bank.

The *cash ratio* shows a firm's ability to meet its current liabilities with cash and marketable securities. Usually this ratio is less than 1.

3.7.2.2 Operating Working Capital Turnover

The operating working capital turnover depends on the trade receivables turnover, trade payables turnover, and the inventory turnover.

Generally, when collection times are shorter than payment times the firm is more efficient. This means that inflows occur before the outflows and, when the firm has to pay its debts, it already has the necessary cash. On the other hand, when payment times are shorter than collection times, a company is forced to borrow money.

The working capital turnover is only partially dependent on management's choices, as it is influenced by various factors such as business model, industry characteristics, commercial policies, contractual strength, and so on. However, working capital provides useful information for managing relations with customers and suppliers and production timing in an informed manner.

The working capital cycle can be broken down into three components:

- the trade receivables turnover;
- the trade payables turnover;
- the inventory turnover.

The sum of these three turnovers defines the average length of the business cycle.

The *trade receivables turnover* measures the average deferral period granted to customers, that is, the period between the moment the revenue is recognized and the moment the price is collected. It is calculated as follows:

$$\text{Trade Receivables Turnover} = 360 / \frac{\text{Sales}}{\text{Trade Receivables}}$$

The trade receivables turnover is calculated by dividing the working days in the year (e.g. 360, but they can be changed according to the sector and the business) by the ratio of sales to trade receivables.

For example, at the end of the year XYZ company recorded sales and trade receivables of $1000 and $120, respectively. By applying the formula, the trade receivables turnover is 43 days, as follows:

$$\text{Trade Receivables Turnover} = 360 \text{ days} / \frac{\$1000}{\$120} = 43 \text{ days}$$

This means that it takes 43 days between the day of sale and the day of collection.

The *trade payables turnover* measures the average deferral period granted by suppliers, that is, the period between the moment the cost is recognized and the moment the price is paid. It is calculated as follows:

$$\text{Trade Payables Turnover} = 360 / \frac{\text{Purchases}}{\text{Trade Payables}}$$

The trade payables turnover is calculated by dividing the working days in the year (e.g. 360) by the ratio of purchases (e.g. raw materials, services) to trade payables.

For example, if XYZ company has purchases and trade payables of $400 and $36, respectively, the trade payables turnover is 32 days, as follows:

$$\text{Trade Payables Turnover} = 360 \text{ days} / \frac{\$400}{\$36} = 32 \text{ days}$$

This means that it takes 32 days between the purchase day and the payment day.

The *inventory turnover* measures for how many days raw materials and finished products are kept idle in the firm before being used for production and sale, respectively. This ratio refers to the inventories of commercial and industrial companies, but is not appropriate to calculate the turnover of specific types of inventories, such as those originating from construction contracts.

The raw material inventory and the products inventory require a distinct calculation.

The raw materials inventory turnover is calculated as follows:

$$\text{Inventory Turnover (Raw Materials)} = 360 / \frac{\text{Cost of Goods Sold}}{\text{Inventory (Raw Materials)}}$$

The cost of goods sold is equal to:

$$\text{Cost of Goods Sold} = \text{Opening stock} + \text{Purchases} - \text{Closing stock}$$

For example, XYZ company has an opening stock of $20, a closing stock (which corresponds to the inventory value) of $25, and purchases of $300. The cost of goods is calculated as follows:

$$\text{Cost of Goods} = \$20 + \$300 - \$25 = \$295$$

The raw materials inventory turnover is 31 days:

$$\text{Inventory Turnover (Raw Materials)} = 360 / \frac{\$295}{\$25} = 31 \text{ days}$$

This means that the raw materials stay in the inventory for 31 days, before "entering" the production cycle.

The products inventory turnover is calculated as follows:

$$\text{Inventory Turnover (Products)} = 360 / \frac{\text{Cost of Sales}}{\text{Inventory (Products)}}$$

The cost of sales is calculated by adding the cost of goods sold, transportation, depreciation, direct labor, commissions, and other direct costs.

For example, at the end of the year, XYZ company recorded products in inventory amounting to $30. Also, transportation costs = $15, direct labor costs = $80, amortization = $200, and maintenance costs = $10. Table 3.1 shows the calculation of the cost of sales.

Therefore, the products inventory turnover is 18 days:

$$\text{Inventory Turnover (Products)} = 360 / \frac{\$600}{\$30} = 18 \text{ days}$$

Table 3.1 Cost of sales

	Cost of goods sold	$295
+	Transportation costs	$15
+	Direct labor costs	$80
+	Amortization	$200
+	Maintenance costs	$10
=	**Cost of sales**	**$600**

Table 3.2 Operating working capital turnover

	Trade receivables turnover	$43
+	Trade payables turnover	$31
+	Inventory turnover (raw materials)	$18
−	Inventory turnover (products)	($31)
=	**Operating working capital turnover**	**$59**

If we consider the trade receivables turnover, the trade payables turnover, and the inventory turnover in combination, we can calculate the operating working capital turnover of XYZ company (Table 3.2).

This means that, on average, it takes 59 days between the time of payment and the time of collection; during this period the company must borrow the necessary liquidity. The higher the number of days, the greater the amount the company needs to borrow to meet the temporary lack of liquidity.

Generally, part of the liquidity generated by a business cycle is used to finance the next one, thereby ensuring the firm's financial balance. In any case, increasingly more favorable commercial conditions must be negotiated and production efficiency must be raised, in order to increase the inventory turnover.

Considering the figures in the example, the firm would greatly benefit if it could postpone the payment of payables from 32 to 40 days and move forward the collection of receivables from 43 to 30 days: the length of the business cycle would decrease from 59 to 39 days, resulting in lower liquidity needs and interest expenses.

Valuers must carefully examine the historic operating working capital turnover, especially when applying the DCF method. Cash flows depend on operating working capital turnover to a large extent and any expected improvements or worsening must be assessed taking into account the trade receivables turnover, the trade payables turnover, and the inventory turnover.

3.7.3 Financial Strategy

The objective of a firm's financial strategy is to analyze the balance between financial sources (equity and debt). The financing mix is a key variable that must be carefully monitored.

Every manager's dream is to mainly conduct business using equity; this provides the company with higher cash flows for investments and saves interest expenses, and higher dividends can be distributed. However, equity alone cannot finance growth, especially in sectors that require a high level of investment and are characterized by high volatility.

A debt-equity mix is therefore essential for the development of a firm. However, there are no hard and fast rules establishing what is optimal financial leverage, as a number of factors come into play, such as risk appetite, characteristics of the business, extent of collateral, structure of the investments.

A management with higher risk appetite is probably more willing to stress financial leverage by resorting to a higher degree of debt. On the one hand, this enables the firm to make higher investments or better support existing ones; on the other hand, it leads to a higher cashout, to the detriment of dividends. A high level of debt can be sustainable in the short term. In the long run, however, investment financed by debt must produce sufficient cash flows to repay it.

The characteristics of the business are another important variable to consider. In theory, capital-intensive firms require greater investment in non-current assets and therefore greater recourse to debt than service companies. In practice, it may happen that the same level of cash flow is absorbed by the day-to-day business in service companies. For example, the cost of human capital in a large consulting firm could be similar to the capital expenditures of a manufacturing company. The difference is that labor cost is recognized in the income statement, while capital expenditures are reported in the balance sheet.

The extent of the guarantees is another aspect to consider. When a bank grants funding, it relies not only on the company's ability to repay it over time, but also on appropriate guarantees. After the subprime crisis, partly caused by loans that were not adequately backed up by guarantees, this aspect has become increasingly relevant. This is especially true in Europe, where guarantees have always been a prerequisite for obtaining financing from banks.

Finally, the financing that best fits the characteristics of the company and the type of investments must be identified. A financial structure is balanced when the length of the investments and that of the loans are consistent. In other words, when:

1. non-current assets are financed by non-current debt;
2. current assets are financed by current debt;

The reason is obvious. For example, to finance the purchase of a plant, the management must take on debt that has repayment terms and methods in line with the characteristics and useful life of the plant: a loan, an operating or finance lease, a corporate bond, and so on. Conversely, to finance the purchase of raw materials, management must consider short-term debt.

This means that there must be a timing correlation between debt and investment. Figure 3.19 shows the theoretical representation of a balanced relation.

In a balanced situation, non-current assets are equal to long-term sources, consisting of both equity and non-current debt. Similarly, current assets are equal to current debt. In this situation, investments are financed with sources of similar duration.

In practice, a "perfect" balance is difficult to achieve. More specifically, two alternative situations may occur.

Long-term sources may finance both non-current assets and part of current assets. This means that a part of current assets is covered by long-term sources, as shown in Fig. 3.20.

Alternatively, current debt may finance both current assets and part of non-current assets. This means that a portion of non-current assets is covered by current debt, as shown in Fig. 3.21.

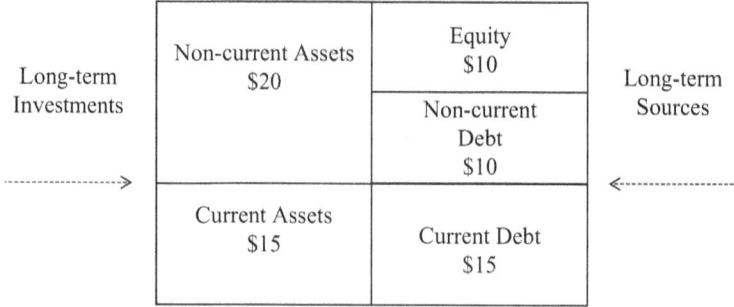

Fig. 3.19 Balance between investments and financial sources

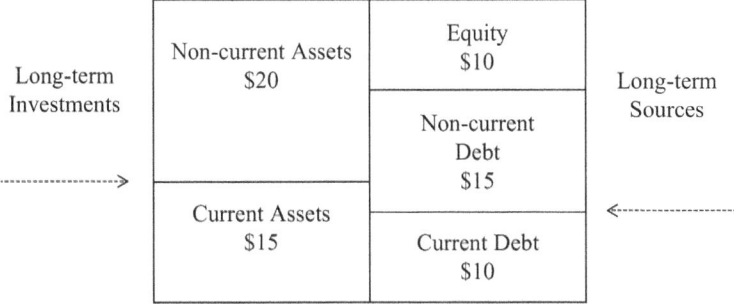

Fig. 3.20 A part of current assets is covered by long-term sources

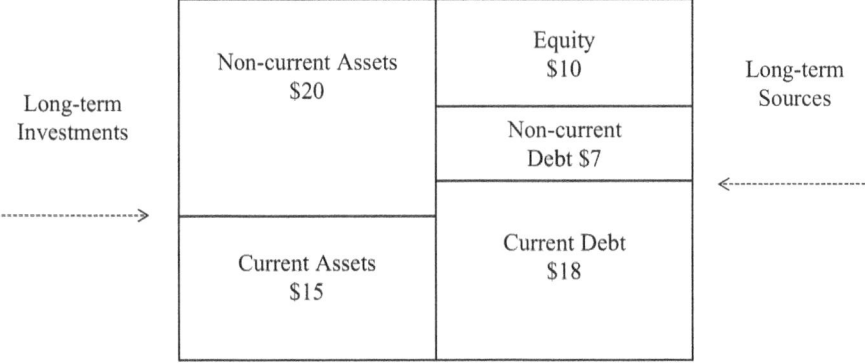

Fig. 3.21 A part of non-current assets is covered by current debt

In both cases the correlation between sources and uses is not "perfectly" balanced.

However, the first case (Fig. 3.20) is preferable to the second (Fig. 3.21), since a part of current assets is covered by long-term sources. This means, for example, that a loan is partially used to finance inventory or trade receivables.

In the second case, a part of current debt covers a portion of non-current assets; this means, for example, that the purchase of a plant is partially financed using current debt. This means that debt that must be repaid within a year is used to purchase an asset that has a life horizon of a few years. In practice, it is like enrolling at university requesting a student loan that must be repaid within 12 months.

Obviously, the former situation is more sustainable than the latter.

Valuers must carefully examine these aspects, in order to assess how the target company's financial structure fits its business model.

Having said that, the firm's financial strategy can be examined through the following ratios:

- Equity-to-capital ratio;
- Debt-to-capital ratio;
- Debt-to-equity ratio;
- Debt-to sales ratio.

3.7.3.1 Equity-to-Capital Ratio

The equity-to-capital ratio is calculated as the ratio of equity and total assets; it measures the portion of investments financed by equity and shows a firm's level of financial self-sufficiency:

$$\text{Equity-to-Capital Ratio} = \frac{\text{Equity}}{\text{Total Assets}}$$

The higher the ratio, the greater its independence from lenders. The result must be read taking into account the specific industry, the characteristics of the business, the level of investments and their turnover, the company's life stage, and so on.

In general, high equity is a positive indicator. A firm with a balanced financial leverage has greater cash flows for its investments and to pay dividends; a firm that places greater emphasis on financial leverage absorbs a higher level of cash flows to repay its debt.

3.7.3.2 Debt-to-Capital Ratio

The debt-to-capital ratio is complementary to the ratio examined above; it is calculated as the ratio of debt (current debt + non-current debt) to total assets:

$$\text{Debt-to-Capital Ratio} = \frac{\text{Current Debt} + \text{Non-current Debt}}{\text{Total Assets}}$$

This ratio measures the part of investments financed by debt. The higher the ratio, the more the firm depends on debt. The level of debt is linked to the business model, the characteristics of the sector, to extent of the guarantees, the ability to produce adequate cash flows.

3.7.3.3 Debt-to-Equity Ratio (D/E)

The debt-to-equity ratio is calculated as the ratio of debt to equity:

$$\text{Debt-to-Equity Ratio} = \frac{\text{Current Debt} + \text{Non-current Debt}}{\text{Equity}}$$

This ratio measures the relationship between debt and equity; the greater the ratio, the higher the exposure to third-party lenders. This ratio must be examined in the light of industry benchmarks.

According to some financial analysis textbooks, the optimal level of this ratio is 1, that is, when equity and debt are equal. In practice, there are sectors in which a structurally high D/E ratio is inherent in the type of business, as is the case for real estate.

The D/E ratio is the most used ratio in financial markets to describe companies' financial strategies.

3.7.3.4 Debt-to-Sales Ratio

Financial leverage is a way to expand the business and achieve a certain level of revenues. Debt, as long as it is sustainable, is necessary for a firm's development and to ensure adequate profits. However, there is a limit beyond which debt reduces its propulsive drive and eats away at income due to interest expenses.

Thus, the relationship between debt and sales must be carefully monitored through the debt-to-sales ratio: this ratio reflects the level of debt necessary to achieve a certain level of sales:

$$\text{Debt-to-Sales Ratio} = \frac{\text{Debt}}{\text{Sales}}$$

The lower the ratio, the lower the need to borrow to support sales. This ratio must be examined in the light of comparable firms.

Interest coverage is another ratio that links the income statement with debt. It is equal to the ratio of EBIT to interest expenses:

$$\text{Interest Coverage} = \frac{\text{EBIT}}{\text{Interest expenses}}$$

This ratio shows the ability of EBIT to repay interest expenses; accordingly, it is positive when it is greater than 1. This is a theoretical measure, as only a portion of EBIT turns into cash flows in time to cover interest expenses.

The total debt coverage is a variant of this ratio and is calculated as follows:

$$\text{Total Debt Coverage} = \frac{\text{Free Cash Flow}}{\text{Debt to be paid in the year} + \text{Interests expenses}}$$

This ratio assesses the firm's ability to repay its short-term debt and interest expenses through the free cash flow. This ratio is positive when it is greater than 1.

3.7.4 Dividend Policies

A company distributes dividends both to remunerate its shareholders and to attract new investors, if it is a publicly traded company.

In business valuations, the distribution of dividends is often disregarded. Only the dividend discount model (DDM) specifically focuses on this aspect (see Sect. 4.6). Indeed:

(a) the DCF method calculates the value of a firm on the basis of the free cash flow (unlevered approach) and the free cash flow to equity (levered approach); neither of the two approaches considers the outflows arising from the payment of dividends in its calculation framework;
(b) the market multiple method tends to disregard the effect of dividends, in both the asset-side approach and the equity-side approach.

However, the potential impact of dividends on the value of a firm is significant. For this reason, valuers should consider the sustainable growth rate, which is measured as:

$$\text{Sustainable Growth Rate} = \text{ROE} \times (1 - \text{Dividend Payout Ratio})$$

The dividend payout ratio is calculated as the ratio of cash outflows arising from the payment of dividends and net income:

$$\text{Dividend Payout Ratio} = \frac{\text{Cash Dividend Paid}}{\text{Net Income}}$$

Table 3.3 Dividend payout ratio and sustainable growth rate

	Company A	Company B	Company C
ROE	10%	10%	10%
Cash dividend paid	$30	$40	$50
Net income	$100	$100	$100
Dividend payout ratio	0.3	0.4	0.5
Sustainable growth rate	7%	6%	5%

This ratio measures how much of net income is distributed to shareholders. The higher the dividend paid, the lower the cash flow available to make investments, pay off debts, and optimize the operating working capital turnover. There is therefore a correlation between the dividends paid and the growth prospects of a company, which the various valuation approaches tend to disregard.

The effect of dividends policies can be easily understood if we consider three companies with the same ROE (10%) and the same net income ($100), but with a different dividend payout ratio (Table 3.3).

Though having the same net income, company A distributes less dividends than B and C. It thus retains a higher amount of cash flow, which it can use to sustain its growth. Therefore, its sustainable growth rate is higher than that of the other two companies.

Of course, it would be too simplistic to say that a lower distribution of dividends facilitates a firm's development, as in the long run shareholders and potential investors could divert their investments elsewhere. Thus, the appropriate trade-off between shareholder remuneration and earnings retention has to be found.

3.8 Financial Statement Analysis in Distressed Firms

The valuation of distressed firms is a complex activity, as the natural cause-effect mechanisms on which valuation methods are based can be significantly altered.

In these situations, the financial statement analysis is all the more essential, as it enables valuers to analyze the state of the crisis, the prospects for turnaround, and the levers that can be used to restore efficiency.

Valuers must be aware that valuation results must be read from a different perspective compared to companies in good health. Notably, the financial statement analysis of distressed firms requires some very specific precautions.

Firstly, the quality of accounting data must be checked. In the periods preceding a crisis, the company managers may adopt different (or even dangerous) accounting policies in an attempt not to alarm investors, lenders, and suppliers.

Secondly, selecting a small number of ratios is preferable, provided they are significant and consistent with the size and complexity of the business. Too high a number of ratios risks producing conflicting data and generates "background noise" that negatively affects the quality of the analysis.

Thirdly, the analysis must be based on an adequate number of years. That is, an adequate number of financial statements must be examined to find elements that can help explain how the crisis originated and how it is evolving.

Finally, again from a comparative perspective, the data must be compared with those of a peer group. Clearly, the way we look at value is different depending on whether the crisis affects the entire industry or just the individual company.

3.8.1 How the Crisis Shows Up

A crisis can originate from a lack of cash flow or from a contraction in revenues. Although it is difficult to generalize, a crisis tends to work its way forward as a vicious circle, as follows:

- investments in non-current assets tend to slow down, or at worst they are stopped; the slowdown negatively affects the asset turnover, causing obsolescence and, consequently, an overall loss of efficiency;
- at the same time, the operating working capital turnover gets worse and meeting short-term debts becomes more difficult;
- the lack of cash flow leads to new debt in order to meet daily obligations;
- failure to meet deadlines with suppliers leads to a progressive worsening of supply conditions (in terms of quantities, payment terms, timing);
- the profit margin tends to decrease and covering fixed costs becomes increasingly difficult; consequent cost cutting can further compromise the business cycle.

As mentioned, a rapid chain of events may sometimes trigger a spiral that rapidly escalates to the point that it becomes impossible to control. Given the circumstances, valuers must be able to examine the main value drivers that affect the firm's value.

3.8.2 Impact of the Crisis on the Main Ratios

As mentioned, the value of a firm is influenced by the ability to:

- operate efficiently (profitability);
- repay debts (liquidity management);
- maintain a balanced financial structure (financial strategy);
- adequately remunerate the shareholders (dividend policies).

The impact of the crisis on the main ratios is examined below.

3.8.2.1 Profitability

The objective of the income statement analysis is to verify the firm's ability to produce sufficient revenues to cover costs, generate profits, and remunerate investments.

Usually, a crisis causes a decrease in revenues and, consequently, covering costs becomes more difficult.

The causes can be linked to inadequate pricing policies compared to those of competitors, obsolete and no longer appealing products, difficulty in achieving minimum sales volumes, and so on. The decrease in revenues triggers consequences that affect the other income statement items.

First, covering fixed costs becomes more difficult, as they are independent of production volumes. In a crisis situation, the contribution margin, which is the difference between revenues and variable costs, tends to decline; consequently, the resources to meet fixed costs also decrease.

The decrease in revenues is not necessarily proportional to the decrease in net income. Indeed, if revenues decrease by 10%, net income does not automatically decrease by 10%, but, depending on the amount of fixed costs, the impact may be non-proportional.

For example (Table 3.4), in "year n" a company shows the following amounts: revenues = $1000; variable costs = 40% of revenues (= $400); fixed costs = $550; net income = $50.

If in "year n + 1" revenues decrease by 10% ($900), variable costs will decrease proportionally ($360), but, with fixed costs being constant, net income falls from + $50 to −$10, contracting by −120%.

To achieve again the break-even point, the firm would have to:

- increase revenues;
- reduce fixed costs.

Table 3.4 Effect of a decrease in revenues

	Year n	Year n + 1	Difference (%)
Revenues	$1.000	$900	−10
Variable costs	($400)	($360)	−10
Fixed costs	($550)	($550)	0
Net income	$50	($10)	−120

Usually, in a crisis situation, the most immediate benefits can be achieved through a reduction in fixed costs, which means disposing of assets and employees and recovering efficiency by focusing on the core business. In these cases, extreme caution should be taken, as the loss of a critical success factor (trademark, plant, specially qualified employee) can have a negative impact on competitiveness and affect the firm's operations.

In a distressed situation some economic ratios may have a negative value as the firm reports losses.

ROE is usually negative, as net income is the first margin to be eroded in a distressed situation. This circumstance is not in itself necessarily alarming, especially if there are prospects for turnaround in the short term and if the amount of the loss is not relevant in proportion to the firm's size. If the ROE is negative, so is the ROA, which reflects the ability of net income to remunerate total assets.

The ROI, which reflects the profitability of the core business, may be either positive or negative. If it is positive, it means that the problem is related to high interest expenses; if it is negative, it means that there is a problem in the core business and the turnaround may be more difficult to implement. If the ROI is positive, so are the EBITDA margin, EBIT margin, and interest coverage; if it is negative, it means that not only is the core business not profitable, but the company is potentially unable to pay its interest expenses and risks becoming insolvent.

3.8.2.2 Liquidity Management

The purpose of a liquidity analysis is to identify the firm's ability to cope with short-term obligations. Liquidity is analyzed through:

- short-term liquidity;
- operating working capital turnover.

In a company in distressed situation both the quick ratio and the current ratio tend to be less than 1. If the value of the inventories is significant, the current ratio may be negative while the quick ratio is positive; in such a case, a company has potentially greater chances for a turnaround. If the quick ratio is also negative, the situation is more alarming, as not even through a hypothetical sale of the inventories will the firm be able to meet its short-term debt.

Operating working capital turnover is influenced by the trade receivables turnover, the trade payables turnover, and the inventory turnover.

These three components measure the average duration of the operating working capital turnover. The shorter the duration, the higher the number of production cycles a company completes in a year. Conversely, the longer the duration, the greater the risk of suffering from "financial stress", which tends to escalate during negative business cycles.

A crisis frequently triggers a contraction of revenues and liquidity, and not necessarily in this order, producing the effects that are summarized below (assuming a manufacturing company):

- first, the firm finds it more difficult to purchase raw materials, as suppliers tend to reduce supplies and impose tighter payment deadlines;
- the reduction in raw materials prevents the firm from regularly fulfilling its orders; this translates into delays in deliveries that can only be offset by offering higher discounts (with consequent negative effects on margins) and/or by extending customers further payment deferrals (which adversely affects short-term liquidity). When these circumstances persist, there is a high risk that customers will turn elsewhere to meet their needs;
- if the lack of liquidity causes delays in the repayment of a loan, the bank might decide to decrease or withdraw the credit lines:
  - in such a scenario, the company is less and less able to meet its obligations and ultimately risks becoming insolvent.

Therefore, valuers must monitor the operating working capital turnover, which is the most effective indicator to gauge the health of a company.

3.8.2.3 Financial Strategy

As mentioned, the firm's financial strategy examines the balance between financing sources (equity and debt) and investments.

The optimal financing mix is linked to the firm's development prospects.

In a distressed situation, financing choices are reduced. Firstly, shareholders are not willing to invest their money in a company unless they are likely to recover the investment. Secondly, banks may not be willing to grant new loans, while they may request the repayment of existing ones.

In this scenario, the equity-to-capital ratio tends to decrease, since the company's financial self-sufficiency is gradually declining. At the same time, due to an increase in payables, both the debt-to-capital ratio and the debt-to-equity ratio increase.

The debt-to-sales ratio may also deteriorate, as debts tend to increase, while sales decrease.

3.8.2.4 Dividend Policies

If net income is zero or significantly downsized, dividend policies are strongly constrained. Thus, calculating the sustainable growth rate and the dividend payout ratio makes little sense.

4

Income-Based Method

4.1 Introduction

According to the *income approach*, the value of the firm is calculated based on the cash flows the firm will be able to generate in the future. This method is also called the discounted cash flow (DCF) method. The value of the firm is equal to:

$$\text{Value of the firm} = \sum_{t=1}^{n} \frac{ECF_t}{(1+i)^t} + \frac{TV}{(1+i)^t}$$

where:

ECF = expected cash flows
i = discount rate
t = numbers of years in the future
TV = terminal value

The logic behind the income approach is that a rational operator is willing to assign a value to a business at least equal to the amount he or she can recover within an acceptable time horizon. In practice, if a person invests $1,000,000 to buy a company, that person expects to recover the investment in "t" years and to receive a reasonable remuneration as of year "t + 1". A time horizon of 5 years can be considered appropriate; few people would be willing to wait 25 years before they can recover their capital.

According to the Theory of Finance, the value of each financial asset depends on the cash flows generated during the remaining useful life of the asset, the distribution of such cash flows over time, and the uncertainty as to their actual realization.

In other words, a person is willing to invest money in a financial asset as long as the associated risk is adequate to his or her risk profile and the remuneration is in line with his or her expectations.

The elements of the formula are examined in the following pages:

1. Expected cash flows (Sect. 4.2);
2. Discount rate (Sect. 4.3–4.6);
3. Terminal value (TV) (Sect. 4.7).

4.2 Expected Cash Flows

The most critical aspect in the application of this method is estimating the ECFs. Since no one has a crystal ball, predicting future values is open to a certain degree of uncertainty. Such uncertainty is linked to various factors:

- characteristics and stability of the industry;
- management's ability to predict how the business will evolve;
- comparability between future and past results.

The *characteristics of the industry* influence the forecast of cash flows. In a stable industry, estimates are more reliable, while in an industry characterized by greater volatility, accurate estimates are difficult to make.

For example, the insurance sector allows for sufficiently reliable forecasts, as people basically tend to annually renew their health, home, and car insurance.

Technology-related sectors do not allow for equally accurate estimates, since changes may take place that suddenly alter development prospects.

Some industries tend to be stable, but may be exposed to short-term volatility, such as real estate; after years of growth and a slowdown due to the subprime crisis, the real estate market has resumed its historical growth trends.

Changes may be linked not only to the intrinsic characteristics of the sector, but to regulatory changes as well. For example, recent legislation has stipulated that only nickel-free metal accessories can be imported into China, as this metal is considered potentially harmful to health; this led firms to explore new alloys and galvanization processes. As a result, in a few years Bluclad, a company formed in 2008, has become the worldwide market leader in the galvanization processes for metal accessories in the fashion business.

Technological developments may also lead to significant changes. For example, in the automotive industry some players outside the industry, such as Google and Apple, are making significant investments to implement self-driving cars. As a result, car manufacturers must enter into alliances with partners that can provide the know-how necessary to develop similar projects.

Sometimes changes can also affect the business model. The development of Amazon and similar platforms, for example, has changed people's buying habits. There are products for which home delivery is easier, cheaper, and more convenient than buying them in a store. Toy's R Us, one of the world's biggest toy chains, closed down in 2017 due to competition from online sales. Some traditional businesses, on the other hand, took advantage of online platforms to increase their turnover. For example, more and more restaurants sign agreements with food delivery companies, such as Deliveroo; this enables them to acquire new customers and optimize their performance.

Based on the foregoing, we may conclude that forecasting future results can be extremely complex in all businesses and that *management must have the necessary skills to foresee potential developments.* An accurate calculation of ECFs starts from historical results and requires identifying development strategies that are consistent with the characteristics of the firm and the industry. Strategies must be translated into figures, which must then be checked for consistency against past trends, financial structure, organizational structure, and so on.

In this regard, defining "who does what" is a necessary step. Many business valuation textbooks dedicate large sections to cash flow prediction, assuming it is the valuer's task to perform this activity. In my opinion, it is not the valuer's task to estimate the ECFs, as valuers are not "insiders" and may not have the necessary information.

At most, valuers can provide support where the management is not able to formalize a business plan, but such contribution should be limited to the technical skills required to build a consistent cash flow statement.

In no case, however, should the valuer replace the management in the formulation of the ECFs. Valuers should merely verify that the assumptions underlying the business plan are consistent and that such plan is formally correct, so as to make sure the cash flows are plausible.

In this respect, one of the greatest risks is not that forecasts may "be wrong"; actually, it is quite normal that the ability to make forecasts does not exceed a period of 12/18 months, especially in highly volatile situations. The greatest risk is to forecast future cash flows that are significantly out of line with past cash flows, when there are no changes justifying them.

This is why the ECFs must be *compared with previous cash flows*.

It is not infrequent to see business plans that, despite modest past results, foresee a scenario where performance improves dramatically, without any plausible reasons justifying such change. Using their professional skepticism, valuers must verify the validity of the assumptions and examine the reasons for a potential improvement.

For example, in calculating free cash flow (FCF), the operating working capital turnover plays a decisive role. As seen in Chap. 3, this metrics depends on three variables: the trade receivables turnover, the trade payables turnover, and the inventory turnover.

An increase in cash flow may result from a reduction in collection days, an increase in payment days, or a faster inventory turnover. If the business plan assumes a decrease in collection days, the grounds for such assumption must be verified, for example, greater bargaining strength with customers, the use of new distribution channels, or a more aggressive discount policy. Likewise, an increase in payment days assumes that a renegotiation of agreements with suppliers has taken place. Finally, a better inventory turnover requires organizational change, the timing of which and required investments may vary according to the characteristics of the business.

Ultimately, a change in the operating working capital turnover that generates a positive impact on cash flows must be based on specific circumstances that are compatible with the characteristics of the firm.

Likewise, an increase in revenues exceeding the company's historical trend, a different impact of variable costs, or a significant reduction in fixed costs must all be adequately justified.

Therefore, an analysis of past results is in order. Through such analysis valuers can:

- understand the relation between past performance and future performance; and
- express an opinion on the consistency of ECFs.

4.2.1 Asset-Side and Equity-Side Valuation

The DCF method is based on the firm's ability to obtain cash flows that offer adequate remuneration. Who benefits from this remuneration? The shareholders are the main beneficiaries.

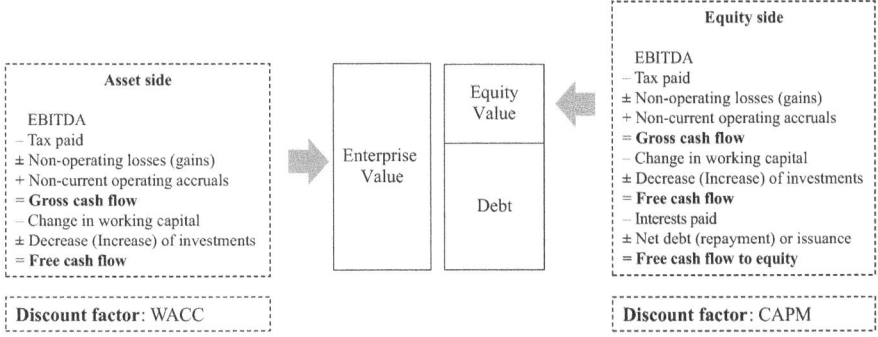

Fig. 4.1 Asset-side and equity-side valuation

Shareholders are remunerated as they contribute their own capital and assume a financial risk by financing a portion of the assets. At the end of the year, they are remunerated through part of the cash flows, which are called free cash flows to equity (FCFEs).

FCFEs provide the basis for directly calculating the equity value. This approach is called equity-side valuation (or levered valuation).

Equity value can also be calculated indirectly, as the difference between the enterprise value, calculated through the FCFs, and debt. This approach is called asset-side valuation (or unlevered valuation) (Fig. 4.1).

In other words, the FCFE measures the remuneration of equity; the FCF measures the remuneration of the company's investments, which are financed in part by equity and in part by debt. The formulas are as follows:

1. Equity-side valuation (levered):

$$\text{Value of the firm} = \sum_{t=1}^{n} \frac{\text{FCFE}_t}{(1+\text{CAPM})^t} + \frac{\text{TV}}{(1+\text{CAPM})^t}$$

2. Asset-side valuation (unlevered):

$$\text{Value of the firm} = \sum_{t=1}^{n} \frac{\text{FCF}_t}{(1+\text{WACC})^t} + \frac{\text{TV}}{(1+\text{WACC})^t} - D$$

The asset-side valuation and the equity-side valuation lead to a similar but not necessarily identical result, as variables combine differently within the two formulas: in the equity-side valuation, the value of the firm is calculated through the FCFEs discounted by the CAPM; in the asset-side valuation, the value of the firm is calculated through the FCFs discounted by the WACC.

4.2.2 The Time Horizon

In the DCF method, the time factor is a relevant variable. As mentioned, according to this method, value is linked to the ECFs that a firm can produce over an appropriate time horizon.

What does appropriate means? It means that forecasts must be consistent with the management's ability to predict the business evolution in a sufficiently reliable manner.

The time horizon may be different depending on the industry and characteristics of the firm. As previously noted, no one has a crystal ball; therefore, the cash flows must be estimated for a plausible number of years. For example, a firm engaged in a stable industry can estimate its cash flows over a period of several years; on the other hand, a firm operating in a volatile industry can reliably estimate its cash flows over a limited time period only.

In practice, a period between three and five years is usually considered as a suitable valuation horizon. Before the subprime crisis, valuations were also made over longer time horizons; the financial crisis, however, taught operators to refrain from overly ambitious programs, since beyond a certain time horizon all forecasts become meaningless.

Realistically, experience suggests that forecasting cash flows over a time horizon of more than 36–48 months is difficult. Given that most listed companies often have difficulty in forecasting results for the next quarter, it is reasonable to assume that results predicted over a five-year horizon look more like good intentions than like reliable estimates.

Since we consider the cash flows for different future periods we also need to consider the different monetary value of time. The Theory of Finance teaches us that a dollar today is not equal to a dollar tomorrow: today's dollar can be invested and thus it may be worth more.

In order to compare the cash flows relating to different periods, such flows must be discounted through a rate (called the discount rate), which considers, inter alia, the different monetary value of time. For this reason, the value of the firm depends on the DCFs rather than on cash flows.

Discounting is the process that enables us to determine today's value, that is, the present value, of results that will occur in future years. Figure 4.2 shows the logic of discounting.

Income-Based Method 83

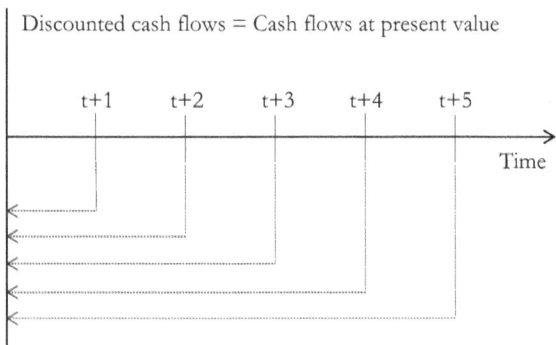

Fig. 4.2 The logic of discounting

If the valuation is carried out in year "t", all future values (t + 1, t + 2, …) must be expressed as present value at year "t" through the following formula:

$$\text{Present Value} = \frac{\text{Expected Cash Flow}_t}{(1+i)^t}$$

Assuming that the cash flow for the year (t + 1) = \$100 and the discount rate i = 5%, the present value at year (t) is calculated as follows:

$$\text{Present Value} = \frac{\$100}{(1+0.05)^1} = \$95.24$$

Assuming that the cash flow for the year (t + 2) = \$100 and the discount rate i = 5%, the present value at year (t) is calculated as follows:

$$\text{Present Value} = \frac{\$100}{(1+0.05)^2} = \$90.70$$

In practice, the further away in time the flows are, the higher the effect of discounting. The same cash flow of \$100 in the fifth year has a present value of \$78.35.

Lastly, it is important to note that, as provided by IVS 105, "a real cash flow does not consider inflation whereas nominal cash flows include expectations regarding inflation. If expected cash flow incorporates an expected inflation rate, the discount rate has to include the same inflation rate."

4.2.3 Risk

A variable to consider when estimating cash flows is risk. According to the Theory of Finance, the valuation of an investment based on expected results cannot ignore risk, for at least two reasons.

First, ECFs are inherently uncertain, as they depend on events that can only partially be controlled by the company. Even when cash flows can be predicted in a sufficiently reliable manner, predicting all the variables affecting a business is impossible.

Second, risk is not the same for all investments. Each firm has its own specific risk profile, which requires a different return. For example, an investment in government bonds requires a lower return than investing in stocks, due to its lower risk. Similarly, two firms that have the same ECFs but are engaged in different sectors and with different risk profiles are not worth the same. The cash flows of a riskier firm must be adjusted to take account of the greater uncertainty linked to the actual realization of such flows. As a matter of fact, the likelihood that the ECFs will actually materialize cannot be the same.

Thus, the value calculated using the DCF method is influenced by the risk that the ECFs do not materialize. Obviously, if the cash flows are lower (higher) than those estimated, the company will be worth less (more) than the estimates.

Valuers must therefore adjust the cash flows according to the associated risk. This is done through a discount rate that considers not only the monetary value of time, but also the risk associated with the firm, the industry, and the market.

The reason that making cash flow projections over a longer than five-year time horizon is not advisable is linked to this circumstance. The adjustment for risk would have to be so high as to considerably reduce the present value of the flow compared to its nominal value.

Finally, according to IVS 105, "different types of cash flow often reflect different levels of risk and may require different discount rates. For example, probability-weighted expected cash flows incorporate expectations regarding all possible outcomes and are not dependent on any particular conditions or events. A single most likely set of cash flows may be conditional on certain future events and therefore could reflect different risks and warrant a different discount rate."

4.3 Discount Rate

The discount rate adjusts the ECFs according to:

- monetary value of time;
- risk of the firm, industry, and country.

As we have seen, the discount rate aligns the cash flows pertaining to different periods and takes into account their volatility based on the firm's riskiness.

For this reason, the discount rate cannot be the same for all companies; otherwise two companies with the same ECFs, but engaged in different sectors, with specific operating methods and with a different risk profile, would have the same value. Thus, the discount rate must be "tailor-made" to take into account the characteristics of the ECFs and the specific situation in which they will be generated.

There are models that consider these variables: they are called "equity risk models" and their objective is to calculate the cost of equity (K_e), that is, the discount rate to be applied to the ECFs in order to estimate the equity value. The most common models are the capital asset pricing model (CAPM), the arbitrage pricing model (APM), the multifactor model, and the proxy models.

Since a firm's funding does not just consist of equity, but also of debt, the cost of debt must also be considered. This cost is linked to the rating of the individual firm and its ability to efficiently finance itself.

The following pages describe the models through which both the cost of equity (Sect. 4.4) and the cost of debt (Sect. 4.5) can be calculated.

4.4 Cost of Equity

The most common model to calculate the K_e is the CAPM, due to its simple calculations and easily identifiable variables. The formula is as follows:

$$\text{CAPM} = K_e = r + (\beta \times \text{ERP})$$

where:

  r = risk-free rate;
  β = measure of a stock's risk of volatility compared to the overall market;

ERP = equity risk premium.

The logic of the model is illustrated in the following pages.

4.4.1 Risk-Free Rate (r)

The minimum return required by shareholders for investing in a firm is equal to the yield of government bonds (sovereign bonds). In sufficiently stable markets, an investment in government bonds can be assumed to be relatively safe, to the point of defining it risk-free (r). In practice, there are no risk-free investments, but for some government bonds the risk may be considered almost zero; this is the case of highly rated government bonds, such as US Treasury Bills, the German Bunds, the UK Gilts, and so on.

The risk-free rate is therefore different for each country and depends on rating. This can be easily understood, if we compare the ten-year yield of countries with different rating (source: S&P, 2017): German bonds (rating AAA), US Treasury bonds (rating AA+), Italian bonds (rating BBB), and Greek bonds (rating B–) (Fig. 4.3).

The return of government bonds is proportional to the risk of the country: the higher the rating, the lower the return. The return on a low-risk (AAA) German bond has historically been very low; in 2017, a ten-year bond had an average return of approximately 0.4%. A Greek bond, which is riskier (B–), has a higher return in order to compensate for the greater risk; in 2017, a ten-year bond had an average return of around 5.0%.

Although a risk-free rate reflects a wide range of macroeconomic variables, in a country where government bonds have a 0.4% return, the monetary value of time is more stable than in a country where the return on bonds is 5%. This has an impact on inflation rates, on country growth rates, as well as on other factors.

In identifying the most appropriate risk-free rate, valuers must consider two aspects:

- the time horizon;
- the geographic relevance.

4.4.1.1 The Time Horizon

The return on a bond changes according to its maturity. In principle, a bond with a longer maturity has a higher yield than a bond with a short maturity. Table 4.1 shows the yields of US Treasuries for different maturities.

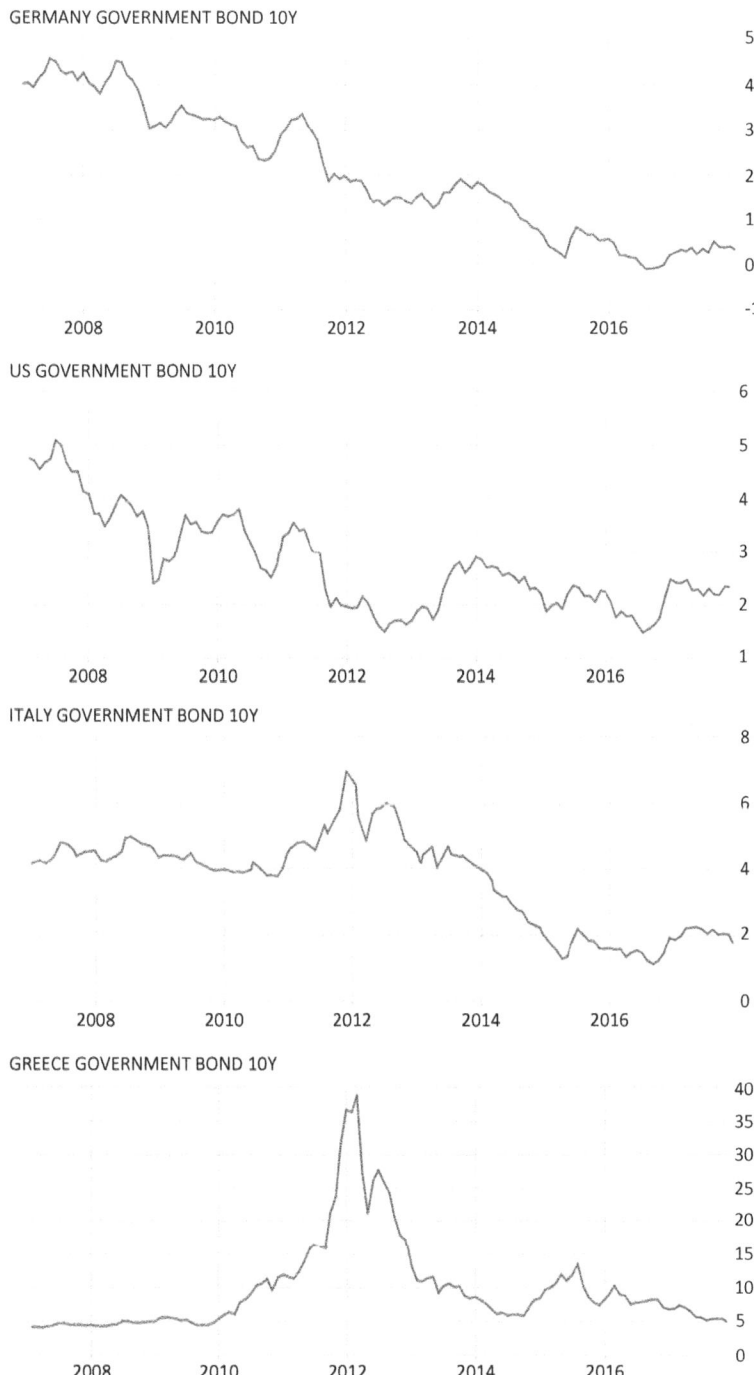

Fig. 4.3 Comparison between the returns of different government bonds

Table 4.1 US Treasuries yields (first semester 2017)

Date	1 month	3 months	6 months	1 year	2 years	3 years	5 years	7 years	10 years	20 years	30 years
3/1/2017	0.52	0.53	0.65	0.89	1.22	1.50	1.94	2.26	2.45	2.78	3.04
1/2/2017	0.50	0.51	0.65	0.83	1.22	1.49	1.93	2.27	2.48	2.80	3.08
1/3/2017	0.46	0.63	0.79	0.92	1.29	1.57	1.99	2.29	2.46	2.81	3.06
3/4/2017	0.73	0.79	0.92	1.02	1.24	1.47	1.88	2.16	2.35	2.71	2.98
1/5/2017	0.67	0.83	0.98	1.09	1.28	1.48	1.84	2.13	2.33	2.71	3.00
1/6/2017	0.82	0.98	1.07	1.16	1.28	1.45	1.76	2.02	2.21	2.60	2.87

Choosing a 5-year bond rather than a 20-year bond obviously affects the risk-free rate and, consequently, the CAPM. Two solutions are possible.

The first solution is to use a risk-free rate with a time horizon that is similar to those of the ECFs. For example, if the ECFs have a time horizon of five years, a five-year bond rate could be used.

The second solution is to use a risk-free rate with a ten-year time horizon regardless of the ECFs. A period of ten years is sufficient to mitigate the effects of short-term volatility and better reflects the length of an economic cycle. Furthermore, when using the DCF method, a TV is always included, which summarizes an average cash flow to be added to the ECFs. A bond with a maturity of less than ten years would not be consistent with the time perspective of a TV.

The latter solution is therefore preferable to the former, subject to the various circumstances to be considered by the valuer.

4.4.1.2 The Geographic Relevance

A second aspect to be taken into consideration concerns the geographic relevance. As we have seen, each country has a specific rating and a different risk-free rate. Thus, it is undisputed that a German company should be assessed using German bonds as the free-risk rate. However, what happens if a company is headquartered in Germany (AAA rating), but exports 100% of its products to a B-rated country? Does the risk-free rate continue to be that of Germany or does it become that of the country to which it exports?

As a matter of fact, there is no single answer. If we consider where the head office is located, the risk-free rate is calculated on the basis of the German bonds; if, on the other hand, if we consider where the company effectively operates, reference should be made to the government bonds of the B-rated country. In general, it is up to the valuer's judgment to make the choice that best reflects operating conditions.

When a company operates in several countries, an average risk-free rate could be used combining the different returns. For example, is it realistic valuing Ferrari using the Italian risk-free rate (BBB rating), when the Italian market accounts for less than 5% of its total sales?

For example, for the Eurozone, the Euro Area Yield Curve shows separately AAA-rated euro area central government bonds and all euro area central government bonds (including AAA rated). The yield curve, daily updated by the European Central Bank (ECB), represents the relationship between market

Table 4.2 Euro Area Yield Curve (November 2017)

Maturity	AAA rated	All bonds	Maturity (years)	AAA rated	All bonds
3 months	−0.795387	−0.622092	15	0.816687	1.517082
6 months	−0.789914	−0.594276	16	0.870813	1.582166
9 months	−0.783867	−0.571758	17	0.918960	1.639912
1 year	−0.776053	−0.551257	18	0.961993	1.691424
2 years	−0.715761	−0.453554	19	1.000635	1.737618
3 years	−0.605966	−0.302938	20	1.035497	1.779251
4 years	−0.460719	−0.107896	21	1.067089	1.816954
5 years	−0.298450	0.108004	22	1.095838	1.851247
6 years	−0.133846	0.324668	23	1.122104	1.882570
7 years	0.023588	0.529317	24	1.146192	1.911288
8 years	0.168699	0.715488	25	1.168358	1.937712
9 years	0.299385	0.881025	26	1.188824	1.962105
10 years	0.415434	1.026304	27	1.207775	1.984693
11 years	0.517683	1.152990	28	1.225374	2.005668
12 years	0.607466	1.263254	29	1.241760	2.025196
13 years	0.686274	1.359338	30	1.257054	2.043423
14 years	0.755567	1.443333			

Source: ECB

remuneration (interest) rates and the remaining time to maturity of debt securities. The information content of a yield curve reflects the asset pricing process on financial markets. Table 4.2 shows the values of the Euro Area Yield Curve.

4.4.2 Beta (β)

Beta measures the specific risk of an investment and consists of two elements: systematic risk and unsystematic risk.

Systematic risk is the part of risk linked to the general market trend. In the same industry, systematic risk is the same for all firms.

Unsystematic risk is the part of risk unrelated to market trends, but linked to the firm's specific characteristics, such as operational efficiency, profitability, ability to make effective investments, and so on.

From a theoretical standpoint, beta is equal to the historic deviations of the security with respect to market performance:

$$\beta_{L(i)} = \frac{\text{Cov}(R_i, R_m)}{\sigma^2(R_m)}$$

where:

$\beta_{L(i)}$	= levered beta of security (i)
R_i	= return on security (i)
R_m	= return on market
$Cov(R_i, R_m)$	= covariance between security (i)'s return and the market return
$\sigma^2(R_m)$	= variance of the market return

Since the covariance of market return with itself $Cov(R_m, R_m)$ is equal to the variance of market return $\sigma^2(R_m)$, the market beta is 1. Beta is less than 1 if the i-th security has lower variance, and therefore is less risky than the market; beta is above 1 when the i-th security is riskier than the market.

Beta can take the following values:

- beta < 0: the security moves opposite to the market, as is the case, for example, for inverse exchange-traded funds (ETFs). However, these are isolated cases that do not concern the beta of firms;
- beta = 0: security movement is uncorrelated to the market. This is the case, for example, of fixed-yield assets. However, a beta of zero does not mean the investment is not risky; it simply means that it has no correlation with the market. For example, walking over a rope between two skyscrapers is certainly risky, but "in economic terms" the beta is zero, as this activity has no correlation with market movements;
- 0 < beta < 1: the security moves in the same direction of the market, but with less volatility and therefore with lower risk. In other words, the investment is affected by market performance to a less than proportional degree;
- beta = 1: the security moves in the same direction as the market, with the same volatility and, therefore, with the same risk.
- beta > 1: the security moves in the same direction as the market, but with higher volatility and therefore with higher risk. In other words, the investment is affected by market performance to a more than proportional degree;

As an example, Table 4.3 shows the betas of some industries.

It is interesting to note that, in a given industry, risk changes according to the geographical area, sometimes to a significant extent.

From a practical standpoint, calculating the beta can be extremely complex and different methodologies can coexist. However, calculating the beta is not the valuer's task, but that of specialized analysis companies, such as Bloomberg and Value Line.

Table 4.3 Beta by industry in the US, Europe, and Japan

Industry name	US Beta	Europe Beta	Japan Beta
Advertising	1.36	0.81	1.17
Apparel	0.88	0.95	0.82
Auto & truck	0.85	1.65	1.47
Banks (regional)	0.47	0.61	1.22
Beverage (alcoholic)	0.79	0.75	0.76
Beverage (soft)	0.91	0.89	0.49
Business & consumer services	1.07	0.85	0.93
Chemical (basic)	1.00	1.12	1.02
Chemical (specialty)	1.20	1.22	0.94
Computer services	0.99	0.83	0.95
Drugs (biotechnology)	1.40	1.30	1.79
Drugs (pharmaceutical)	1.02	1.10	1.00
Electrical equipment	1.14	1.12	1.02
Electronics (general)	0.86	0.97	1.15
Entertainment	1.20	0.77	0.85
Environmental & waste services	0.85	0.87	1.19
Food processing	0.75	0.76	0.53
Healthcare products	1.04	1.04	0.88
Homebuilding	1.08	1.00	0.97
Hotel/gaming	0.96	0.80	0.90
Insurance (general)	0.90	1.12	0.67
Insurance (life)	1.03	1.63	1.42
Investments & asset management	0.90	0.79	1.86
Machinery	1.06	1.08	1.01
Metals & mining	1.30	1.38	1.29
Oil/gas distribution	1.20	2.17	1.14
Packaging & container	0.84	0.82	0.61
Precious metals	1.25	0.95	0.99
Publishing & newspapers	1.32	0.89	0.88
Real estate (development)	0.68	1.05	1.31
Real estate (operations & services)	0.99	0.63	1.14
Software (Internet)	1.13	0.98	1.45
Software (system & application)	1.13	0.65	1.30
Steel	1.60	1.46	1.30
Telecom. services	1.04	0.99	1.08
Transportation	1.01	1.06	0.90

Source: Damodaran On Line, 2017

For instance, Bloomberg calculates both raw beta and adjusted beta.

Raw beta, also known as historical beta, is calculated by a linear regression of the historical trading prices of the stock (dependent variable) against the S&P 500 (independent variable), using weekly data over a two-year period. The beta is leveraged if the firm has had long-term debt on its balance sheet for the past two fiscal years.

On the other hand, adjusted beta is an estimate of a security's future beta. It is initially derived from historical data, but modified by the assumption that a security's beta will move toward the market average (=1) over time. The formula used to adjust raw beta is:

$$\text{Adjusted Beta} = \left[(0.67) \times \text{Raw Beta}\right] + \left[(0.33) \times 1\right]$$

For example, if a raw beta of 1.2 results from the linear regression based on historical data, the adjusted beta is calculated as follows:

$$\text{Adjusted Beta} = \left[(0.67) \times 1.2\right] + \left[(0.33) \times 1\right] = 1.13$$

Value Line calculates the beta similarly to Bloomberg, but with some differences. Specifically, Value Line uses the NYSE index as the independent variable, using quarterly data over a five-year period.

Obviously, Value Line's results are partially different from Bloomberg's results, but this is inevitable. If we could identify a unique and certain way to measure risk, we would have solved all finance problems. Aside from the different treatment of some variables, the reliability of these models rests on the large database employed and their widespread use in the financial markets.

4.4.2.1 Levered and Unlevered Beta

Depending on the source they use, valuers may have a sector beta or a comparable firm beta.

Sector beta is an aggregate figure provided by databases, analyst reports, sector publications; often, neither the sample from which the aggregate data is drawn nor the method of calculation is known. If the source is authoritative, the data can be considered reliable and does not require the valuer to perform any specific checks.

On the other hand, comparable firm betas are obtained from a peer group of selected companies similar to the target company (by sector, size, financial structure, number of employees, or other relevant variables). In this case, the aggregate data is processed by the valuer through the choice of the sample and an appropriate calculation methodology.

In both cases the levered beta is an aggregate figure based on the beta of listed companies. The levered beta reflects total risk, which includes both operating risk and financial risk. Operating risk is specific to the sector.

Conversely, financial risk reflects the average financial structure of the sector that is required to sustain a certain level of investments.

Valuers must first cleanse the levered beta from financial risk and then calculate the unlevered beta. In other words, unlevered beta is a measure of operating risk alone, irrespective of the financial structure of the aggregate data, which could be different from that of the target company. The formula is as follows:

$$\beta_U = \frac{\beta_L}{1+\left[(1-t)\times D/E\right]}$$

where:

β_L = levered beta
t = tax rate
D/E = the last fiscal year sector's average debt-to-equity ratio

For example, assuming sector beta = 1.24, tax rate = 22%, and industry average D/E = 0.65, the unlevered beta can be calculated as follows:

$$\beta_U = \frac{1.24}{1+\left[(1-0.22)\times 0.65\right]} = 0.82$$

This means that, if the sector beta = 1.24, the operating risk is equal to 0.82.

The valuer can subsequently calculate the levered beta of the target company according to its specific debt-to-equity ratio through the following formula:

$$\beta_L = \beta_U \times \left\{1+\left[(1-t)\times D/E\right]\right\}$$

Assuming that the debt-to-equity ratio of the target company = 0.55, the levered beta is calculated as follows:

$$\beta_L = 0.82 \times \left\{1+\left[(1-0.22)\times 0.55\right]\right\} = 1.17$$

Due to a more favorable debt-to-equity ratio (0.55 compared to 0.65), the total risk of the target company, measured through the levered beta, is lower than the industry average (1.17 compared to 1.24).

Table 4.4 Peer group beta

Company	Levered beta	D/E	Unlevered beta
Peer 1	0.90	0.76	0.57
Peer 2	0.96	0.65	0.64
Peer 3	1.02	0.82	0.62
Peer 4	0.84	0.69	0.55
Peer 5	0.95	0.62	0.64
Peer 6	1.04	0.74	0.66
Mean	0.95	0.71	0.61
Median	0.96	0.72	0.63

In calculating the levered beta of the target company, two aspects should be considered: one regards the tax rate and the other the debt-to-equity ratio.

First, the tax rate is included in the formula to take into account the benefits arising from the tax deductibility of interest expenses. However, in heavily indebted companies, the tax benefits become uncertain; in this case, using an alternative formula that eliminates the effect of these benefits is preferable:

$$\beta_L = \beta_U \times (1 + D/E)$$

As regards the debt-to-equity ratio, the effective financial structure must be used in an equity-side valuation; conversely, in an asset-side valuation, the most appropriate financial structure should be used with respect to planned investments, based on the (equity and debt) "weights" included in the WACC formula (Sect. 4.6).

If the beta is calculated on the basis of comparable companies, it is necessary to:

1. identify a homogeneous peer group;
2. calculate the unlevered beta for each peer group company through the debt-to-equity ratio;
3. calculate the mean and the median of the sample.

The larger the sample, the more significant the beta is.

Table 4.4 shows the levered beta and the debt-to-equity ratio of a sample of comparable companies.

Assuming a tax rate = 22%, the unlevered beta for each company is calculated.

Supposing that the debt-to-equity ratio of the target firm = 0.85 and taking the average value of the unlevered beta (0.61) as a reference, the levered beta is calculated as follows:

$$\beta_L = 0.61 \times \{1 + [(1 - 0.22) \times 0.85]\} = 1.01$$

In this case, the levered beta of the target company is higher than the average of the peer group due to the higher debt-to-equity ratio.

4.4.2.2 Multibusiness Company Beta

The above description is valid for a company that operates in a single business. What happens if a company is engaged in more than one business? In this case, the beta of each business must be calculated and weighted according to a representative variable (e.g. investments, number of employees, FCF, revenues). In practice, this is not a simple process, since an efficient segment reporting system is required to calculate the debt-to-equity ratio of each business unit (BU).

Table 4.5 shows the unlevered beta of a peer group, the debt-to-equity ratio, and the revenues of the individual BUs.

Assuming a tax rate = 22%, the levered beta for each BU is calculated using the formula previously examined (Table 4.6):

Finally, the weighted average levered beta of the firm can be calculated on the basis of revenues realized by each BU:

Table 4.5 Business unit key data

Business units	Unlevered sector beta	BU D/E	BU revenues
Business Unit 1	0.91	0.64	$20,000
Business Unit 2	0.87	0.52	$32,000
Business Unit 3	0.63	0.57	$18,000
Business Unit 4	0.75	0.78	$25,000

Table 4.6 Business unit's levered betas

Business units	BU levered beta
Business Unit 1	1.36
Business Unit 2	1.22
Business Unit 3	0.91
Business Unit 4	1.21

$$\text{Levered Beta} = \frac{\left[(1.36 \times 20{,}000) + (1.22 \times 32{,}000) + (0.91 \times 18{,}000) + (1.21 \times 25{,}000)\right]}{(20{,}000 + 32{,}000 + 18{,}000 + 25{,}000)} = 1.19$$

The weighted average levered beta of the four BUs (and therefore of the firm) is 1.19.

4.4.2.3 The Main Weaknesses of Beta

Beta has essentially two main weaknesses.

The *first weakness* is that the market is considered as the only benchmark for calculating risk. In theory, the *Arbitrage Pricing Theory* (APT) could be used as an alternative; unlike the CAPM—which assumes that the risk is summarized by the market only—the APT admits multiple sources of risk (consisting in unexpected changes in the fundamental macroeconomic variables, called "factors") and measures the sensitivity of the investment to each of these changes with a specific beta.

In short, the APT assumes that investors take advantage of every arbitrage opportunity: if two assets (or two portfolios) have the same exposure to risk, but different expected returns $E(r_j)$, investors will buy the asset with the higher expected returns, thereby increasing its price (thus lowering the expected returns) and restoring balance.

According to the APT the cost of equity is calculated as follows:

$$K_e = r + \beta(1) \times RP(1) + \beta(2) \times RP(2) + \cdots + \beta(n) \times RP(n)$$

where:

r = risk-free rate
β = sensitivity of the asset to the particular factor
RP = risk premium associated with the particular factor

The number of factors depends on how detailed the analysis is and on whether an adequate sensitivity can be identified for each of them. Let us assume that four factors have been identified as well as the sensitivity associated with each of them:

- GDP growth: β = 0.6, RP = 3%
- Stock index growth: β = 0.4, RP = 4%
- Inflation rate: β = 1.2, RP = 2%
- Industrial production growth: β = 1.1, RP = 3%

Assuming the risk-free rate = 2%, K_e according to the APT model is calculated as follows:

$$K_e = 2\% + (0.6 \times 3\%) + (0.4 \times 4\%) + (1.2 \times 2\%) + (1.1 \times 3\%) = 11.10\%$$

Subject to the difficulty of identifying the factors and estimating the sensitivity and risk premium for each of them, the APT, unlike the CAPM, measures market risk with respect to multiple macroeconomic variables.

In any case, valuers must be aware that if they replace the CAPM with the APT or with other models, the objectivity and demonstrability of the valuation may decrease as a result, since the CAPM is widely used in the financial markets and is a reference standard due to the ease of calculation and wide information base.

The *second weakness* is that, for small businesses, a sector beta or a comparable firm beta may not be representative, as it assumes a risk-return ratio similar to that of a large company.

Both the valuation practice and some textbooks suggest making adjustments to the beta to take account of the greater riskiness of a small company. If this choice is not supported by adequate sources, there is a risk that the CAPM will reflect the valuer's sensitivity rather than being based on objective elements. In my opinion, it is preferable not to make any adjustments, rather than assuming percentage increases or decreases based on subjective assumptions.

In practice, there is no entirely rational criterion for adjusting the beta according to the size of the firm.

4.4.3 Equity Risk Premium (ERP)

The equity risk premium (ERP), or risk premium, measures the expected return required by investors on top of the risk-free rate in order to offset the risk of an investment.

Investors are exposed to two risks: specific risk and generic risk.

Specific risk is that of the industry (unlevered beta) and of the firm (levered beta). It is related to the characteristics of the specific business and reflects a wide range of variables. As shown in Table 4.6 (beta by industry), for example, the steel industry beta is on average high in Europe (1.46), the US (1.60), and

Japan (1.30); conversely, the beta of the soft beverage industry has a moderately low beta of 0.89 in Europe, 0.91 in the US, and 0.49 in Japan.

On the other hand, generic risk is linked to the country in which the company conducts its business. It is reasonable to assume that a high-rating country is more stable than a low-rating country; this has a positive impact on a series of financial ratios, such as the tax rate, the interest rate, the country growth rate, and so on.

For example, in 2017 the ERP of Germany (AAA rating), 5.7% on average, was lower than that of Italy (BBB rating), which was about 8.4%. This means that, all other conditions being equal, an investment in Germany requires a lower remuneration for risk than the same investment made in Italy: in other words, the return on an investment made in Italy must be approximately 2.7% higher (8.4–5.7%) than the return on an investment made in Germany.

From a logical standpoint, the specific risk of the industry (beta) adjusts the country's risk (ERP). For example, if beta is 1.2 and the risk premium is 6.5%, the total risk of the investment is equal to 1.2 times the risk of the country, namely:

$$\text{Total Risk} = \beta \times \text{ERP} = 1.2 \times 6.5\% = 7.80\%$$

On the other hand, a modest industry risk, that is, a beta of less than 1, has a reductive effect on total risk. For example, if beta is 0.7 and the risk premium is 6.5%, the total risk of the investment is equal to 0.7 times the risk of the country:

$$\text{Total Risk} = \beta \times \text{ERP} = 0.7 \times 6.5\% = 5.55\%$$

A beta of less than 1 reduces the risk of the country; in other words, the low volatility of an industry or company partially compensates for country risk.

Conversely, a beta of 1 is neutral with respect to country risk.

Table 4.7 shows the ERPs of some countries. For more details, we recommend consulting the specific databases that provide this information.

The ERP can be calculated in various ways, the complexity being proportional to the number of variables. Multiple methods can be used to determine the ERP. Specifically:

1. historical averages method;
2. modified historical averages method;
3. implied method.

Table 4.7 ERP by country

Country	Moody's rating	ERP (%)
Argentina	B3	14.94
Australia	Aaa	5.69
Austria	Aa1	6.25
Belgium	Aa3	6.55
Brazil	Ba2	9.96
Canada	Aaa	5.69
China	Aa3	6.55
Denmark	Aaa	5.69
Finland	Aa1	6.25
France	Aa2	6.40
Germany	Aaa	5.69
Greece	Caa3	19.90
Iceland	A3	7.40
Ireland	A3	7.40
Italy	Baa2	8.40
Liechtenstein	Aaa	5.69
Luxembourg	Aaa	5.69
Netherlands	Aaa	5.69
Norway	Aaa	5.69
Portugal	Ba1	9.24
Russia	Ba1	9.24
Spain	Baa2	8.40
Sweden	Aaa	5.69
Switzerland	Aaa	5.69
Turkey	Ba1	9.24
UK	Aa1	6.25
US	Aaa	5.69

Source: Damodaran On Line, 2017

According to the *historical averages method*, the ERP is equal to the spread between the return on market (r_m) and the risk-free rate (r):

$$ERP = r_m - r$$

Therefore, the ERP is equal to the difference between the return on a high-volatility investment (stock market) and the return on a low-volatility investment (default-free securities) over the long term. To avoid short-term effects, which could distort results, the ERP is calculated based on a historical series relating to a reasonable number of years, rather than just one year. Countries that have reliable statistics determine the ERP over a period of 50 years or more, using arithmetic or geometric means.

The *modified historical averages method* consists in making an adjustment to a base premium for mature equity markets. In practice, assuming the minimum possible risk for a stable country, a default spread is added that takes into account the greater risk of a less stable country:

ERP = Mature equity market risk premium + Default spread

The US risk premium is often taken as base premium, although the risk premium of other countries with similar rating could also be used. The default spread is calculated by rating agencies on the basis of a wide range of economic variables, starting from a default spread of 0.00% for countries with the highest rating.

For example, considering that the US ERP is 5.69%, if a country has a default spread of 2.50%, that country's ERP is calculated as follows:

$$ERP = 5.69\% + 2.50\% = 8.19\%$$

This method has some methodological foundation, but it is excessively empirical, as the same formula contains variables that pertain to different economic environments.

The *implied method* is not based on historical series, but on an analytical model, according to which the stock value (V) is equal to the ratio between:

1. the expected dividends (ED) in next period; and
2. the difference between the required return on equity (RROE) and the expected growth rate (g).

In practice:

$$V = \frac{ED}{RROE - g}$$

Solving for RROE:

$$RROE = \frac{ED}{V} - g$$

The calculation methods given here are for mere information purposes. Valuers are not required to independently calculate the risk premium, as there are various sources that can be relied on. However, valuers must carefully consider which country they should refer to. For example, if a company is headquartered in Germany (ERP = 5.69%) and exports 100% of its production to Brazil (ERP = 9.96%), which ERP should the valuer refer to? In this case, the risk premium of the company is more likely to be that of Brazil than that of Germany. An intermediate solution is to calculate the arithmetic average or the weighted average of the ERPs of both countries. If we use an arithmetic average, the ERP is calculated as follows:

$$ERP = \text{Mean}\left(ERP_{Germany}; ERP_{Brazil}\right) = 7.82\%$$

4.4.4 An Overview of CAPM

In light of the above analysis, the cost of equity, calculated using the CAPM formula, is equal to the sum of the risk-free rate and the risk rate (Fig. 4.4).

The first component, equal to the return of free-risk securities (r), is the minimum remuneration required by an investor to invest his or her capital. Since investing in a business involves a certain degree of risk, both the specific risk of the industry and the firm (β) as well as the risk of the country in which the activity is carried out (ERP) must be considered.

The variables that make up the formula are subject to some uncertainty.

The risk-free rate may vary depending on both the sovereign bond used and its duration. The ability of beta to measure the risk of the business sector is linked to the reliability of the reference sample. Finally, risk premium is an approximate measure of country risk, which can be calculated using various methods.

For these reasons, valuers are advised to perform a sensitivity analysis on the CAPM, in order to analyze how the CAPM changes as the formula variables change.

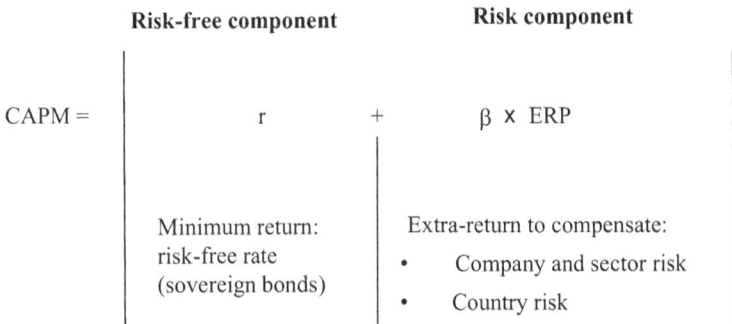

Fig. 4.4 CAPM at a glance

Table 4.8 Sensitivity analysis on CAPM

			Risk-free rate		
			Min (%)	Mean (%)	Max (%)
			2.5	3.0	3.5
Beta	Min	0.7	7.40	7.90	8.40
	Mean	0.8	8.10	8.60	9.10
	Max	0.9	8.80	9.30	9.80

Table 4.9 Sensitivity analysis on total value

Variables	n + 1	n + 2	n + 3	Total value
ECF	$100.00	$120.00	$140.00	
CAPM = 7.40%	$93.11	$104.03	$113.01	$310.15
CAPM = 8.60%	$92.08	$101.75	$109.30	$303.13
CAPM = 9.80%	$91.07	$99.54	$105.76	$296.37

For example, if the valuer estimates that:

- the risk-free rate is between 2.5% and 3.5%;
- the beta is between 0.7 and 0.9;
- the ERP is equal to 7%;

the valuer can perform a sensitivity analysis to examine the effects of a risk-free rate and beta change, by using the minimum, mean, and maximum values (Table 4.8). In this way, the valuer can combine the variables and examine the effects of the changes on the CAPM and, consequently, on the overall value of the firm.

Of course, valuers must show the effects of the sensitivity analysis and justify their choice in the selection of values. The effects of the discount rate on the value of a business can be significant. If we apply the minimum, mean, and maximum values of Table 4.8 to ECFs of $100, $120, $140, the DCFs are significantly different (Table 4.9).

4.4.5 Adjusted CAPM: Do We Really Need It?

According to some authors, the CAPM should be adjusted since it assumes a perfectly diversified portfolio, which is not the case in practice, especially in unlisted companies. Specifically, two adjustments are proposed:

1. a small stock premium (SSP);
2. a company-specific premium (CSP).

The *first adjustment* concerns smaller listed companies, as there is evidence that small cap stocks outperform their large cap counterparts over the long run. In the US market, in 2015, the average return was 10.30% for small caps, 10.00% for mid caps, and 8.50% for large caps. An SSP should adjust the CAPM to take into account both the higher return and the greater volatility of small cap companies.

Although this adjustment has theoretical foundations, in practice it is difficult to calculate. Moreover, the cost of identifying suitable CAPM adjustments is probably higher than the benefit. Empirical studies show that the adjustment is usually modest, while the analyses that must be carried out to achieve an appreciable result require robust analyses and detailed information.

A good compromise to account for the different return of small caps is to calculate the beta based on a peer group composed of small caps only. The limit of this approach is related to the smaller number of publicly traded small caps and the greater volatility of beta. Therefore, a beta calculated on this peer group could have a higher standard error than a beta calculated on a larger peer group, also comprising less volatile large caps.

In conclusion, if we consider both the costs and the benefits, an adjustment based on the SSP could have a modest impact while increasing the discount rate uncertainty.

The *second adjustment* concerns a CSP. This adjustment assumes that companies with different characteristics compared to the average of comparables have a different risk profile. Risk may be adversely influenced by the firm's dependence on one or few customers/suppliers, inappropriate management, obsolete products, and so on.

There are two critical issues in this adjustment. First, the adjustment is too subjective; although adverse elements that theoretically affect the discount rate can be detected, the valuer may find it difficult to quantify such higher degree of risk. Second, any adverse variables should already be accounted for in the cash flows, if these have been reliably determined. If the business plan does not correctly detect this circumstance, there is an issue that is not related to a potential premium, but to the reliability of the cash flows and their ability to adequately reflect the firm's prospects.

In conclusion, any adjustments are likely to introduce greater subjectivity if they are not based on a consistent methodology and on assumptions that can also be verified by third parties.

4.5 Cost of Debt

The cost of debt (also called the after-tax cost of debt) is the cost that a company has to incur to remunerate lenders. It is influenced by three variables: the risk-free rate, the spread, and the tax rate (t):

$$\text{Cost of Debt} = \text{Pre-tax Cost of Debt}(1-t)$$

The pre-tax cost of debt is calculated as the sum of the risk-free rate and a spread:

$$\text{Pre-tax Cost of Debt} = K_d = r + \text{spread}$$

The *risk-free rate* is analyzed in detail in Sect. 4.4.1. It is the basis of the cost of debt, as the minimum return expected by a lender is precisely that of a risk-free investment. All loans are linked to the performance of interest rates as reflected in a yield curve.

The *spread*, that is, the greater return lenders require to remunerate risk, is calculated based on the risk of default of the target company. The risk of default can be defined as the exposure to loss due to non-payment by a borrower of a financial obligation when it becomes payable. Default risk relates to the creditworthiness of the borrower and is taken into account when setting the interest rate on the loan.

The easiest way to calculate the risk of default is to refer to the company's rating, if a rating has been assigned (Table 4.10). Companies with a higher rating are less exposed to the risk of default; accordingly, the spread applied to the risk-free rate is low. On the other hand, companies with a low rating are more exposed to the risk of default; to compensate for and remunerate such higher risk, lenders apply a higher spread.

The spread associated with the rating class depends on various factors, including the characteristics of the lender, the characteristics of the borrower, the credit history, the guarantees provided, and so on.

For example, a large cap rated AAA and an excellent credit history will probably obtain a smaller spread than a privately held company that has recently been upgraded to AAA.

In general, the spread can change over time, including within the same rating class, and each lender has developed its own calculation system. Thus, identifying an average spread associated with each rating class is a complex activity, especially for non-investment-grade classes, the upper threshold of

Table 4.10 Rating definitions

Moody's	S&P	Fitch	Definition
Aaa	AAA	AAA	The obligor's capacity to meet its financial commitment on the obligation is extremely strong
Aa	AA	AA	The obligor's capacity to meet its financial commitment on the obligation is very strong
Aa	A	A	An obligation rated "A" is somewhat more susceptible to the adverse effects of changes in circumstances and economic conditions than obligations in higher-rated categories. However, the obligor's capacity to meet its financial commitment on the obligation is still strong
Baa	BBB	BBB	Adverse economic conditions or changing circumstances are more likely to lead to a weakened capacity of the obligor to meet its financial commitment on the obligation
Ba	BB	BB	The obligation is less vulnerable to non-payment than other speculative issues. However, it faces major ongoing uncertainties or exposure to adverse business, financial, or economic conditions which could lead to the obligor's inadequate capacity to meet its financial commitment on the obligation
B	B	B	The obligation is more vulnerable to non-payment than the previous obligations, but the obligor currently has the capacity to meet its financial commitment on the obligation. Adverse business, financial, or economic conditions will likely impair the obligor's capacity or willingness to meet its financial commitment on the obligation
Caa	CCC	CCC	The obligation is currently vulnerable to non-payment, and is dependent upon favorable business, financial, and economic conditions for the obligor to meet its financial commitment on the obligation. In the event of adverse business, financial, or economic conditions, the obligor is not likely to have the capacity to meet its financial commitment on the obligation
Ca	CC	CC	The obligation is currently highly vulnerable to non-payment. This rating is used when a default has not yet occurred, but it is expected to be a virtual certainty, regardless of the anticipated time to default
	C	C	The obligation is currently highly vulnerable to non-payment, and it is expected to have lower relative seniority or lower ultimate recovery compared to obligations that are rated higher
C	D	D	The obligation is in default or in breach of an imputed promise
NR	NR	NR	No rating has been requested, or that there is insufficient information on which to base a rating

which usually coincides with a BBB rating. In such cases, there are so many variables that can affect the calculation that the spread is all the more "tailor-made".

If a company is not rated, alternative methods should be found, based on the following information:

- the company's credit history for the last few years. The time horizon depends on the average duration of the loans. For a company that only uses short-term debt (i.e. with an average duration of less than one year), a time horizon of two/three years can be considered. On the other hand, for a company that uses long-term debt, reference should be made to the average duration of its loans;
- the debt composition and cost. Different interest rates apply to short-term and long-term debt, respectively. Short-term debt is generally more expensive;
- the average return on debt (ROD) of the last few years. The ROD is calculated on an annual basis and is equal to the ratio of interest expenses to average debt; the ROD measures the interest rate. For example, assuming an initial debt of $1,000, a final debt of $1,400, and interest expenses of $52, the ROD is calculated as follows:

$$ROD = \frac{\text{Interest Expenses}}{\text{Average Debt}} = \frac{\$52}{(\$1000 + \$1400)/2} = 4.33\%$$

The result obtained is an average figure that takes into account both short-term debt and long-term debt, which—as mentioned—may have a different cost. Nevertheless, the ROD is a good approximation of the average interest rate of the target company;

- the financial ratios of the target company based on the guideline provided in Chap. 3. They help understand the firm's "state of health" and identify a summary rating based on multiple ratios. For example, the Altman Z Score Plus (updated in 2012) estimates the risk of default through the sum of weighted financial ratios. The model can be applied to different types of firms:

$$Z' - \text{score}_{\text{Manufacturing}} = 0.717X_1 + 0.847X_2 + 3.107X_3 + 0.420X_4 + 0.998X_5$$

$$Z' - \text{score}_{\text{Private general companies}} = 6.56X_1 + 3.26X_2 + 6.72X_3 + 1.05X_4$$

where:

X_1 = working capital/total assets
X_2 = retained earnings/total assets
X_3 = EBIT/total assets
X_4 = book value of equity/total liabilities
X_5 = sales/total assets

The risk of default is measured as follows:

- private manufacturing companies: above 2.90: bankruptcy is not likely; from 1.23 to 2.90: bankruptcy cannot be predicted (gray area); below 1.23 bankruptcy is likely;
- private general companies: above 2.6: bankruptcy is not likely; from 1.10 to 2.60: bankruptcy cannot be predicted (gray area); below 1.10 bankruptcy is likely.

Empirical evidence confirms the model is substantially consistent, although it is optimistic to assume that a formula based on four or five ratios can be universally used to predict insolvency.

Finally, we must consider that interest expenses are tax deductible for the firm. Thus, the pre-tax cost of debt must be stated net of the *statutory tax rate* (t). Using the effective tax rate, equal to the ratio of taxes due to income before taxes, is not correct as this figure can vary yearly based on the tax treatment of costs.

4.6 Weighted Average Cost of Capital (WACC)

As mentioned, according to the asset-side approach, the discount rate is composed of both the cost of equity and the cost of debt.

Discount Rate = Cost of Equity + Cost of Debt

However, the weight of equity and debt may not be the same. Therefore, their cost must be weighted based on the amount of equity and debt. The formula is called weighted average cost of capital (WACC):

$$WACC = K_e \frac{E}{D+E} + K_d(1-t)\frac{D}{D+E} =$$

$$= [r + (\beta \times ERP)]\frac{E}{D+E} + K_d(1-t)\frac{D}{D+E}$$

where:

E/D + E = weight of equity;
D/D + E = weight of debt.

Let us assume that a French company engaged in the steel business has equity and debt of €400 and €600, respectively. Furthermore, r = 2.2%, spread = 1.8%, t = 25%; sector's average D/E = 1.4. The WACC is calculated as follows.

The CAPM can be calculated based on the following information:

- European beta of the steel industry (Table 4.3): 1.46
- French ERP (Table 4.7): 6.40%

First, the unlevered beta is calculated using the industry average D/E of 1.4:

$$\beta_U = \frac{\beta_L}{1 + [(1-t) \times D/E]} = \frac{1.46}{1 + [(1-0.25) \times 1.4]} = 0.71$$

Secondly, the levered beta is calculated considering the D/E of the target company ($600/$400 = 1.5):

$$\beta_L = \beta_U \times \{1 + [(1-t) \times D/E]\} = 0.71 \times \{1 + [(1-0.25) \times 1.5]\} = 1.51$$

The company's beta is higher than the industry average due to the higher D/E. The CAPM is therefore equal to:

$$CAPM = K_e = r + (\beta \times ERP) = 2.2\% + (1.51 \times 6.40\%) = 11.86\%$$

The pre-tax cost of debt (K_d) is calculated as follows:

$$\text{Pre-tax cost of debt} = K_d = r + \text{spread} = 2.2\% + 1.8\% = 4.00\%$$

The weight of equity and debt is calculated as follows:

- E/D + E = $400/$1000 = 0.40
- D/D + E = $600/$1000 = 0.60

Finally, the WACC is equal to:

$$WACC = \left[r + (\beta \times ERP)\right]\frac{E}{D+E} + K_d(1-t)\frac{D}{D+E} =$$

$$= (11.86\% \times 0.4) + \left[4.00\%(1-0.25)\right] \times 0.6 = 4.75\% + 1.08\% = 5.83\%$$

4.7 The Terminal Value

There are two types of ECFs:

- ECFs during the explicit forecast period (three to five years);
- ECFs beyond the explicit forecast period, since the company "does not end" in the last year envisaged by the business plan, but hopefully will continue in future years.

This means that a detailed yearly representation of the near-term ECFs is required. While for those that are further away in time, since we do not have a crystal ball, identifying a summary cash flow, or TV, is sufficient.

According to IVS 105, the TV should consider:

(a) whether the asset is deteriorating/finite-lived in nature or indefinite-lived, as this will influence the method used to calculate a TV;
(b) whether there is future growth potential for the asset beyond the explicit forecast period;
(c) whether there is a predetermined fixed capital amount expected to be received at the end of the explicit forecast period;
(d) the expected risk level of the asset at the time the TV is calculated;
(e) for cyclical assets, the TV should consider the cyclical nature of the asset and should not be performed in a way that assumes "peak" or "trough" levels of cash flows in perpetuity; and
(f) the tax attributes inherent in the asset at the end of the explicit forecast period (if any) and whether those tax attributes would be expected to continue into perpetuity.

Table 4.11 Example of expected cash flows series

	t + 1	t + 2	t + 3	t + 4	St. Dev.
Expected cash flows (series 1)	$100	$110	$120	$130	12.91
Expected cash flows (series 2)	$100	$140	$190	$230	56.86

The TV is usually calculated through the perpetuity formula:

$$\text{Terminal Value} = \frac{\text{Cash Flow}_{t+x}}{i - g}$$

where:

Cash flow$_{t+x}$ = ECFs beyond the explicit forecast period
i = Discount rate
g = Growth rate

Let us examine each component.

Cash flow$_{t+1}$ shows a result that the firm could achieve steadily in the future. This result may theoretically be estimated in different ways.

In practice, the possible solutions are as follows:

1. if the cash flows contained in the business plan are consistent and in line with historical results, the cash flow of the last year of the business plan can be used as the basis for calculation;
2. if the cash flows contained in the business plan are not consistent with historical results, it is preferable to use a simple or weighted average of said cash flows.

For example, let us assume two ECFs on a four-year time horizon (Table 4.11): the first series forecasts a conservative cash flow growth (from $100 to $140), while the second series foresees a rapid growth (from $100 to $230).

For each series the standard deviation is calculated, in order to quantify the amount of dispersion of both the sets of data values. A low standard deviation (series 1) indicates that the data points tend to be close to the mean (also called the expected value) of the set, while a high standard deviation (series 2) indicates that the data points are spread out over a wider range of values.

The standard deviation of series 1 is relatively low and indicates a modest dispersion around the mean. Therefore, the TV can be calculated using the cash flow of the last year (t + 4), which is considered representative of a stable value over time.

On the other hand, the standard deviation of series 2 is high and indicates greater dispersion around the mean. Therefore, if the cash flow of the last year were used, the TV would be based on the higher and further away in time amount of the time series; this TV would risk not being representative of a stable value. In this case, it is preferable to calculate the TV through an arithmetic average or a weighted average of the ECFs:

$$\text{Arithmetic Average} = \frac{\sum_{i=1}^{n} x_i}{n}$$

$$\text{Weighted Average} = \frac{\sum_{i=1}^{n} x_i p_i}{\sum_{i=1}^{n} p_i}$$

where:

n = number of years in the business plan
x_i = ECF of year i
p_i = weight attributed to each year i

With reference to the series 2 values in Table 4.11, the arithmetic average is $165.

Assuming that we assign a greater weight to the nearest ECF over time (t + 1), for example, 4, and a lower weight to the furthest ECF over time (t + 1), for example, 1, the weighted average is calculated as follows:

$$\text{Weighted Average} = \frac{(\$100 \times 4) + (\$140 \times 3) + (\$190 \times 2) + (\$230 \times 1)}{(4 + 3 + 2 + 1)} = \$143$$

Within the $143–$165 range, valuers can identify the amount of the stable cash flow, which, based on an integrated valuation approach, they consider as more representative and more suitable to interpret the value of the firm.

The *discount rate (i)* is used to discount the cash flow according to the perpetuity formula.

According to the asset-side approach, the FCF is discounted using the WACC. According to the equity-side approach, the FCFE is discounted using the CAPM:

$$\text{Terminal Value} = \frac{\text{Free Cash Flow}}{(\text{WACC} - g)}$$

$$\text{Terminal Value} = \frac{\text{Free Cash Flow to Equity}}{(\text{CAPM} - g)}$$

Finally, the *growth rate (g)* is used to adjust the discount rate, to take account of the growth prospects of the business. Some authors, including Damodaran, calculate the growth rate as follows:

$$\text{Growth Rate} = \text{Return on Capital} \times \text{Reinvestment Rate} =$$

$$= \frac{\text{Adjusted EBIT}(1-t)}{\text{BV of Debt} + \text{BV of Equity} - \text{Cash}} \times \frac{\text{CapEx} - \text{Depreciation} + \text{Change in non cash WC}}{\text{Adjusted EBIT}(1-t)} =$$

$$= \frac{\text{CapEx} - \text{Depreciation} + \text{Change in non cash WC}}{\text{Business Assets}} =$$

Essentially the growth rate reflects the firm's investments necessary to maintain a competitive advantage. In other words, the ECFs must at least allow for an adequate level of investment to be maintained.

That said, my personal opinion about the growth rate is: handle with care!

As highlighted in Sect. 4.7.2, the limit of the DCF model is that the value of the firm depends to a large extent on the TV. Now, the growth rate makes the value of the firm even more dependent on the TV, since a reduction in the denominator further increases the TV.

For example, let us assume the following values: free cash flow$_{\text{5th year}}$ = \$100; WACC = 7%; g = 3%.

The TV without the growth rate is as follows:

$$\text{Terminal Value} = \frac{\$100}{7\%} = \$1428$$

The TV with the growth rate is as follows:

$$\text{Terminal Value} = \frac{\$100}{7\% - 3\%} = \$2500$$

In the latter case, the TV increases by 75% due to the growth rate effect.

Damodaran also introduced a two-stage growth model and a three-stage growth model to predict growth patterns other than stable growth (Gordon model); this approach does not reduce the uncertainty of the result.

The DCF model already has an element of uncertainty, as it is based on ECF. The growth rate only adds to the uncertainty, because, by increasing the "weight" of the TV, it makes the value of the firm even more dependent on a summary formula, thereby further increasing the uncertainty of the result.

Including a growth rate is acceptable for large caps as, due to their diversified investment portfolio and large scale, they can grow at a steady pace in the long term. In small businesses, such a circumstance is unrealistic, especially as the model predicts perpetual growth.

4.7.1 Cash Flow or EBIT?

As we saw in Chap. 3, in the short run, FCF and EBIT may differ significantly due to the misalignment between revenues and inflows on the one hand and costs and outflows on the other. In the long run, however, FCF and EBIT tend to align.

For this reason, EBIT can be used as an alternative to cash flow in the calculation of the TV.

EBIT, compared to cash flow, is more easily predictable, as it is more stable over time. EBIT is not influenced by Operating Working Capital, investment and disinvestment policies, and financial policies.

For example, a worsening of the trade receivables turnover or trade payables turnover directly affects the cash flow, while, given the same revenues and operating costs, this circumstance is totally irrelevant for EBIT.

Likewise, an investment affects the cash flow to its full extent, while it influences EBIT to the extent of the amortization/depreciation rate only. For example, the purchase of a $1000 plant is reflected in an outflow of $1000 in the cash flow statement. Assuming that this plant is depreciated over 10 years, the impact on EBIT is $100 (i.e. $1000/10 years).

Finally, taking on or reimbursing a loan also affects the cash flow, but not the EBIT.

By way of example, Table 4.12 shows a typical cash flow and EBIT trend.

Table 4.12 Cash flows versus EBIT

	t + 1	t + 2	t + 3	t + 4	t + 5
Cash flows	$120	$90	$180	$125	$200
EBIT	$110	$140	$150	$165	$180

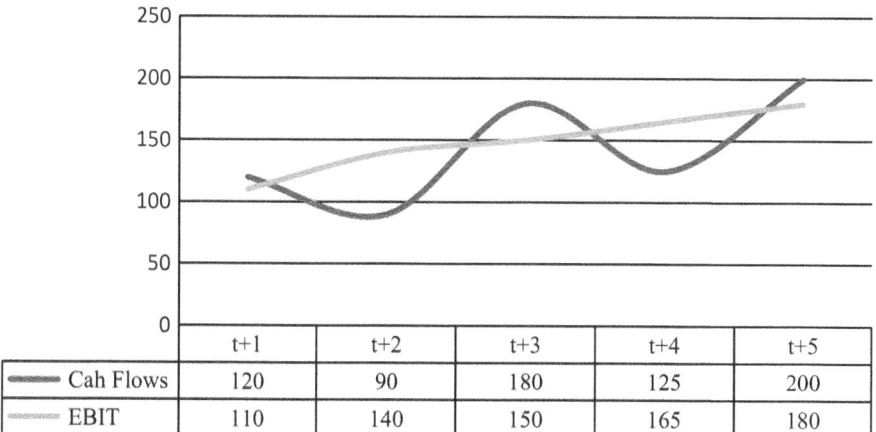

Fig. 4.5 Cash flows and EBITs trend

As can be easily inferred from the graph in Fig. 4.5, the growth of the cash flows is more volatile than the growth of EBITs, although they follow the same trend.

The decision to use the cash flow rather than EBIT or vice versa as the basis for calculating the TV is at the valuer's discretion, who must identify the performance measure that best reflects the stable value of the firm.

4.7.2 The Role of the Terminal Value

As mentioned above, one of the main limitations of the DCF model is the weight of the TV with respect to the value of the firm.

In business valuation textbooks, great emphasis is usually placed on the need to develop a reliable business plan. However, the most significant part of the value of the firm is left to a summary measure, that is, the TV.

Various studies show that, in the DCF model, the TV accounts for 60–90% of the value of the firm. This means that most of the value of the firm depends on an ECF calculated through the perpetuity formula.

For example, let us assume that the ECFs are those in Table 4.12. Furthermore, WACC = 7%; g = 3%; debt = $500. Let us now calculate the total value with and without the growth rate, considering the TV equal to the cash flow of t + 4.

First, the TV is calculated with and without a growth rate:

Table 4.13 Value of the firm without growth rate

WACC	7%				
	t + 1	t + 2	t + 3	t + 4	TV
FCFs	$100.00	$110.00	$120.00	$130.00	$1857.14
DCFs	$93.46	$96.08	$97.96	$99.18	$1416.81
Asset value	$1803.47				
Debt	($500)				
Value of the firm	**$1303.47**				
TV/asset value	78.56%				

Table 4.14 Value of the firm with growth rate

WACC	7%				
g	3%				
	t + 1	t + 2	t + 3	t + 4	TV
FCFs	$100.00	$110.00	$120.00	$130.00	$3250.00
DCFs	$93.46	$96.08	$97.96	$99.18	$2479.41
Asset value	$2866.08				
Debt	($500)				
Value of the firm	**$2366.08**				
TV/asset value	86.51%				

$$\text{Terminal Value}_{\text{without g}} = \frac{\$130}{7\%} = \$1857.14$$

$$\text{Terminal Value}_{\text{with g}} = \frac{\$130}{7\% - 4\%} = \$3250.00$$

In Table 4.13 the value of the firm is calculated without a growth rate.

In Table 4.14 the value of the firm is calculated by taking into account the growth rate.

From this simple example we can draw some conclusions:

1. most of the value of the firm depends on the TV: 78.56% without growth rate and 86.51% with the growth rate;
2. if the ECFs had been forecast in the business plan for three years rather than four, the TV would have had an even greater weight;
3. the value of the firm with a growth rate of 3% ($2266.08) is 81.50% higher than the value of the firm without a growth rate ($1303.47).

These three simple observations are enough to understand that the value of the firm is subject to a high degree of uncertainty, depending on the parameters used. Theoretically, both values are plausible, since the DCF method has been developed in compliance with the theoretical reference model.

Thus, identifying the most appropriate value does not depend on the formula but on the valuer. Based on their sensitivity and their ability to interpret the firm according to an integrated valuation approach, valuers can judge which of the two values is more representative of the firm.

4.7.3 Alternative Methods for Calculating the TV

The TV can also be calculated through two alternative methods. They are based on:

1. market value;
2. salvage value.

According to a *market value* perspective, the TV is calculated as a multiple (see Chap. 5). In the asset-side valuation, an asset-side multiple is used (such as EV/revenue, EV/EBITDA, EV/EBIT); in the equity-side valuation, an equity-side multiple is used (such as P/E, P/BV, etc.).

This method of calculating the TV is most frequently used in the asset-side valuation. The formula is as follows:

$$\text{Value of the firm} = \sum_{t=1}^{n} \frac{\text{FCF}_t}{(1+\text{WACC})^t} + \left(\text{EBITDA}_t \times j_t\right) - D$$

where j is the EBITDA multiple in year t-th, following the explicit forecast period. EBITDA can be replaced with any other asset-side multiple.

Taking again the example in Table 4.12 and assuming an EBITDA $_{t+5}$ = \$250 and an EV/EBITDA = 5.5×, the TV is calculated as follows:

$$\text{Terminal Value} = \$250 \times 5.5 = \$1375.00$$

The value of the firm is shown in Table 4.15.

The market value approach can be used if it is reasonably certain that the business will be sold at the end of the explicit forecast period. In this case the TV corresponds to the exit value that an asset is expected to have at the time it is sold at a predetermined point in the future.

In other situations, the market value approach has two weaknesses. First, there is the risk of valuing the business twice, as the value of the firm is calcu-

Table 4.15 Value of the firm using an EBITDA multiple

WACC	7%			
	t + 1	t + 2	t + 3	t + 4
FCFs	$100.00	$110.00	$120.00	$130.00
DCFs	$93.46	$96.08	$97.96	$99.18
Cash flow present value	$386.67			
TV (EBITDA × 5.5)	$1375.00			
Asset value	$1761.67			
Debt	($500)			
Value of the firm	**$1261.67**			

lated partly with the DCF method and partly with the market multiple method; in doing so, some overlapping is inevitable. Second, the multiple refers to the date on which the valuation is made and not to the TV date; since multiples can vary significantly over time, it is unlikely that today's multiple can be applied to a revenue/EBITDA/EBIT that will take place in the future.

The *salvage value* is the amount a company expects to receive from the sale of an asset at the end of that asset's useful life. This approach can be used when the TV may have little or no relationship to the preceding cash flow. Examples of such assets include wasting assets such as a mine or an oil well.

As specified by IVS 105, "in such cases, the Terminal Value is typically calculated as the salvage value of the asset, less costs to dispose of the asset. In circumstances where the costs exceed the salvage value, the terminal value is negative and referred to as a disposal cost or an asset retirement obligation."

The formula is as follows:

$$\text{Value of the firm} = \sum_{t=1}^{n} \frac{FCF_t}{(1+WACC)^t} + (SV - TC) - D$$

where:

SV is the salvage value
TC are the transaction costs

This approach is only used in specific cases.

4.8 A Summary Example

The cash flow statement in Table 4.16 summarizes what we have examined so far.

Income-Based Method

Table 4.16 Cash flow statement

Cash flow statement	t + 1	t + 2	t + 3	t + 4
EBITDA	$60,000	$65,400	$69,500	$75,300
Tax paid	(−$12,000)	(−$13,734)	(−$14,595)	(−$15,813)
Gross cash flow	**$47,400**	**$51,666**	**$54,905**	**$59,487**
Change in working capital	$6800	$3200	$7500	$8200
Increase of long-term investment	$5400	$4800	$6900	$5200
Decrease of long-term investment	(−$2500)	0	(−$4,300)	0
FCF	**$37,700**	**$43,666**	**$44,805**	**$46,087**
Interest paid	(−$3600)	(−$3900)	(−$3800)	(−$3500)
Net debt repayment	(−$7200)	(−$8900)	(−$6500)	(−$6600)
FCFE	**$26,900**	**$30,866**	**$34,505**	**$35,987**

Table 4.17 Asset-side valuation

Asset-side valuation	t + 1	t + 2	t + 3	t + 4	TV
FCFs	$37,700	$43,666	$44,805	$46,087	$736,670.70
DCFs	$35,623.17	$38,987.54	$37,800.72	$36,740.35	$588,864.93
Asset value	$738,016.70				
Debt	(−$45,000)				
Value of the firm	**$693,016.70**				
TV/asset value	79.79%				

Let us assume CAPM = 11.86%; WACC 5.83%; debt = $45,000; no growth rate is considered. The TV according to an asset-side and an equity-side approach is calculated on the basis of the arithmetic average of the FCFs and the FCFEs, respectively:

$$\text{Terminal Value}_{\text{asset side}} = \frac{\$43,065}{5.83\%} = \$738,670.70$$

$$\text{Terminal Value}_{\text{equity side}} = \frac{\$32,065}{11.86\%} = \$281,319.56$$

The value of the firm according to the asset-side approach is shown in Table 4.17.

The value of the firm according to the equity-side approach is shown in Table 4.18.

The value of the firm can differ, depending on whether the asset-side or the equity-side approach is used. This is inevitable, as each approach uses different values discounted at a different rate. As mentioned several times, both values are plausible and it is up to the valuer to identify the approach that best reflects the value of the firm.

Table 4.18 Equity-side valuation

Equity-side valuation	t + 1	t + 2	t + 3	t + 4	TV
FCFEs	$26,900	$30,866	$34,505	$35,987	$281,319.56
DCFs	$24,047.92	$24,667.82	$24,652.31	$22,985.10	$179,680.39
Value of the firm	**$276,033.53**				
TV/value of the firm	65.09%				

4.9 The Dividend Discount Model (DDM)

The dividend discount model (DDM) is a variant of the DCF model. It considers the expected dividends per share rather than the ECFs. The logic of the DDM is similar to that of the DCF: the value is calculated based on the ability to pay dividends to the shareholders.

The formula is as follows:

$$\text{Value per share} = \sum_{t=1}^{n} \frac{\text{EDpS}_t}{(1+\text{CAPM})^t}$$

where:

EDpS = expected dividend per share

The formula does not calculate the value of the firm, but the value per share. Therefore, the value of the firm can be determined by multiplying the value per share by the number of shares.

To calculate the expected dividend per share, the payout ratio of the earnings per share (EPS) must be calculated based on:

(a) a prospective payout ratio; or
(b) the actual payout ratio of prior years.

For example, let us assume that a company's shareholder equity consists of 10,000 shares and the payout ratio of the last few years was 45% of earnings. The expected earnings estimated in the business plan are shown in Table 4.19.

Based on the expected earnings, we may calculate first the EPS and then the expected dividend per share, by using the payout ratio of previous years (Table 4.20).

Assuming CAPM = 9.50%, in Table 4.21 both the value per share and the value of the firm are calculated (multiplying the value per share by the number of shares).

Income-Based Method

Table 4.19 Expected earnings

	t + 1	t + 2	t + 3	t + 4
Expected earnings	$32,000	$35,000	$42,000	$48,000

Table 4.20 Expected dividend per share

	t + 1	t + 2	t + 3	t + 4
Expected earnings	$32,000	$35,000	$42,000	$48,000
EPS	$3.20	$3.50	$4.20	$4.80
Payout ratio	0.45	0.45	0.45	0.45
Expected dividend per share	$1.44	$1.57	$1.89	$2.16

Table 4.21 Value per share

DDM	t + 1	t + 2	t + 3	t + 4
Expected dividend per share	$1.44	$1.57	$1.89	$2.16
Present value	$1.31	$1.31	$1.44	$1.50
Value per share	$5.57			
Number of shares	10,000			
Value of the firm	$55,706.02			

A variant of the model considers the expected dividend per share of year t + 1 and discounts it according to the perpetuity formula, using the CAPM and (possibly) the growth rate (g):

$$\text{Value per share} = \frac{\text{EDpS}_{t+1}}{\text{CAPM} - g}$$

The growth rate can be calculated by multiplying the retention ratio by the return on equity (ROE).

The retention ratio refers to the percentage of net income that is retained to grow the business, rather than being paid out as dividends. It is the opposite of the payout ratio, which measures the percentage of earnings paid out to shareholders as dividends:

$$g = \text{Retention Ratio} \times \text{ROE} = (1 - \text{Payout ratio}) \times \text{ROE}$$

Using the data of the previous example and assuming ROE = 8%, the value per share can be calculated as follows:

$$g = (1 - 0.45) \times 8\% = 4.40\%$$

$$\text{Value per share} = \frac{\$1.44}{9.50\% - 4.40\%} = \$28.24$$

The value of the firm is calculated by multiplying the value per share ($28.24) by the number of shares (10,000):

$$\text{Value of the firm} = \$28.24 \times 10{,}000 = \$282{,}353$$

The difference in value between the two methods does not come as a surprise. In the first case the value of the firm is calculated on a four-year time horizon; in the second case on an infinite perspective.

Some business valuation textbooks consider the DDM as an alternative valuation method to those that are most commonly used in financial markets, such as the DCF and the market multiples methods.

It is not so for at least two reasons.

First, the DDM is a special version of the DCF and calculates the value of the firm exclusively from the perspective of the shareholders and is based on their expectations to maximize invested capital. As the sustainable growth rate suggests (see Sect. 3.7.4), there is a trade-off between maximizing income and developing the business, with the paradoxical consequence that a short-term increase in value (from a higher dividend payout) may lead to a decrease in value in the medium term (due to a reduction in growth rate).

Second, the DDM is based on the forecast of dividend payouts, which have a high degree of uncertainty. The amount of potentially distributable dividends is based on net income, but the amount of actually payable dividends depends on the cash flows available. For example, a worsening of the operating working capital turnover does not affect net Income, but adversely affects cash flows. Forecasting dividends is therefore a complex exercise and experience shows that, over the long term, especially in small caps, there may be a significant difference between shareholder expectations and actually distributed dividends.

5

Market-Based Method

5.1 Introduction

In the market approach, the value of the firm is calculated by comparing it with similar businesses, for which significant and recent indications on price are available; this method is called market multiple method.

The DCF method is based on the fact that an investor is willing to acknowledge a value equal to expected cash flows. The market multiple method is based on the fact that an investor is unwilling to acknowledge a value other than the current market price as expressed by comparable businesses.

According to IVS 105, the market approach should be applied under the following circumstances:

(a) "the subject asset or substantially similar assets are actively publicly traded; and/or
(b) the subject asset has recently been sold in a transaction appropriate for consideration under the basis of value;
(c) there are frequent and/or recent observable transactions in substantially similar assets".

IVS 105 also specifies circumstances in which the market approach cannot be used directly, but can help corroborate a value calculated using other methods, or to provide evidence. These circumstances include:

- "transactions involving the subject asset or substantially similar assets are not recent enough considering the levels of volatility and activity in the market.
- the asset or substantially similar assets are publicly traded, but not actively.
- information on market transactions is available, but the comparable assets have significant differences to the subject asset, potentially requiring subjective adjustments.
- information on recent transactions is not reliable (i.e. hearsay, missing information, synergistic purchaser, not arm's-length, distressed sale, etc.).
- the critical element affecting the value of the asset is the price it would achieve in the market rather than the cost of reproduction or its income-producing ability."

In the following pages, we are going to analyze circumstances (b) and (c) only, which concern:

1. the comparable companies method;
2. the comparable transactions method.

In both cases, the method is based on the following assumptions:

- there are performance measures (such as sales, EBITDA, EBIT, cash flow, etc.) that have a correlation with the value of the firm;
- this correlation tends to be homogenous across companies in the same industry that are comparable in terms of size, profitability, debt-to-equity ratio, and other relevant parameters:

$$\text{Value of the firm} = f\left(\text{performance measure}\right)$$

- by adequately selecting a peer group of comparable firms for which the enterprise value (EV) is known, a constant (i.e. a multiple) between the EV and a performance measure can be identified:

$$\text{Market multiple} = \frac{\text{Enterprise Value}}{\text{Performance measure}}$$

In practice:

$$\text{Market multiple} = \frac{\text{Numerator} = \text{What you are paying for the asset}}{\text{Denominator} = \text{What you are getting in return}}$$

- such constant (or market multiple) can be applied to the target company:

$$\text{Enterprise Value}_{\text{Target}} = \text{Market multiple} \times \text{performance measure}_{\text{Target}}$$

For example, if a peer group has the following multiple:

$$\frac{\text{Enterprise Value}}{\text{EBITDA}} = 7\times$$

the value of the target company is:

$$\text{Enterprise Value}_{\text{Target}} = 7 \times \text{EBITDA}_{\text{Target}}$$

In practice, to calculate the EV of the target company, the market multiple (7) must be multiplied (×) by the EBITDA of the target company, on the assumption that the correlation between EV and EBITDA is the same as that of the peer group.

In the comparable companies method, the market multiple is calculated based on the market value of comparable publicly traded companies. In the comparable transactions method, the market multiple is calculated based on the prices recorded in similar transactions.

5.2 Widespread Use of the Multiple Method

Multiples are one of the most widespread valuation methods. Since multiples are based on the values of comparable companies or comparable transactions, they are affected by market conditions: in a positive economic cycle, multiples tend to have higher values; in a recession, they are affected by price contraction.

For example, the EV/EBITDA multiple of the luxury business in 2009—at the height of the subprime crisis—was on average 5.4×, below the multiples of traditional sectors, such as the food sector (7.7×) and manufacturing (6.3×). As soon as the recovery got under way in 2012, the same multiple rose to 14.6×.

Some deals were even closed at higher EBITDA multiples, as in the case of the acquisitions of Valentino (25.4×), Pomellato (25.6×), and Loro Piana (21.8×).

Therefore, multiples are quite obviously not independent of market volatility; rather, they reflect volatility trends, sometimes amplifying the effect.

In some specific cases, the EV can be calculated through the multiples of other sectors. For example, in the Ferrari IPO in 2015, an EV/EBITDA multiple of approximately 16× prevailed; this multiple was closer to the luxury industry than to the automotive industry and slightly lower than that of the best in class, Hermes (17.5×).

The reasons the market multiple method is so widely used in financial markets are the following:

1. ease of use;
2. objectivity.

The market multiple method is undeniably *easy to handle*. In addition to specific databases, there are many qualified open sources that provide reliable information on both comparable companies and comparable transactions.

Information on comparable transactions, once difficult to obtain, are now the subject of research and market analyses carried out by consulting firms, research centers, universities, and so on. Therefore, data that up until a few years ago required significant investments to obtain are now available with little effort, or better, are now "apparently available".

The risk of open sources is that they provide information on the main market deals only, which involve multinational companies or, in any case, large-size transactions. Sometimes the only element these companies have in common with the target company is the industry; their size, cost structure, financial structure, ROI, and many other performance measures can be very different. As mentioned in Chap. 1, a Smart and a Ferrari both have a steering wheel, four wheels, and an engine: but the similarities end there. Likewise, valuing a company based on the performance of another company is not possible if their characteristics are not homogeneous.

Furthermore, open sources provide very little information on the performance measures of comparable companies. Usually they report the market cap (comparable companies) or the transaction value (comparable transactions), the multiples, the name of the acquirer, the name of the target company, and little else. Such information, at least in most cases, is not sufficient to make a meaningful comparison.

On the other hand, through the professional databases it is possible to conduct a search based on several relevant parameters and to select a peer group made up of companies that have similar characteristics. For example, one can follow a search strategy based on variables such as EBIT margin, debt-to-equity ratio, ROI, turnover, and so on. Compatibility is guaranteed by the comparative analysis of a series of performance measures.

Thus, ease of use should not be confused with oversimplification. The market multiple method can provide significant values only if the peer group is selected using a consistent methodology, based on an adequate number of parameters. Otherwise, as mentioned, a valuer risks measuring the performance of a Smart based on a peer group made up of sports cars. The strengths of a Smart are its compact size and manageability; a valuation based on speed and acceleration leads to a meaningless result.

A second reason that explains the spread of the market multiple method is its *objectivity*.

Through this method the value of the firm can be calculated on the basis of external parameters. By themselves, they do not guarantee the best possible value, but they enable the valuer to define a range of plausible values, acknowledged by the market.

For example, if we look at apartment transactions in the same neighborhood, we can identify a range of prices. Price variability depends on various factors, including the view, condition of the building, location, floor, maintenance condition, and so on. Despite the specificities of each apartment, a significant misalignment in the values identified in the same area is unlikely. Therefore, a nice apartment in a degraded area can be positioned in the upper part of the price range, but it will hardly be worth twice or three times the price of the other houses in the neighborhood; similarly, a lousy apartment in a high standing area can be positioned in the lower part of the range, but it will hardly be worth half the price of the other houses.

Business valuations follow the same logic: if the peer group is built in a consistent and reliable manner, the market multiple method will lead to a plausible range of values. Obviously, valuers must ascertain whether the target company is in the upper, middle, or lower part of the range, by comparing its characteristics with those of the peer group. However, it is unlikely that a firm may have a value significantly different from that of a peer group, as the firm tends to reflect the characteristics of the industry of which it is part.

We may wonder if, in doing so, the market multiple method increases the risk of excessive flattening. In other words, is it an oversimplification to evaluate a firm based on the value determined by others?

This approach may be reductive for companies that are "unique" and have outstanding characteristics compared to the industry average, such as Ferrari, which—as we said—was assigned a multiple typical of the luxury industry.

For the majority of firms, however, a consistently calculated market multiple may be a good approximation of the value of the firm.

However, not all methods have the same degree of objectivity. As a matter of fact, the comparable companies methods are more reliable, as they refer to homogeneous transactions. In the short term, market price may be affected by contingent circumstances. In the long run, however, market price tends to reflect the characteristics of the firm and the industry.

Prices derived from comparable transactions are often heterogeneous in nature, deal size, conditions, and timing. Moreover, if the transaction concerns only a part of the stocks, the price paid to acquire an equity stake may not necessarily apply to the entire company. In a transaction, in general, the price may depend on various elements: characteristics of the buyer and the seller; reasons underlying the transaction; transaction type; sale of a controlling interest or a minority interest; payment timing and methods; guarantees; synergies achievable by the buyer; and so on.

For example, in 2016 the market price of Whole Food Market, Inc. fluctuated in the range between $28 and $34 per share; the EV/EBITDA was about 7×. At the beginning of 2017 the company reported its sixth consecutive quarter of declining sales, announcing the closure of nine stores. In June 2017, Amazon acquired Whole Food, paying $42 per share. The total amount of the deal was $13.7 billion, with an EV/EBITDA of 10.4×. Amazon therefore paid a premium of about 30% compared to the market value of Whole Food, taking into account the potential synergies it may obtain from the deal: thus, the EV/EBITDA multiple of 10.4× does not reflect a market value, but just the value of the synergies according to Amazon.

If a valuer used this multiple to evaluate a firm in the same industry, it would probably overestimate it by an amount equal to the premium paid by Amazon. The price calculated using the comparable transactions method ultimately contains a more significant subjective component than the price calculated using the comparable companies method.

In general, the comparable transactions method is influenced by the control premium, that is, the amount a buyer is sometimes willing to pay over the current market price of a publicly traded company in order to acquire a controlling share in that company (see Chap. 8). On the other hand, the comparable companies method is more affected by the liquidity premium, that is, the premium demanded by investors when any given security cannot be easily converted into cash for its fair market value.

5.3 Asset-Side and Equity-Side Approach

The value of the firm can be calculated through an asset-side approach and an equity-side approach (Fig. 5.1).

According to the asset-side approach, the market multiple is equal to the ratio of the EV to an unlevered performance measure (such as sales, EBITDA, EBIT, free cash flow [FCF]):

$$\text{Market multiple} = \frac{\text{Enterprise Value}}{\text{Unlevered performance measure}}$$

According to the equity-side approach, the equity value can be calculated directly through a levered performance measure (such as P/E, P/BV [price/book value], FCF to equity):

$$\text{Market multiple} = \frac{\text{Equity Value}}{\text{Levered performance measure}}$$

To calculate the equity value indirectly starting from the EV, net debt must be deducted:

$$\text{Equity Value} = \text{Enterprise Value} - \text{Net Debt}$$

Net debt is equal to:

$$\text{Net Debt} = \text{Debt} + \text{Financial Leases} + \text{Other Interest Bearing Liabilities}$$
$$+ \text{Minority Interests} - \text{Cash} - \text{Liquid Short} - \text{Term Investments}$$

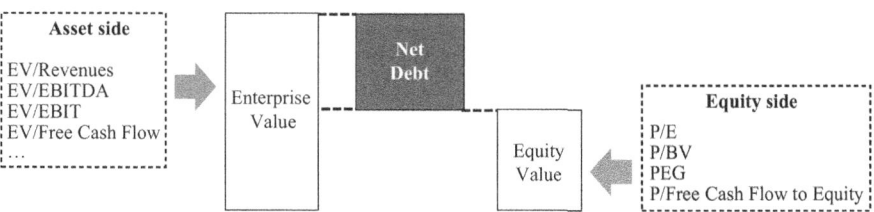

Fig. 5.1 Asset-side and equity-side approaches

5.4 Application of the Market Multiple Method

The application of the market multiple method involves the following steps:

1. selection of peer group (Sect. 5.5);
2. choice of multiple (Sects. 5.6, 5.7, 5.8, and 5.9);
3. application of multiple to the target company (Sect. 5.10).

5.5 Selection of the Peer Group

In the market multiple method, the selection of a homogeneous peer group is essential to obtain a reliable value of the target company. Valuers must therefore make an accurate selection based on several parameters.

In the following pages, we show a value map for the selection of the peer group, with a view to minimize randomness. The following aspects are examined in detail:

1. selection of peer group in the comparable companies method;
2. selection of peer group in the comparable transaction method;
3. application tools in the selection of the peer group.

5.5.1 Selection of Peer Group in the Comparable Companies Method

In the comparable companies method, the choice of the sample requires analyzing both quantitative and qualitative variables. The following parameters must be taken into consideration:

1. industry;
2. geographical scope;
3. competitive positioning;
4. dimension and performances;
5. part of a group;
6. maturity;
7. time;
8. tax rate.

Table 5.1 Key statistics of food and beverage industry

	Industry and segment	Stock price % change 1 year	EV/EBITDA % change 1 year	Current EV/EBITDA
Inputs	Protein processing	17.3%	28.7%	7.9×
	Fruit and vegetables	32.1%	(0.6%)	9.9×
	Ingredients/flavors	(0.2%)	(6.6%)	14.6×
	Agribusiness	27.1%	21.1%	10.3×
Food and beverage	Branded processed foods	8.0%	(7.6%)	13.5×
	Private label foods and beverages	5.5%	1.9%	10.4×
	Natural/organic food	17.9%	(2.6%)	17.1×
	Baked goods	(4.5%)	(23.5%)	9.5×
	Dairy	14.1%	8.4%	13.7×
	Non-alcoholic beverages	1.8%	(5.4%)	12.5×
	Alcoholic beverages	1.7%	(11.3%)	13.5×
	Snacks	14.0%	4.3%	15.0×

Source: Harris Williams & Co., Jan 2017

The first analysis regards the *industry*, as it is logical to assume that companies engaged in the same industry have a similar operating risk. Sometimes, classifying a company within a specific industry is difficult as it may be engaged in several businesses. For example, Montblanc has four business units: writing items, leather goods, jewelry, and watches. Thus, Montblanc is engaged in unrelated sectors that require specific strategies, production methods, management of company processes, and know-how. Given that writing items, once the company's main business, today account for about 50% of revenues, it is not easy to identify which is Montblanc's core industry.

The same boundaries between the sectors, moreover, may be blurred, a circumstance that must be kept in mind when selecting the peer group. For example, it is not infrequent for companies such as Montblanc to be positioned across different industries, comprising fashion, jewelry, and automotive companies, inter alia (luxury goods sector), on the assumption that homogeneity is ensured not so much by the products, but by the target customers.

Furthermore, valuers must pay attention to oversimplifications. For example, food and beverages are commonly treated as a homogeneous industry, while they actually consist of various segments that are quite different from each other. Table 5.1 shows the key statistics of the food and beverage industry.

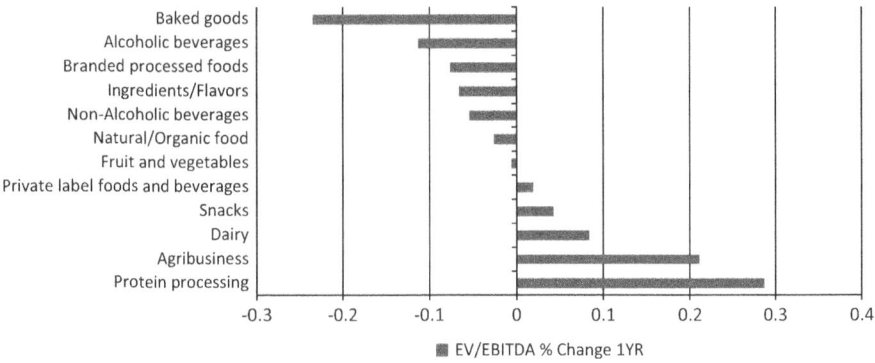

Fig. 5.2 EV/EBITDA % change over one year

The values of the segments included in the food and beverage industry have little or no correlation between them, as can be seen by comparing the percentage changes in the EV/EBITDA multiple over one year (Fig. 5.2).

The representativeness of the sample is also linked to its *geographical scope*.

There are companies that have a small number of comparables on a national basis, especially in countries with few publicly traded companies. For example, it is far easier to identify an adequate number of comparables in the NYSE or Nasdaq than in any single European Stock Exchange.

In addition, there are companies that, on the domestic level, are engaged in a sector with few competitors, such as car manufacturers or telephone operators.

This is why, taking into account the characteristics of the business, it is advisable to consider a wider geographical scope, which includes a higher number of firms and, therefore, a higher number of comparables. There are several options that depend on the perspective of the analysis and the type of business—for example, Western Europe, Europe, Europe and the US, G8 countries, G20 countries, and so on.

Obviously, the valuer must select countries that are comparable from a legislative, macroeconomic, and market standpoint. For example, following the commencement of the Brexit process, one has to understand whether British companies may in the future be included in a panel of European firms or otherwise.

Another aspect to be considered is the *competitive positioning* of comparable companies. Competitive positioning is a complex variable to be examined, since, in the abstract, there are no suitable metrics to quantify it. In general, many variables must be compared, such as customers and suppliers, turnover, sourcing markets, end markets, production characteristics, distribution channels, and so on, provided, of course, that such information is available and easily accessible.

Although companies in the same industry respond to similar logics and operate according to similar business models, not all operators have the same characteristics. For example, when evaluating a small cap of the food and beverage industry, using the multiples of Nestlé, Unilever, or the Kraft Heinz Company does not make sense, as the latter are large caps with global operations. Rather, companies operating in the same segment and with turnover and performance similar to those of the target company must be identified.

In addition to the competitive positioning, the *size and the performance* of the target company must also be considered. Usually, these variables provide the basis for a research strategy aimed at identifying a group of homogeneous comparables. Selecting suitable parameters is more complex than it may at first appear.

Indeed, valuers must:

(a) identify the parameters that best represent the characteristics of the target company; and
(b) identify comparable companies based on these parameters.

As mentioned in Chap. 3, there may be more than one parameter to measure the size and performance of the company. A firm may be analyzed on the basis of profitability (revenues, EBIT margin, ROI, ROE, distribution of revenues by geographical area, and market segment), solvency (quick ratio, debt-to-equity ratio, FCF), growth prospects (EBIT growth, revenues growth), or a mix of them. However, sometimes parameters are not aligned.

For example, some companies may be comparable in terms of revenues, but have significantly different EBIT margins; or they may have the same profitability, but a different financial structure. The potential combinations are endless and using too many parameters may result in no comparable companies at all.

For this reason, valuers must identify no more than two to three parameters they consider essential for their research strategy, taking into account the specifics of the business. For example, in the biotechnology sector, two relevant parameters are R&D expenses and capital expenditures. On the other hand, working capital turnover and the FCF are relevant factors in the valuation of service companies.

From a practical point of view, revenues and the number of employees are usually used as first-level parameters; they enable the search to be circumscribed to companies of similar size. As second-level parameters, all other performance measures can be used, depending on the type of analysis the valuer intends to focus on.

Furthermore, it is advisable to make sure that all the firms in the peer group have adopted the same accounting standards.

Another aspect to consider is whether the target company is a pure player or if it acts as part of a group. The performance of a company that is part of a *group of companies* is different from that of a pure player, as within a group various factors may come into play, such as synergies with other subsidiaries, economies of scale and scope, cash pooling, and so on. The effects of these factors can be significant and difficult to eliminate from the analysis.

In general, it is preferable for the peer group of comparable companies to be formed by pure players, including when the target company is part of a group. Obviously, there are sectors where this is not possible, for example, in the automotive industry, where all players are multinational groups.

Another aspect to consider is the *maturity* of both the target company and the peer group companies. Start-ups, especially in the fastest-growing businesses, can have extremely volatile performances. In such cases the correlation between EV and performance measure may be weak. The experience of speculative bubbles suggests that market euphoria can lead to the overestimation of comparable companies and, consequently, of the target company.

The choice of the multiple also depends also on the reference *time frame*. Valuers can choose from among different types of multiples: current, trailing, forward.

Current multiples are obtained by comparing stock prices and the last available balance sheet.

Trailing multiples are obtained by comparing stock prices and the results of the last 12 months before the date chosen to calculate the index. Results on the previous 12 months are taken by the four-quarterly report or the last biyearly report provided by the companies.

Forward multiples are obtained by comparing stock prices and the expected results of the following year or those of the next ones. Estimations are usually taken by the consensus forecast, published by financial analysts' associations.

In very volatile markets, using multiples based on historical data (current and trailing) is preferable.

Finally, in an equity-side valuation it is necessary to select comparables that have the same *tax rate*. For example, earnings taxed at 15%, 25%, or 35%, respectively, lead to significantly different P/E values. To prevent non-homogeneous comparisons, it is advisable to compare companies that are subject to equivalent tax systems.

5.5.2 Selection of Peer Group in the Comparable Transaction Method

In the comparable transaction method, the choice of the sample requires analyzing several parameters, both quantitative and qualitative. More specifically—as mentioned—one has to consider that this method can be based on prices that reflect premiums linked to transaction-related synergies or specific competitive advantages, which cannot be extended to the target company. The following parameters must be taken into consideration:

1. industry;
2. geographical scope;
3. dimension and performance;
4. reference time period;
5. type of transaction;
6. target of the transaction;
7. suspensive conditions of the contract.

The first parameter to consider is the firm's *industry*. While in the comparable companies method there is only one subject to be compared, that is, the publicly traded company, in the comparable transaction method there are three subjects: the target company, the seller, and the buyer. Since the buyer and seller may not be industry players—but rather holding companies, private equity funds, pension funds—the reference industry should always be that of the target company. Otherwise, the same considerations set out in Sect. 5.5.1 also apply to this method.

Geographical scope is often a relevant parameter, especially in cross-border deals. The fact that several legal systems may come into play may affect the technicalities as well as the pricing. For example, in some countries, foreign companies cannot hold the entire share capital of a company; this circumstance obviously affects the price of the transaction and, therefore, the multiples.

As regards *dimension* and *performance*, the same considerations set out in Sect. 5.5.1 fully apply to this method. As to the search strategy intended to identify the peer group, using the revenues and the number of employees as first-level parameter is again advisable; as second-level parameters, the other available performance measures can be used, depending on the analytical perspective the valuer intends to focus on. However, in most cases, the performance measures reported by both databases and open sources are EV/Sales, EV/EBITDA, and EV/EBIT.

A further issue concerns the *time period* in which the transaction took place, which should be close to the valuation reference date. Again, the considerations set out in Sect. 5.5.1 apply here, considering that, if there are no recent significant transactions, other transactions carried out over a wider period of time can be used, provided that the methodology remains essentially consistent.

Other aspects to consider are the *type of transaction*, the payment method, and the level of control achieved in the target company. All these variables affect the value of the deal and, therefore, on the multiples. There are numerous options, such cash payment, business combinations, buyouts, assumption of liabilities, and so on.

A cash payment tends to provide the best evidence of value, since, although it is affected by the negotiating contingency, it is a good approximation of a fair value. On the other hand, in business combinations, it is not just the value of the deal that matters, but also the competitive advantages achieved through the deal. The assumption of liabilities is a fairly common form of price, which, however, may not be fully representative of the theoretical value of the target company, as it may also reflect the buyer's advantage from obtaining a payment deferral on the debt assumed by the counterparty.

The relationships between buyer, seller, and target company also play a role in the transaction. A transaction between independent parties is likely to reflect a reliable market price, while the price determined in a related party transaction might not be fully representative of value, especially if the companies involved in the transaction are not regulated by a supervisory authority.

Finally, the price paid for the acquisition of a stake could be influenced by valuation discounts and premiums for business interests (see Chap. 8). The purchase of a controlling interest gives rise to a control premium, while the purchase of a minority interest could result in a discount, since a partial ownership interest may be less than its proportional share of the total business.

Another aspect to be considered when selecting the peer group is the *target of the transaction*. For example, in November 2015, Albertsons signed an agreement with Heggen to acquire a business unit that comprised 30 food outlets, for an amount of $14.4 million; in January 2016, Sezarc Company formalized the acquisition of the Southern Comfort and Tuaca business units from the Brown-Forman Corporation for $540 million. In the former case, 30 retail outlets were the target of the transaction; in the latter case, two well-known brands in the spirits sector. The data from these transactions may not be suitable to evaluate a target company operating in the food and beverage industry, as the deal concerned specific assets (30 stores in the first case and 2 brands in the second).

A further analysis should then be carried out regarding any *suspensive conditions of the contract* that may affect the value of the transaction and, consequently, the multiple; such conditions are however difficult to identify. For example, a residual part of the price could be linked to the occurrence of circumstances not yet defined when the deal was closed, which could change the overall value of the transaction.

5.5.3 Selection of Peer Group: Application Tools

In the market multiple method, the selection of a homogeneous peer group is essential to obtain a reliable value of the target company. The valuer must especially consider two aspects:

1. the number of elements composing the peer group;
2. the standard deviation of the multiples in the peer group.

The *number* of firms or transactions that make up a peer group cannot be determined a priori.

In some cases, a large peer group can be built as a large number of comparable companies are available. In other cases, the number of comparables may be very limited; this is common for companies in niche sectors, with outstanding performance measures and a non-replicable business model.

In general, the larger the sample size, the lower the standard error, which is calculated as follows:

$$\text{Standard Error} = \frac{\text{Standard deviation}_{\text{Comparable firms}}}{\sqrt{n}}$$

where n is the number of companies in the peer group.

Table 5.2 shows two peer groups (A and B) that contain multiples for a specific sector. Peer group A consists of five comparable firms (C_1, ..., C_5), while peer group B is composed of ten comparable firms (C_1, ..., C_{10}).

The average value of the multiples of peer group A is the same as the multiples of peer group B, that is, 7.54. The standard deviation is also almost the same: 0.52 for peer group A and 0.51 for peer group B. The standard error, however, differs significantly: 0.23 for peer group A and 0.16 for peer group B. In other words, peer group B has a lower standard error compared to peer group A, due to the higher number of companies in the group.

Table 5.2 Comparison between two peer groups

	C_1	C_2	C_3	C_4	C_5	C_6	C_7	C_8	C_9	C_{10}	Mean	St. Dev.	St. Error
Peer group A	7.5×	8.2×	6.9×	7.2×	7.9×	–	–	–	–	–	7.54×	0.52	0.23
Peer group B	7.5×	8.2×	6.9×	7.2×	7.9×	7.9×	7.1×	8.1×	6.8×	7.8×	7.54×	0.51	0.16

This simple example illustrates the importance of constructing a peer group with a large number of comparable companies, since the standard error decreases as the number of comparables increases.

For this reason, the use of specific databases is recommended, as they enable the construction of a more consistent and larger peer group than that obtainable from open sources.

In general, the comparable companies method has a lower standard error than the comparable transactions method, as the number of publicly traded comparable companies is statistically higher and temporally more homogeneous than that of comparable transactions.

A further aspect to consider is the *standard deviation* of multiples of the peer group. In general, the lower the standard deviation, the greater the homogeneity of the peer group. Table 5.3 shows peer group A and peer group B, each consisting of six comparable firms; both groups are homogeneous in terms of industry, size, performance, and so on. For each peer group the EV/EBITDA multiple is reported.

The mean and the median of the two peer groups are substantially identical. However, the values that make up the peer groups are different. Peer group A has a higher dispersion, as the EV/EBITDA values range from 4.9× to 12.9×. Peer group B, on the other hand, has a smaller dispersion; the values are more homogeneous, with a range between 7.8× and 8.5×.

This is confirmed by the standard deviation, which is 2.95 for peer group A and 0.27 for peer group B. The standard deviation shows how the data are distributed in a peer group with respect to the average; in other words, the standard deviation tells us whether the average is a reliable figure, that is, if it provides a meaningful representation of the data. The closer the value is to 0, the more the peer group is reliable, as it has less dispersion.

Companies belonging to the same industry may have significantly different values. Take for example the top five companies by capitalization of the food and beverage industry (data as of January 2016). They are homogeneous from

Table 5.3 Peer group's standard deviation

Peer group A	EV/EBITDA	Peer group B	EV/EBITDA
C_1	5.7×	C_1	8.5×
C_2	7.9×	C_2	8.1×
C_3	4.9×	C_3	8.2×
C_4	10.2×	C_4	7.9×
C_5	7.8×	C_5	8.4×
C_6	12.9×	C_6	7.8×
Mean	8.2×	Mean	8.2×
Median	7.9×	Median	8.2×
Max	12.9×	Max	8.5×
Min	4.9×	Min	7.8×
St. Dev.	2.95	St. Dev.	0.27

Table 5.4 Standard deviation of EV/EBITDA

Company	Market cap ($mil)	EBITDA margin %	EV/EBITDA
Nestlé	229.670	19%	10.0×
Unilever	122,484	17%	13.6×
The Kraft Heinz Company	92,198	22%	38.6×
Mondelez International	65,712	16%	16.8×
Danone	40,173	16%	12.6×
Mean	110,047	0.18	18.32×
Median	92,198	0.17	13.60×
St. Dev.	–	0.03	11.60

various standpoints: they are multinational, are engaged in the same markets, have a comparable EBITDA margin (between 16% and 22%), own well-known brands. Nevertheless, the dispersion of the EV/EBITDA multiplier is quite significant (from 10.0× to 38.6×), as shown in Table 5.4.

Although the standard deviation of the EBITDA margin is quite modest, confirming the consistency of the peer group, the standard deviation of the multiple is significantly high.

5.6 Correlation Between Multiple and Performance Measure

The choice of a multiple is a delicate step, as each multiple examines a different perspective, such as profitability (EV/Sales, EV/EBITDA, EV/EBIT, etc.), solvency (EV/FCF, etc.), the attitude to innovate (EV/R&D expenses), and so on; thus, each multiple inevitably leads to different results.

Table 5.5 Correlation between multiples and EBITDA margin

Peer group	EV/FCF	EV/Sales	EBITDA margin %
C_1	9.2×	3.4×	12.3
C_2	8.5×	2.9×	11.2
C_3	9.1×	3.1×	11.8
C_4	7.5×	2.6×	9.7
C_5	8.9×	3.2×	10.5
C_6	8.1×	2.9×	10.2
C_7	8.8×	2.6×	11.6
C_8	9.1×	3.5×	12.1
C_9	8.2×	2.8×	10.9
C_{10}	9.5×	3.0×	12.6
Mean	8.69×	3.00×	11.3
Median	8.85×	2.95×	11.4
St. Dev.	0.61	0.31	0.01
Min	7.5×	2.6×	9.7
Max	9.5×	3.5×	12.6
ρ (EBITDA margin)	0.90	0.54	–
R^2	0.80	0.28	–

Once the peer group has been selected, the multiple that best reflects the value map of the target company must be identified. To this end, the theoretically most suitable multiple should be identified, taking also into account the correlation with one or more significant performance measures.

Correlation (ρ) helps understand the relationship between a multiplier and a performance measure. This, in turn, helps identify the multiple that better depicts the business, with respect to a parameter that is considered significant.

Assume that the EBITDA margin % is considered as an essential parameter and that the valuer must choose whether to use EV/FCF or the EV/Sales. The multiple that has a greater correlation with the EBITDA margin % should be chosen. In the example in Table 5.5, the EV/FCF multiple has a higher correlation and coefficient of determination (R^2) with the EBITDA margin % than the EV/Sales multiple.

This means that, despite the standard deviation being higher, EV/FCF has a closer "relationship" with the EBITDA margin than with EV/Sales. Therefore, in a value map perspective, the EV/FCF more reliably reflects the value of the target company. Figure 5.3 shows the regression line of both EV/FCF and EV/Sales.

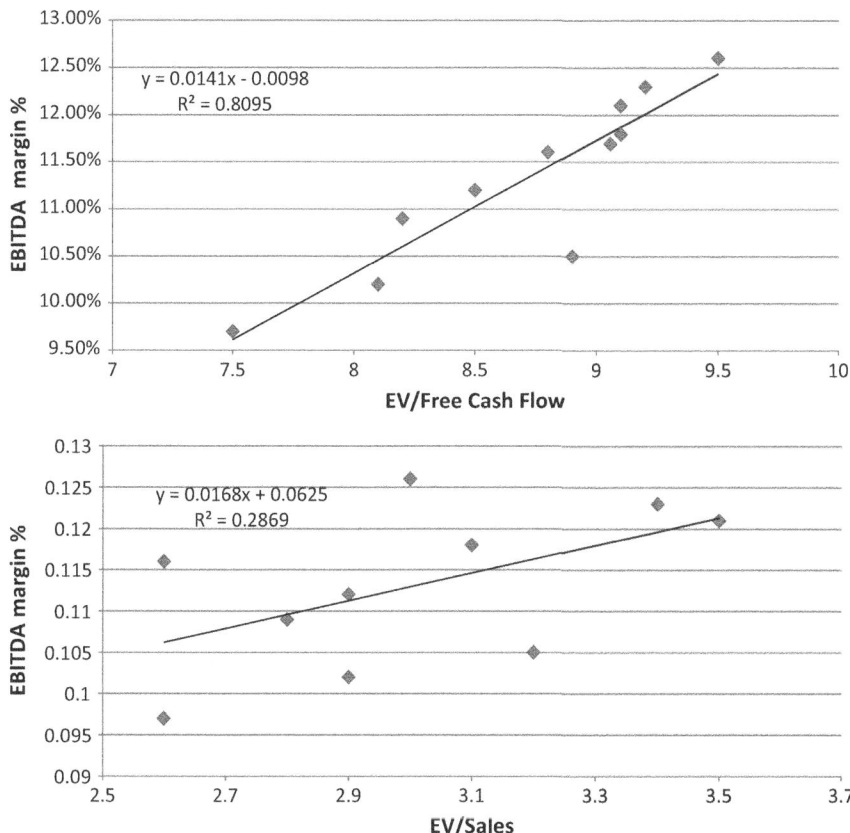

Fig. 5.3 EV/FCF and EV/Sales regression

5.7 Asset-Side Multiples

According to the asset-side approach, the market multiple is equal to the ratio of the EV to an unlevered performance measure.

$$\text{Market multiple} = \frac{\text{Enterprise Value}}{\text{Unlevered performance measure}}$$

The most commonly used performance measures are sales, EBITDA, EBIT, FCF.

Table 5.6 Application of the EV/Sales

Income statement	Company A	Company B
Sales	$850,000	$850,000
Operating expenses	($750,000)	($550,000)
Gross margin	**$100,000**	**$300,000**
Labor cost	($130,000)	($130,000)
EBITDA	**($30,000)**	**$170,000**
Amortization	($20,000)	($20,000)
EBIT	**($50,000)**	**$150,000**
Interest	($10,000)	($10,000)
Earnings before taxes	**($60,000)**	**$140,000**

5.7.1 EV/Sales

The EV/Sales multiple measures the value of a business based on sales:

$$\text{Multiple} = \frac{\text{Enterprise Value}}{\text{Sales}}$$

Sales are a first-level parameter when selecting a peer group. Therefore, a sales-based multiple has a good correlation with the multiples of companies in the peer group.

Nevertheless, a business valuation exclusively based on EV/Sales may be limiting, as revenues do not provide sufficient feedback on the firm's efficiency, attitude to generate cash flows, and ability to meet its obligations.

This is easy to understand, if we consider the income statements of company A and company B shown in Table 5.6.

Both companies have the same sales and the same costs, except for operating expenses, which are higher in company A than in company B. Therefore, company A reports a loss while company B makes a profit. Assuming that the companies are engaged in the same industry and that the average EV/Sales = 1.2×, we obtain:

$$EV_{\text{Company A}} = \$850,000 \times 1.2 = \$1,020,000$$

$$EV_{\text{Company B}} = \$850,000 \times 1.2 = \$1,020,000$$

The two companies have the same value, regardless of cost structure and profitability. From a logical standpoint this is not correct.

This means that EV/Sales does not independently provide a feedback on value, as it is not able to grasp the complexity of a company. However, it may be used as a second-level multiple that provides feedback with respect to another multiple used as main valuation parameter.

The EV/Sales multiple may only be used as a stand-alone parameter if the target company and the peer group have numerous elements in common, such as the EBITDA margin, the debt-to-equity, and so on.

Typically, the sales multiple is a popular valuation shortcut to quickly evaluate both technology and high-growth companies with negative profits and cash flows for which reversing this trend in the short term is unlikely. For these companies, sales are a more stable performance measure than profit or cash flow. In many cases they are also the only performance measure.

Some authors argue that sales are a more neutral parameter than others, since they are not influenced by accounting standards. This is actually not true. The International Financial Reporting Standards (IFRS) and Financial Accounting Standard Board (FASB) have developed common revenue recognition standards (IFRS 15 and Topic 606) with the aim of: removing inconsistencies and weaknesses in existing revenue requirements; providing a more robust framework for addressing revenue issues; improving comparability of revenue recognition practices across entities, industries, jurisdictions, and capital markets.

Ultimately, in business valuations, EV/Sales is rarely used as a single multiple and is more frequently used as a control multiple.

5.7.2 EV/EBITDA

The EV/EBITDA multiple measures the value of a business based on EBITDA:

$$\text{Multiple} = \frac{\text{Enterprise Value}}{\text{EBITDA}}$$

Being calculated gross of amortization and depreciation, this multiple is widely used, as it is not significantly influenced by accounting policies. EV/EBITDA is therefore a relatively neutral multiple through which firms in the same industry can be easily compared.

This is an advantage, but also a limitation: since investments are not taken into account, EV/EBITDA may lead to an over- or undervaluation, depending on the amount of depreciation/amortization.

Consider the income statements of company A and company B shown in Table 5.7.

Both companies have the same EBITDA.

Assuming the average EV/EBITDA = 5.4, we obtain:

Table 5.7 Application of the EV/EBITDA

Income statement	Company A	Company B
Sales	$850,000	$850,000
Operating expenses	($550,000)	($550,000)
Gross margin	**$300,000**	**$300,000**
Labor cost	($130,000)	($130,000)
EBITDA	**$170,000**	**$170,000**
Amortization	($60,000)	($20,000)
EBIT	**$110,000**	**$150,000**
Interest	($10,000)	($10,000)
Earnings before taxes	**$100,000**	**$140,000**

$$EV_{\text{Company A}} = \$170,000 \times 5.4 = \$918,000$$

$$EV_{\text{Company B}} = \$170,000 \times 5.4 = \$918,000$$

The companies have the same value. However, the amortization/depreciation amount of company A is three times that of company B ($60,000 vs. $20,000). This means that the employed capital of company A is higher than that of company B. There are two possible reasons for this:

- Company A is less efficient and is unable to adequately use its employed capital; although it makes higher investments, Company A has the same EBITDA as company B;
- Company B does not make sufficient investments and runs the risk of a potential operating gap with respect to company A.

The scenario is quite different. In the first case, company A is likely to be overvalued, as its results are the same of a company that requires less investment. On the contrary, in the second case, company B risks being overvalued, as it has the same EV of a company that is regularly investing.

The integrated valuation approach encourages a valuer not to slavishly apply a formula, but to weigh results according to a larger number of parameters. This simple example shows how reductive it is, in a valuation based on EV/EBITDA, to merely look at the EBITDA, without considering the "lower part" of the income statement.

5.7.3 EV/EBIT

The EV/EBIT multiple measures the value of a business based on EBIT:

$$\text{Multiple} = \frac{\text{Enterprise Value}}{\text{EBIT}}$$

Compared to EV/EBITDA, this multiple also considers the effects of amortization and depreciation; it therefore provides more complete information, as it also takes into account the firm's investments and evaluates a business based on operating profit.

On the other hand, EV/EBIT is more exposed to the influence of accounting policies, as each company may have different levels of amortization as a result of different accounting standards, different investment policies, and different business models. For example, according to the local accounting standards of some European countries, leased assets are not recorded as assets, as they are not owned by the firm. Accordingly, they are not subject to depreciation/amortization.

Different levels of depreciation/amortization may also depend on investment policies. A company that conducts its business with more obsolete assets incurs lower depreciation charges, while a company that keeps its assets regularly up to date has a higher level of depreciation charges.

The business model also affects the level of depreciation/amortization. For example, capital expenditures are lower in companies that outsource part of their production activities; as a result, these companies have lower depreciation charges, but higher costs for services.

Consider the income statements of company A and company B shown in Table 5.8.

Table 5.8 Application of the EV/EBIT

Income statement	Company A	Company B
Sales	$850,000	$850,000
Operating expenses	($650,000)	($550,000)
Gross margin	**$200,000**	**$300,000**
Labor cost	($130,000)	($130,000)
EBITDA	**$70,000**	**$170,000**
Amortization	($10,000)	($110,000)
EBIT	**$60,000**	**$60,000**
Interest	($10,000)	($10,000)
Earnings before taxes	**$50,000**	**$50,000**

Both companies have the same EBIT. Company A outsources some of its production activities and requires a low level of investments; on the other hand, company B produces internally and has made significant investments. Thus, what differentiates the two companies is their business model. The multiples of the peer group are as follows: EV/EBITDA = 4.8×; EV/EBIT = 8.2×.

If the companies are valued with the EV/EBITDA, the results are as follows:

$$EV_{Company\ A} = \$70,000 \times 4.8 = \$336,000$$

$$EV_{Company\ B} = \$170,000 \times 4.8 = \$816,000$$

If the companies are valued with the EV/EBIT, the results are as follows:

$$EV_{Company\ A} = \$60,000 \times 8.2 = \$492,000$$

$$EV_{Company\ B} = \$60,000 \times 8.2 = \$492,000$$

The EV/EBITDA valuation shows two significantly different values; taking into account that the two companies have the same sales, the same EBIT, and the same earnings before taxes, this difference cannot be justified; EBITDA, in this case, is probably not the performance measure that better interprets the value of the company. The EV/EBIT valuation, on the other hand, does justice to the substantial homogeneity of the values, which the EBITDA is not able to capture.

In general, companies that require a high level of investments have EV/EBIT multiples significantly different from the EV/EBITDA multiples. Table 5.9 shows the multiples of some automotive industry manufacturers.

We can see that for investment-intensive companies, the level of amortization/depreciation has a significant impact. Conversely, for companies that have a low level of investments, the EV/EBIT and the EV/EBITDA tend to coincide.

Ultimately, EV/EBIT has the advantage of measuring value based on operating profit; to obtain consistent results, the selected peer group must be made up of companies that have adopted the same accounting standards and must be sufficiently numerous to mitigate the effects of different investment policies.

Table 5.9 EV/EBITDA and EV/EBIT in automotive industry (Q1 2016, Source: Capital IQ)

Manufacturer	Market cap ($mil)	EV/EBITDA	EV/EBIT
Toyota Motor Corporation	$160,909	6.8×	10.2×
Daimler AG	$82,085	6.9×	12.2×
Ford Motor Co.	$53,758	9.2×	16.6×
Volkswagen AG	$68,949	6.6×	13.0×
Bayerische Motoren Werke A.	$59,989	9.7×	13.1×
Nissan Motor Co.	$41,144	6.9×	13.5×
Honda Motor Co.	$49,500	10.1×	13.4×
General Motor Company	$48,653	5.8×	10.1×
Hyundai Motor Company	$24,067	7.1×	8.8×
Fiat Chrysler Automobiles N.V.	$10,423	2.1×	4.5×
Kia Motor Corp.	$16,958	3.6×	4.6×
Peugeot S.A.	$13,670	2.5×	3.9×
Mazda Motor Corporation	$9292	3.6×	4.7×
Mean	$46,698	6.2×	9.9×
Median	$41,144	6.8×	10.2×

5.7.4 EV/Free Cash Flow

The EV/FCF multiple calculates the EV taking into account the ability to generate cash flow:

$$\text{Multiple} = \frac{\text{Enterprise Value}}{\text{Free Cash Flow}}$$

As a performance measure, cash flow:

- is neutral, since it is not influenced by either accounting standards or accounting policies;
- is objective, because it measures value based on data that are certain.

The main limitation of cash flow is that it is subject to a certain degree of volatility over time, as it is influenced by various elements, such as trade receivables turnover, trade payables turnover, inventory turnover, CapEx, and so on. Ultimately, cash flow does not have the same stability as EBIT and EBITDA.

For this reason, although it is a multiple based on objective data, its application is less widespread than income statement multiples.

The inverse of EV/FCF is the FCF yield, which is the ratio of FCF to EV:

$$\text{FCF Yield} = \frac{\text{Free Cash Flow}}{\text{Enterprise Value}}$$

The FCF yield is a return evaluation ratio of a stock, which indicates the FCF a company is expected to earn against its market price. Generally, the lower the ratio, the less attractive the investment is, and vice versa. The logic behind this is that investors are willing to pay as little price as possible for as many cash flows as possible.

The FCF yield establishes the relationship between the money an investor puts in a company compared to the returns it generates. Specifically, it investigates if the capital expenditures are justified by fixed asset investment. For example, if a firm's CapEx is high, yet the asset turnover ratio does not indicate a relative intensive use of the assets, the company spends more money than the income it generates.

5.8 Comparison Between EV/EBITDA and EV/EBIT

The EV/EBITDA and EV/EBIT multiples are different indicators. Thus, an in-depth analysis is proposed which sets two objectives:

1. verifying how the EV/EBITDA and the EV/EBIT evolved in the 2005–2015 period through the comparable companies method;
2. identifying the multiple that has the lower level of volatility.

From a methodological standpoint:

(a) the analysis concerns multiples that refer to the North American market, as it constitutes a relatively homogeneous context from regulatory and Generally Accepted Accounting Principles (GAAP)-application points of view, and a reliable and comprehensive time series is available;
(b) multiples do not refer to specific companies, but to average sector values, as identified by Bloomberg, Datastream, and Damodaran On Line;
(c) the sectors have been selected considering their relevance; however, it is possible that a larger sample may lead to partially different results.

Furthermore, it should be noted that the multiples refer to an extremely long period of time; during that period many changes took place, which inevitably have an impact on the volatility of the markets and, therefore, on values.

5.8.1 The Peer Group

As stated, the peer group is made up of the North American market. For each of these and for every year considered (2005–2015), the EV/EBITDA and EV/EBIT multiples and beta coefficient have been identified (Table 5.10):
The data show that:

(a) multiples vary across sectors; this is due to differences in the competitive environment, in the business model, in the financial structure, and so on;
(b) on average, the beta coefficient is 1: this confirms that the peer group has a "neutral" risk level; therefore, any volatility in the value of multiples does not depend on high-risk sectors;
(c) the EV/EBIT multiple has a higher standard deviation than the EV/EBITDA multiple, presumably due to the different level of investment in the various sectors.

5.8.2 Evolution and Volatility in Multiples Over Time

As mentioned, the first objective is to verify how the average value of multiples evolved over the 2005–2015 period (Tables 5.11 and 5.12). For each sector the mean, median, min, max, and standard deviation have been calculated.

In both cases, it can be observed that the value of multiples changes from one year to another, sometimes significantly, especially in sectors characterized by a higher degree of volatility.

For example, the EV/EBITDA of the "power" industry shows a significant interval between minimum and maximum value: the maximum value (in 2006) is about seven times the minimum value (in 2011). An even greater volatility can be observed for the EV/EBIT multiple.

For a more intuitive understanding of the changes in multiples over time, Tables 5.13 and 5.14 show year-on-year percentage changes (YoY).

Almost all the changes are significant, confirming that multiples are affected by market trends. It is interesting to note that the most significant change took place in 2008, at the onset of the subprime crisis.

Table 5.10 The peer group

Business sector	2005 EV/EBITDA	2005 EV/EBIT	2005 Beta	2006 EV/EBITDA	2006 EV/EBIT	2006 Beta	2007 EV/EBITDA	2007 EV/EBIT	2007 Beta	2008 EV/EBITDA	2008 EV/EBIT	2008 Beta	2009 EV/EBITDA	2009 EV/EBIT	2009 Beta	2010 EV/EBITDA	2010 EV/EBIT	2010 Beta
Air transport	11.0x	22.4x	1.03	8.5x	14.0x	1.03	6.4x	9.5x	1.01	4.8x	7.2x	0.72	7.9x	14.4x	0.67	10.2x	20.7x	0.85
Apparel	8.8x	11.2x	0.77	10.9x	13.4x	0.84	8.9x	11.0x	0.76	4.9x	6.2x	0.83	8.1x	10.4x	1.09	9.8x	12.9x	1.20
Auto and truck	7.9x	14.0x	0.50	10.0x	21.4x	0.64	6.5x	12.2x	0.87	3.8x	6.1x	0.56	10.7x	91.2x	0.74	11.2x	112.1x	0.83
Bank	NA	NA	0.39	6.0x	6.0x	0.43	4.9x	4.9x	0.39	3.8x	3.8x	0.30	5.6x	5.6x	0.28	4.8x	4.8x	0.30
Beverage (alcoholic)	11.0x	13.7x	0.46	12.2x	16.3x	0.55	16.0x	21.5x	0.77	8.7x	11.7x	0.78	11.0x	14.4x	0.84	11.8x	14.8x	0.74
Beverage (soft drink)	12.5x	15.9x	0.54	13.2x	16.9x	0.63	16.9x	22.3x	0.85	9.9x	12.5x	0.83	11.9x	15.0x	0.90	12.6x	15.4x	0.83
Biotechnology	43.8x	61.2x	1.58	29.4x	38.6x	1.50	20.3x	25.8x	1.39	20.6x	27.1x	1.15	21.8x	32.3x	0.96	15.9x	20.9x	1.01
Broadcasting	11.3x	34.9x	1.20	12.8x	31.1x	1.31	9.1x	18.5x	1.08	6.3x	13.4x	0.94	6.2x	12.4x	1.02	6.6x	12.7x	0.95
Building materials	8.1x	10.5x	0.79	7.6x	9.8x	0.78	7.7x	10.1x	0.83	6.0x	9.0x	0.75	8.3x	14.1x	0.84	11.7x	29.3x	0.83
Chemical (specialty)	10.0x	14.7x	0.76	10.0x	14.4x	0.84	10.5x	14.9x	0.93	6.4x	9.1x	0.92	8.3x	12.8x	1.03	11.8x	19.2x	1.15
Coal	16.7x	30.4x	0.82	10.2x	16.0x	1.53	13.7x	21.4x	1.52	6.9x	13.0x	1.39	8.6x	12.3x	1.39	11.2x	17.5x	1.39
Computer services	13.9x	17.3x	2.00	14.6x	18.1x	1.79	15.4x	19.0x	1.51	7.4x	8.8x	1.14	11.3x	13.6x	0.97	11.8x	13.9x	1.01
Drug	13.2x	16.7x	1.47	13.6x	18.2x	1.46	11.8x	15.9x	1.67	8.6x	11.5x	1.03	9.3x	12.0x	0.99	9.0x	11.7x	0.97
Electronics	11.8x	19.6x	1.48	11.6x	20.0x	1.33	11.6x	18.2x	1.17	4.1x	6.1x	0.93	7.6x	11.4x	0.94	10.1x	16.1x	0.98
Entertainment	9.7x	14.4x	1.17	11.4x	15.2x	1.07	9.9x	13.8x	1.17	5.3x	7.1x	1.01	7.0x	9.4x	1.21	10.1x	13.1x	1.36
Environmental	8.7x	14.5x	0.51	10.1x	17.1x	0.60	9.3x	14.7x	0.71	7.8x	11.9x	0.78	8.5x	12.8x	0.68	9.5x	14.5x	0.62
Food processing	10.3x	14.4x	0.50	11.0x	14.1x	0.61	12.3x	15.6x	0.66	8.4x	10.4x	0.63	9.1x	11.0x	0.69	10.0x	12.6x	0.72
Furnishings/home furnishings	8.9x	12.2x	0.82	9.0x	12.0x	0.71	7.3x	9.9x	0.88	4.2x	5.8x	0.86	8.71x	14.6x	1.16	11.9x	22.2x	1.37
Hotel/gaming	14.5x	21.4x	0.63	18.1x	26.5x	0.60	15.0x	20.9x	0.96	6.48x	9.1x	0.78	10.4x	17.1x	1.00	20.3x	48.7x	1.24
Internet	48.0x	75.8x	2.73	29.3x	20.2x	2.25	30.6x	41.0x	1.94	11.5x	15.9x	1.36	20.2x	27.8x	1.02	19.8x	26.7x	1.09
Machinery	10.3x	14.5x	0.65	10.2x	13.7x	0.81	11.0x	14.2x	1.00	5.1x	6.5x	0.97	7.5x	10.0x	0.96	14.0x	22.2x	0.99

Market-Based Method   151

Maritime	6.3x	8.5x	0.44	8.0x	11.6x	0.55	12.0x	17.5x	0.59	7.2x	10.9x	0.48	7.0x
Packaging and container	8.3x	14.2x	0.53	9.1x	15.2x	0.61	8.0x	12.3x	0.80	5.4x	8.1x	0.77	7.1x
Paper/forest products	6.9x	11.5x	0.53	8.3x	15.7x	0.57	7.7x	12.8x	0.68	6.0x	13.18x	0.60	10.1x
Power	26.7x	43.5x	1.78	45.5x	85.0x	2.05	43.6x	66.1x	1.71	7.8x	11.95x	0.77	8.5x
Publishing	8.6x	13.4x	0.57	10.1x	15.1x	0.70	10.7x	4.0x	1.05	5.0x	6.5x	0.58	7.1x
Shoe	10.5x	12.3x	0.98	10.3x	11.9x	1.05	11.1x	2.6x	1.48	6.4x	7.7x	1.22	10.3x
Steel (general)	5.4x	6.5x	0.85	6.4x	7.6x	1.05	6.4x	7.4x	1.57	4.4x	5.2x	1.39	5.2x
Telecom. equipment	16.4x	21.2x	2.52	14.7x	18.3x	2.24	15.1x	18.7x	1.88	6.4x	8.8x	1.34	11.0x
Mean	13.5x	20.8x	1.00	13.2x	19.8x	1.04	12.7x	17.8x	1.10	6.9x	9.8x	0.89	9.4x
Median	10.4x	14.6x	0.79	10.32x	15.7x	0.84	11.0x	14.9x	1.00	6.4x	9.0x	0.83	8.5x
Min	5.4x	6.5x	0.39	6.0x	6.1x	0.43	4.9x	4.9x	0.39	3.8x	3.8x	0.30	5.2x
Max	48.0x	75.8x	2.73	45.5x	85.0x	2.25	43.6x	66.1x	1.94	20.6x	27.1x	1.39	21.84x
Standard deviation	10.02	15.75	0.62	8.28	14.80	0.52	7.85	11.47	0.41	3.22	4.45	0.28	3.63

10.2x	10.2x	0.57	10.3x	20.1x	0.59
11.2x	0.80	8.1x	12.58x	0.78
28.9x	0.91	7.2x	13.9x	0.96
12.6x	0.63	8.3x	12.6x	0.65
9.0x	0.90	6.2x	8.3x	0.94
12.4x	1.30	13.2x	15.8x	1.30
6.3x	1.30	8.9x	10.2x	1.32
17.12x	1.05	10.4x	14.5x	0.94
16.6x	0.92	10.9x	20.4x	0.96
12.6x	0.96	10.3x	14.8x	0.96
5.6x	0.28	4.8x	4.8x	0.30
91.2x	1.39	20.3x	112.6	1.39
15.57	0.23	3.46	19.46	0.26

(continued)

Table 5.10 (continued)

Business sector	2011 EV/EBITDA	2011 EV/EBIT	2011 Beta	2012 EV/EBITDA	2012 EV/EBIT	2012 Beta	2012 EV/EBITDA	2013 EV/EBIT	2013 Beta	2014 EV/EBITDA	2014 EV/EBIT	2014 Beta	2015 EV/EBITDA	2015 EV/EBIT	2015 Beta
Air transport	12.9x	20.2x	1.02	6.0x	9.3x	0.70	9.64x	14.6x	0.48	8.1x	22.2x	0.59	5.8x	9.7x	0.81
Apparel	8.6x	10.8x	1.13	11.7x	14.6x	1.23	14.1x	16.0x	0.96	12.3x	18.4x	0.84	10.8x	16.3x	0.85
Auto and truck	5.8x	10.4x	0.79	7.4x	13.9x	0.93	11.7x	24.0x	0.66	14.5x	41.1x	0.54	10.0x	20.9x	0.44
Bank	4.3x	4.3x	0.33	4.8x	4.8x	0.37	NA	NA	0.43	NA	NA	0.31	NA	NA	0.43
Beverage (alcoholic)	11.2x	13.9x	0.65	11.8x	14.6x	0.72	18.7x	22.7x	0.91	17.3x	21.2x	0.88	19.9x	24.1	0.81
Beverage (soft drink)	12.0x	14.8x	0.73	12.7x	15.5x	0.80	13.9x	16.8x	1.17	14.2x	17.6x	0.93	15.8x	19.6x	0.95
Biotechnology	NA	NA	0.91	22.4x	30.7x	1.07	22.8x	49.9x	1.02	19.0x	36.3x	1.02	13.6x	21.0x	1.12
Broadcasting	6.2x	11.2x	0.92	7.1x	12.3x	0.92	13.5x	15.5x	1.08	9.2x	14.8x	0.67	9.3x	15.1x	0.87
Building materials	10.9x	29.2x	0.82	14.4x	35.8x	0.99	14.4x	19.6x	1.02	11.8x	17.6x	0.88	11.4x	16.1x	0.94
Chemical (specialty)	9.8x	14.0x	1.09	10.8x	15.2x	1.00	10.8x	13.3x	0.89	11.8x	16.1x	0.86	10.6x	14.8x	0.97
Coal	7.3x	11.1x	1.22	5.9x	9.3x	0.91	9.2x	43.1x	0.69	8.9x	66.8x	0.78	6.0x	184.3x	0.36
Computer services	8.6x	9.8x	0.98	9.7x	11.1x	0.92	9.5x	11.0x	0.78	8.3x	10.7x	0.93	8.2x	10.8x	0.94
Drug	9.3x	13.0x	0.98	8.9x	12.1x	0.94	11.5x	15.6x	0.97	13.5x	18.7x	0.91	13.6x	19.3x	0.90
Electronics	5.8x	7.8x	0.89	6.6x	9.2x	1.01	11.8x	19.5x	0.89	11.2x	18.0x	0.91	9.4x	15.2x	0.87
Entertainment	8.0x	10.6x	1.21	9.5x	12.2x	1.24	12.6x	15.1x	0.95	11.7x	15.7x	0.95	10.3x	13.1x	0.94
Environmental	8.7x	13.5x	0.58	8.4x	12.7x	0.48	10.7x	17.1x	0.80	9.9x	17.1x	0.93	10.1x	18.5x	0.81
Food processing	9.5x	11.9x	0.74	10.1x	12.5x	0.74	12.2x	14.6x	0.69	11.9x	15.1x	0.80	14.9x	19.1x	0.72
Furnishings/home furnishings	9.6x	14.3x	1.52	8.3x	11.2x	1.37	11.2x	14.8x	0.99	10.3x	15.4x	0.89	9.9x	15.0x	0.98
Hotel/gaming	12.4x	20.5x	1.20	10.6x	15.6x	1.21	14.1x	22.0x	0.87	12.9x	22.5x	0.80	11.8x	20.0x	0.65

Internet	17.0x	21.4x	1.06	23.1x	31.6x	1.15	22.8x	33.6x	1.01	21.1x	33.7x	1.22	23.8x	39.0x	1.28
Machinery	9.1x	12.4x	1.04	9.9x	12.9x	1.11	12.0x	14.8x	0.91	10.4x	13.5x	1.05	9.6x	12.6x	1.16
Maritime	9.6x	18.1x	0.53	10.3x	21.6x	0.57	13.0x	21.0x	0.92	9.4x	19.5x	0.91	6.4x	13.5x	0.83
Packaging and container	7.1x	10.5x	0.83	7.5x	11.2x	0.84	9.1x	12.8x	0.71	9.0x	13.7x	0.68	9.4x	14.2x	0.88
Paper/forest products	5.4x	8.8x	0.89	7.2x	11.3x	0.99	9.7x	15.6x	0.90	9.0x	14.9x	0.58	9.1x	15.4x	0.87
Power	6.6x	10.1x	0.57	8.9x	21.7x	0.53	9.7x	16.8x	0.40	9.8x	18.1x	0.52	8.9x	15.3x	0.49
Publishing	6.4x	9.4x	0.82	8.7x	13.1x	0.92	10.1x	16.3x	0.82	9.5x	17.1x	0.82	8.8x	16.4x	1.01
Shoe	11.6x	13.4x	1.23	14.1x	16.9x	1.24	16.1x	18.9x	0.78	15.1x	20.2x	0.80	17.2x	23.2x	0.78
Steel (general)	7.1x	13.3x	1.23	5.6x	8.8x	1.16	10.3x	18.0x	0.85	8.6x	16.1x	0.85	7.4x	NA	0.79
Telecom. equipment	8.4x	11.5x	0.91	6.7x	8.5x	0.96	11.6x	14.6x	1.04	12.0x	15.8x	1.12	10.6x	13.6x	10.09
Mean	8.9x	13.2x	0.92	10.0x	14.8x	0.93	12.8x	19.6x	0.85	11.8x	21.0x	0.83	11.2x	23.6x	0.85
Median	8.7x	12.1x	0.91	8.9x	12.7x	0.94	11.7x	16.5x	0.89	11.3x	17.6x	0.86	10.1x	16.1x	0.87
Min	4.3x	4.3x	0.33	4.8x	4.8x	0.37	9.1x	11.0x	0.40	8.1x	10.7x	0.31	5.8x	9.7x	0.36
Max	17.x	29.2x	1.52	23.1x	35.8x	1.37	22.8x	49.9x	1.17	21.1	66.8x	1.22	23.8x	184.3x	1.28
Standard deviation	2.75	4.93	0.26	4.30	7.15	0.25	3.62	8.83	0.19	3.26	11.30	0.19	4.10	32.60	0.22

Table 5.11 Evolution of the EV/EBITDA multiple

Business sector	2005 EV/EBITDA	2006 EV/EBITDA	2007 EV/EBITDA	2008 EV/EBITDA	2009 EV/EBITDA	2010 EV/EBITDA	2011 EV/EBITDA	2012 EV/EBITDA	2013 EV/EBITDA	2014 EV/EBITDA	2015 EV/EBITDA	Mean	Median	Min	Max	St. Dev.
Air transport	11.0x	8.5x	6.4x	4.8x	7.9x	10.2x	12.9x	6.0x	9.6x	8.1x	5.8x	8.3x	8.1x	4.8x	12.9x	2.49
Apparel	8.8x	10.9x	8.9x	4.9x	8.1x	9.8x	8.6x	11.7x	14.1x	12.3x	10.8x	9.9x	9.8x	4.9x	14.1x	2.47
Auto and truck	7.9x	10.0x	6.5x	3.8x	10.7x	11.2x	5.8x	7.4x	11.7x	14.5x	10.0x	9.0x	10.0x	3.8x	14.5x	3.07
Bank	NA	6.0x	4.9x	3.8x	5.6x	4.8x	4.3x	4.8x	NA	NA	NA	4.9x	4.8x	3.9x	6.1x	0.74
Beverage (alcoholic)	11.0x	12.2x	16.0x	8.7x	11.0x	11.8x	11.2x	11.8x	18.7x	17.3x	19.9x	13.6x	11.8	8.8x	19.9x	3.70
Beverage (soft drink)	12.5x	13.2x	16.9x	9.9x	11.9x	12.6x	12.0x	12.7x	13.9x	14.2x	15.8x	13.2x	12.7x	9.9x	16.9x	1.92
Biotechnology	43.8x	29.4x	20.3x	20.6x	21.8x	15.9x	NA	22.4x	22.8x	19.0x	13.6x	23.0x	21.2x	13.6x	43.8x	8.46
Broadcasting	11.3x	12.8x	9.1x	6.3x	6.2x	6.6x	6.2x	7.1x	13.5x	9.2x	9.3x	8.9x	9.1x	6.2x	13.5x	2.69
Building materials	8.1x	7.6x	7.7x	6.0x	8.3x	11.7x	10.9x	14.4x	14.4x	11.8x	11.4x	10.2x	10.9x	6.0x	14.4x	2.86
Chemical (specialty)	10.0x	10.0x	10.5x	6.4x	8.3x	11.8x	9.8x	10.8x	10.8x	11.8x	10.6x	10.11x	10.5x	6.4x	11.8x	1.56
Coal	16.7x	10.2x	13.7x	6.9x	8.6x	11.2x	7.3x	5.9x	9.2x	8.9x	6.0x	9.55x	8.9x	5.9x	16.7x	3.31
Computer services	13.9x	14.6x	15.4x	7.4x	11.3x	11.8x	8.6x	9.7x	9.5x	8.3x	8.2x	10.8x	9.7x	7.4x	15.4x	2.82
Drug	13.2x	13.6x	11.8x	8.6x	9.3x	9.0x	9.3x	8.9x	11.5x	13.5x	13.6x	11.1x	11.5x	8.6x	13.6x	2.13
Electronics	11.8x	11.6x	11.6x	4.1x	7.6x	10.1x	5.8x	6.6x	11.8x	11.2x	9.4x	9.2x	10.1x	4.1x	11.8x	2.76
Entertainment	9.7x	11.4x	9.9x	5.3x	7.0x	10.1x	8.0x	9.5x	12.6x	11.7x	10.3x	9.6x	9.9x	5.3x	12.6x	2.13
Environmental	8.7x	10.1x	9.3x	7.8x	8.5x	9.5x	8.7x	8.4x	10.7x	9.9x	10.1x	9.2x	9.3x	7.8x	10.7x	0.89
Food processing	10.3x	11.0x	12.3x	8.4x	9.1x	10.0x	9.5x	10.1x	12.2x	11.9x	14.9x	10.9x	10.3x	8.4x	14.9x	1.85

Market-Based Method 155

Industry														
Furnishings/home furnishings	8.9x	9.0x	7.3x	4.2x	8.71x	11.9x	9.6x	8.3x	11.2x	10.3x	9.9x	9.0x	9.0x	4.2x	11.9x	2.07
Hotel/gaming	14.5x	18.1x	15.0x	6.48x	10.4x	20.3x	12.4x	10.6x	14.1x	12.9x	11.8x	13.3x	12.9x	6.4x	20.3x	3.79
Internet	48.0x	29.3x	30.6x	11.5x	20.2x	19.8x	17.0x	23.1x	22.8x	21.1x	23.8x	24.3x	22.8x	11.5x	48.0x	9.46
Machinery	10.3x	10.2x	11.0x	5.1x	7.5x	14.0x	9.1x	9.9x	12.0x	10.4x	9.6x	9.9x	10.2x	5.1x	14.0x	2.30
Maritime	6.3x	8.0x	12.0x	7.2x	7.0x	10.3x	9.6x	10.3x	13.0x	9.4x	6.4x	9.1x	9.4x	6.3x	13.0x	2.27
Packaging and container	8.3x	9.1x	8.0x	5.4x	7.1x	8.1x	7.1x	7.5x	9.1x	9.0x	9.4x	8.0x	8.1x	5.4x	9.4x	1.19
Paper/forest products	6.9x	8.3x	7.7x	6.0x	10.1x	7.2x	5.4x	7.2x	9.7x	9.0x	9.1x	7.9x	7.7x	5.4x	10.1x	1.50
Power	26.7x	45.5x	43.6x	7.8x	8.5x	8.3x	6.6x	8.9x	9.7x	9.8x	8.9x	16.8x	8.9x	6.6x	45.5x	14.81
Publishing	8.6x	10.1x	10.7x	5.0x	7.1x	6.2x	5.4x	8.7x	10.1x	9.5x	8.8x	8.3x	8.7x	5.1x	10.7x	1.85
Shoe	10.5x	10.3x	11.1x	6.4x	10.3x	13.2x	11.6x	14.1x	16.1x	15.1x	17.2x	12.4x	11.6x	6.4x	17.2x	3.19
Steel (general)	5.4x	6.4x	6.4x	4.4x	5.2x	8.9x	7.1x	5.6x	10.3x	8.6x	7.4x	6.9x	6.4x	4.4x	10.3x	1.79
Telecom. equipment	16.4x	14.7x	15.1x	6.4x	11.0x	10.4x	8.4x	6.7x	11.6x	12.0x	10.6x	11.2x	11.1x	6.4x	16.4x	3.28

Table 5.12 Evolution of the EV/EBIT multiple

Business sector	2005 EV/EBIT	2006 EV/EBIT	2007 EV/EBIT	2008 EV/EBIT	2009 EV/EBIT	2010 EV/EBIT	2011 EV/EBIT	2012 EV/EBIT	2013 EV/EBIT	2014 EV/EBIT	2015 EV/EBIT	Mean	Median	Min	Max	St. Dev.
Air transport	22.4x	14.0x	9.5x	7.2x	14.4x	20.7x	20.2x	9.3x	14.6x	22.2x	9.7x	14.9x	14.4x	7.2x	22.4x	5.66
Apparel	11.2x	13.4x	11.0x	6.2x	10.4x	12.9x	10.8x	14.6x	16.0x	18.4x	16.3x	12.8x	12.9x	6.2x	18.4x	3.44
Auto and truck	14.0x	21.4x	12.2x	6.1x	91.2x	112.1x	10.4x	13.9x	24.0x	41.1x	20.9x	33.4x	20.9x	6.1x	112.6x	35.42
Bank	NA	6.0x	4.9x	3.8x	5.6x	4.8x	4.3x	4.8x	NA	NA	NA	4.9x	4.8x	3.8x	6.1x	0.74
Beverage (alcoholic)	13.7x	16.3x	21.5x	11.7x	14.4x	14.8x	13.9x	14.6x	22.7x	21.2x	24.1	17.2x	14.8x	11.7x	24.1x	4.32
Beverage (soft drink)	15.9x	16.9x	22.3x	12.5x	15.0x	15.4x	14.8x	15.5x	16.8x	17.6x	19.6x	16.6x	15.9x	12.5x	22.3x	2.61
Biotechnology	61.2x	38.6x	25.8x	27.1x	32.3x	20.9x	NA	30.7x	49.9x	36.3x	21.0x	34.3x	31.5x	20.9x	61.2x	12.86
Broadcasting	34.9x	31.1x	18.5x	13.4x	12.4x	12.7x	11.2x	12.3x	15.5x	14.8x	15.1x	17.4x	14.8x	11.2x	34.9x	7.99
Building materials	10.5x	9.8x	10.1x	9.0x	14.1x	29.3x	29.2x	35.8x	19.6x	17.6x	16.1x	18.3x	16.1x	9.0x	35.8x	9.27
Chemical (specialty)	14.7x	14.4x	14.9x	9.1x	12.8x	19.2x	14.0x	15.2x	13.3x	16.1x	14.8x	14.4x	14.7x	9.1x	19.2x	2.43
Coal	30.4x	16.0x	21.4x	13.0x	12.3x	17.5x	11.1x	9.3x	43.1x	66.8x	184.3x	38.7x	17.5x	9.3x	184.3x	51.30
Computer services	17.3x	18.1x	19.0x	8.8x	13.6x	13.9x	9.8x	11.1x	11.0x	10.7x	10.8x	13.1x	11.1x	8.8x	19.0x	3.58
Drug	16.7x	18.2x	15.9x	11.5x	12.0x	11.7x	13.0x	12.1x	15.6x	18.7x	19.3x	15.0x	15.6x	11.5x	19.3x	3.03
Electronics	19.6x	20.0x	18.2x	6.1x	11.4x	16.1x	7.8x	9.2x	19.5x	18.0x	15.2x	14.7x	16.1x	6.15x	20.0x	5.13
Entertainment	14.4x	15.2x	13.8x	7.1x	9.4x	13.1x	10.6x	12.2x	15.1x	15.7x	13.1x	12.7x	13.2x	7.1x	15.7x	2.73
Environmental	14.5x	17.1x	14.7x	11.9x	12.8x	14.5x	13.5x	12.7x	17.1x	17.1x	18.5x	15.0x	14.5x	11.9x	18.5x	2.19
Food processing	14.4x	14.1x	15.6x	10.4x	11.0x	12.6x	11.9x	12.5x	14.6x	15.1x	19.1x	13.7x	14.1x	10.4x	19.1x	2.46

Market-Based Method 157

Industry														
Furnishings/home furnishings	12.2x	12.0x	9.9x	5.8x	14.6x	22.2x	14.3x	11.2x	14.8x	15.4x	15.0x	13.4x	14.3x	5.8x	22.2x	4.09
Hotel/gaming	21.4x	26.5x	20.9x	9.1x	17.1x	48.7x	20.5x	15.6x	22.0x	22.5x	20.0x	22.2x	20.9x	9.1x	48.7x	9.86
Internet	75.8x	20.2x	41.0x	15.9x	27.8x	26.7x	21.4x	31.6x	33.6x	33.7x	39.0x	35.2x	33.6x	15.9x	75.8x	15.60
Machinery	14.5x	13.7x	14.2x	6.5x	10.0x	22.2x	12.4x	12.9x	14.8x	13.5x	12.6x	13.4x	13.5x	6.5x	22.2x	3.78
Maritime	8.5x	11.6x	17.5x	10.9x	10.2x	20.1x	18.1x	21.6x	21.0x	19.5x	13.5x	15.7x	17.5x	8.5x	21.6x	4.82
Packaging and container	14.2x	15.2x	12.3x	8.1x	11.2x	12.58x	10.5x	11.2x	12.8x	13.7x	14.2x	12.4x	12.5x	8.1x	15.2x	2.05
Paper/forest products	11.5x	15.7x	12.8x	13.18x	28.9x	13.9x	8.8x	11.3x	15.6x	14.9x	15.4x	14.7x	13.9x	8.8x	28.9x	5.16
Power	43.5x	85.0x	66.1x	11.95x	12.6x	12.6x	10.1x	21.7x	16.8x	18.1x	15.3x	28.5x	16.8x	10.1x	85.1x	25.33
Publishing	13.4x	15.1x	14.0x	6.5x	9.0x	8.3x	9.4x	13.1x	16.3x	17.1x	16.4x	12.6x	13.4x	6.5x	17.1x	3.68
Shoe	12.3x	11.9x	12.6x	7.7x	12.4x	15.8x	13.4x	16.9x	18.9x	20.2x	23.2x	15.0x	13.4x	7.4x	23.2x	4.51
Steel (general)	6.5x	7.6x	7.4x	5.2x	6.3x	10.2x	13.3x	8.8x	18.0x	16.1x	NA	9.9x	8.2x	5.2x	18.0x	4.41
Telecom. equipment	21.2x	18.3x	18.7x	8.8x	17.12x	14.5x	11.5x	8.5x	14.6x	15.8x	13.6x	14.8x	14.6x	8.5x	21.2x	4.04

Table 5.13 YoY percentage change of the EV/EBITDA multiple

Business sector	2005 EV/EBITDA	2006 EV/EBITDA (%)	2007 EV/EBITDA (%)	2008 EV/EBITDA (%)	2009 EV/EBITDA (%)	2010 EV/EBITDA (%)	2011 EV/EBITDA (%)	2012 EV/EBITDA (%)	2013 EV/EBITDA (%)	2014 EV/EBITDA (%)	2015 EV/EBITDA (%)
Air transport		−22.72	−24.70	−25.31	64.36	29.09	26.22	−53.49	60.48	−16.07	−28.27
Apparel		23.27	−17.75	−45.21	64.42	22.38	−12.45	35.53	20.38	−12.26	−12.52
Auto and truck		27.03	−34.77	−41.80	181.67	4.18	−48.08	28.36	57.04	24.01	−31.00
Bank		–	−19.17	−21.26	45.42	−13.81	−10.03	11.55	–	–	–
Beverage (alcoholic)		10.87	31.11	−45.28	25.68	7.99	−5.72	6.07	57.96	−7.76	15.02
Beverage (soft drink)		6.11	27.69	−41.26	20.28	5.93	−5.08	5.87	9.47	2.25	10.95
Biotechnology		−32.72	−31.14	1.67	5.81	−27.17	–	–	1.83	−16.66	−28.65
Broadcasting		13.12	−28.60	−30.37	−2.13	6.45	−5.90	13.38	91.21	−32.06	1.30
Building materials		−6.54	0.98	−21.78	38.28	41.59	−6.81	31.56	0.09	−18.37	−3.32
Chemical (specialty)		−0.14	4.92	−39.07	30.23	41.43	−16.67	10.41	−0.35	9.44	−9.87
Coal		−38.53	33.59	−49.06	23.27	30.33	−34.59	−18.38	54.99	−4.02	−32.27
Computer services		4.86	5.28	−51.94	52.90	4.27	−27.05	12.32	−1.90	−11.77	−1.49
Drug		2.31	−13.26	−26.66	7.77	−2.83	3.18	−4.43	29.14	17.71	0.34
Electronics		−1.49	−0.06	−64.32	83.44	33.12	−42.63	14.04	78.66	−7.01	−13.97
Entertainment		16.49	−12.58	−46.41	31.10	45.54	−21.15	18.65	32.32	−7.16	−11.47
Environmental		15.95	−8.05	−15.50	9.18	11.13	−8.05	−3.79	27.79	−7.58	1.62
Food processing		6.45	12.10	−31.91	8.36	10.23	−4.91	5.91	21.38	−2.83	25.33

Furnishings/home furnishings	1.07	−18.41	−42.40	105.54	37.21	−19.06	−13.83	34.86	−7.90	−3.70
Hotel/gaming	25.35	−17.35	−56.82	61.39	94.86	−38.88	−14.34	32.84	−8.59	−8.33
Internet	−38.86	4.45	−62.48	75.66	−1.73	−14.14	35.78	−1.55	−7.45	12.83
Machinery	−1.31	8.01	−53.84	48.36	86.10	−35.45	9.38	21.10	−13.06	−8.23
Maritime	26.91	49.76	−39.84	−3.21	47.77	−7.12	7.60	25.86	−27.60	−32.22
Packaging and container	10.01	−12.22	−32.60	32.17	14.03	−11.98	5.48	20.44	−0.24	3.92
Paper/forest products	19.46	−6.87	−22.36	68.58	−28.55	−24.65	32.25	34.48	−6.70	0.29
Power	70.51	−4.20	−82.09	9.52	−3.17	−20.14	34.68	9.58	1.20	−9.88
Publishing	16.77	5.97	−52.68	40.59	−12.04	2.40	36.00	16.23	−6.03	−7.55
Shoe	−1.90	7.15	−41.59	59.59	28.86	−12.43	21.13	17.13	−8.10	13.72
Steel (general)	16.74	0.45	−30.50	17.25	71.54	−21.20	−20.46	83.38	−16.41	−14.17
Telecom. equipment	−10.1	2.53	−57.33	71.23	−5.31	−19.31	−20.36	72.89	3.16	−11.78

Table 5.14 YoY percentage change of the EV*EBIT multiple

Business sector	2005 EV/EBIT	2006 EV/EBIT (%)	2007 EV/EBIT (%)	2008 EV/EBIT (%)	2009 EV/EBIT (%)	2010 EV/EBIT (%)	2011 EV/EBIT (%)	2012 EV/EBIT (%)	2013 EV/EBIT (%)	2014 EV/EBIT (%)	2015 EV/EBIT (%)
Air transport		−37.33	−32.46	−23.96	100.45	43.40	−2.59	−53.89	57.49	51.31	−56.29
Apparel		19.97	−18.04	−43.91	67.91	24.35	−16.33	35.56	9.16	15.35	−11.36
Auto and truck		53.07	−43.06	−49.80	1386.32	23.37	−90.77	34.16	72.57	70.88	−49.12
Bank		–	−19.17	−21.26	45.42	−13.81	−10.03	11.55	–	–	–
Beverage (alcoholic)		19.01	31.89	−45.21	22.41	2.64	−5.61	5.01	55.07	−6.41	13.32
Beverage (soft drink)		6.41	31.52	−43.84	20.26	2.37	−4.01	5.26	8.42	4.36	11.52
Biotechnology		−36.97	−33.13	5.14	19.24	−35.18	–	–	62.33	−27.15	−42.25
Broadcasting		−10.88	−40.56	−27.13	−7.89	2.54	−11.55	9.59	25.73	−4.54	2.27
Building materials		−6.54	2.62	−10.18	56.06	107.71	−0.37	22.58	−45.06	−10.58	−8.58
Chemical (specialty)		−2.58	3.73	−38.92	40.36	49.92	−26.79	8.35	−12.69	21.52	−8.35
Coal		−47.20	33.45	−39.27	−5.46	42.08	−36.39	−16.18	362.54	54.70	175.87
Computer services		4.46	4.87	−53.79	55.13	2.37	−29.82	13.27	−0.40	−2.50	0.98
Drug		9.20	−13.04	−27.32	4.16	−2.10	10.46	−7.04	28.92	20.45	3.00
Electronics		1.78	−8.57	−66.39	86.62	40.85	−51.50	18.44	110.62	−7.86	−15.11
Entertainment		2.55	−9.27	−48.69	33.07	39.86	−19.03	14.44	23.57	4.58	−16.35
Environmental		17.23	−13.52	−18.86	7.18	13.19	−6.53	−5.89	34.27	0.05	8.22
Food processing		−2.33	11.16	−33.27	5.49	14.62	−5.67	5.04	16.74	3.07	27.07
Furnishings/home furnishings		−1.38	−17.58	−41.07	150.84	52.12	−35.78	−21.57	32.47	3.70	−2.53

Hotel/gaming	23.58	−21.11	−56.63	88.57	184.69	−57.91	−23.65	41.01	2.19	−11.12
Internet	−46.96	2.08	−61.23	74.68	−3.81	−19.98	47.77	6.30	0.36	15.69
Machinery	−5.69	3.75	−54.14	53.46	121.85	−44.24	4.24	14.67	−8.59	−7.08
Maritime	36.41	50.36	−37.59	−6.52	96.95	−9.86	19.42	−3.02	−7.17	−30.71
Packaging and container	7.17	−19.36	−34.00	38.37	11.98	−16.49	6.62	14.77	7.17	3.74
Paper/forest products	36.02	−18.44	2.89	119.31	−51.61	−36.84	28.85	37.68	−4.74	3.24
Power	95.56	−22.31	−81.93	5.73	0.24	−19.67	113.35	−22.33	7.66	−15.53
Publishing	11.90	−7.16	−52.98	37.70	−8.27	13.94	38.70	24.36	5.11	−4.26
Shoe	−3.47	6.38	−41.11	66.05	27.59	−15.26	26.70	11.27	7.22	14.61
Steel (general)	17.51	−2.31	−29.01	19.40	61.41	30.35	−33.11	103.12	−10.67	–
Telecom. equipment	−13.42	1.81	−52.90	94.33	−15.30	−20.70	−26.00	71.88	8.42	−13.72

Table 5.15 Multiples standard deviation (2005–2015)

Business sector	EV/EBITDA St. Dev.	EV/EBIT St. Dev.
Air transport	2.49	5.66
Apparel	2.47	3.44
Auto and truck	3.07	35.42
Bank	0.74	0.74
Beverage (alcoholic)	3.70	4.32
Beverage (soft drink)	1.92	2.61
Biotechnology	8.46	12.86
Broadcasting	2.69	7.99
Building materials	2.86	9.27
Chemical (specialty)	1.56	2.43
Coal	3.31	51.3
Computer services	2.82	3.58
Drug	2.13	3.03
Electronics	2.76	5.13
Entertainment	2.13	2.73
Environmental	0.89	2.19
Food processing	1.85	2.46
Furnishings/home furnishings	2.07	4.09
Hotel/gaming	3.79	9.86
Internet	9.46	15.6
Machinery	2.30	3.78
Maritime	2.27	4.82
Packaging and container	1.19	2.05
Paper/forest products	1.50	5.16
Power	14.81	25.33
Publishing	1.85	3.68
Shoe	3.19	4.51
Steel (general)	1.79	4.41
Telecom. equipment	3.28	4.04

To identify the multiple with the lower volatility, the standard deviation of EV/EBITDA and EV/EBIT is compared (Table 5.15).

As is immediately apparent, the EV/EBIT multiple has a higher standard deviation than the EV/EBITDA. Hence, we can infer that the EV/EBIT ratio has a higher average volatility than the EV/EBITDA ratio.

5.9 Equity-Side Multiples

According to the equity-side approach, the market multiple is equal to the ratio of price to a levered performance measure.

$$\text{Market multiple} = \frac{\text{Price}}{\text{Levered performance measure}}$$

The most commonly used performance measures are earnings, earnings growth, BV, FCF to equity.

5.9.1 Price/Earnings (P/E)

The Price/Earnings (P/E) multiple measures the value of a business based on earnings per share (EPS):

$$\text{Multiple} = \frac{\text{Price}}{\text{Earnings Per Share}} = \frac{P}{E}$$

This multiple is simple to calculate, as both price and earnings are easily available performance measures. This is also why it is a widespread multiple in the financial community.

We can show that the P/E ratio is a restatement of the constant growth dividend discount model (DDM, see Sect. 4.6). Assuming that value is equal to market price, the latter is calculated as follows:

$$P_0 = \frac{D_1}{k_e - g}$$

where:

P_0 = actual price of a share
D_1 = expected dividend in period 1
k_e = cost of equity
g = growth rate

The expected dividend (D_1) shall be expressed as follows:

$$D_1 = D_0 \times (1+g)$$

where D_0 is the dividend of the current year; D_0 may be also expressed as:

$$D_0 = EPS_0 \times (1-RR)$$

where:

EPS_0 = earnings per share in period 0
RR = retention ratio
(1 − RR) = payout ratio

Substituting D_1 in the first formula:

$$P_0 = \frac{EPS_0 \times \text{Payout ratio} \times (1+g)}{k_e - g}$$

Dividing both sides by EPS_0:

$$\frac{P_0}{EPS_0} = \frac{P}{E} = \frac{\text{Payout ratio} \times (1+g)}{k_e - g}$$

The equation shows that the determinants of the P/E ratio are:

(a) the expected dividend payout ratio: payout ratio × (1 + g)
(b) the cost of equity: k_e
(c) the expected growth rate of dividends: g

The P/E ratio shows how much the market is willing to pay for one dollar of expected earnings.

There are three main limits to this multiple.

First, earnings just like EBIT are considerably more exposed to the influence of accounting policies, as each company may have different levels of amortization as a result of different accounting standards, different investment policies, and different business models.

Secondly, earnings are influenced by the financial structure. A company with high interest-bearing debt has higher interest expenses; conversely, in a company with limited interest-bearing debt, interest expenses may be modest.

Finally, earnings are influenced by the different tax rate. Other conditions being equal, companies operating in different countries and subject to a different marginal tax rate have a different P/E multiple.

Take, for example, two companies, A and B, that have the same EBIT but different interest expenses (Table 5.16).

Assuming that the peer group P/E = 9.5, we obtain:

$$P_{\text{Company A}} = \$1.50 \times 9.5 = \$14.25$$

$$P_{\text{Company A}} = \$1.00 \times 9.5 = \$9.50$$

Table 5.16 Application of P/E ratio

Income statement	Company A	Company B
Sales	$850,000	$850,000
Operating expenses	($650,000)	($550,000)
Gross margin	**$200,000**	**$300,000**
Labor cost	($130,000)	($130,000)
EBITDA	**$70,000**	**$170,000**
Amortization	($10,000)	($110,000)
EBIT	**$60,000**	**$60,000**
Interest	($10,000)	($30,000)
Earnings before taxes	**$50,000**	**$30,000**
Taxes	($20,000)	($10,000)
Earnings	**$30,000**	**$20,000**
Number of share	20,000	20,000
EPS	$1.50	$1.00

The EV is calculated by multiplying the price of each company by the number of shares:

$$EV_{Company\ A} = \$14.25 \times 20,000 = \$285,000$$

$$EV_{Company\ B} = \$9.50 \times 20,000 = \$190,000$$

It is interesting to note that if the companies had been valued using another multiple, such as the EV/EBIT, both the EV and the price per share would have been the same. Assuming, for example, EV/EBIT = 4.4, the EV of both is $264,000 ($60,000 x 4.4). The price per share of both is $13.2 ($264,000/20,000 shares).

5.9.2 PEG Ratio

The PEG ratio (price/earnings to expected growth rate) allows for better contextualization of the P/E ratio. It is especially useful for identifying overvalued and undervalued stocks based on the expected growth rate of EPS. Indeed:

- companies with a P/E ratio lower than the expected growth rate, that is, with a PEG < 1, can be considered undervalued;
- companies with a P/E ratio higher than the expected growth rate, that is, with a PEG > 1, can be considered overvalued.

Table 5.17 Application of P/E ratio

	Company A	Company B
Current price	$15.0	$15.0
Current EPS	$2.0	$1,5
P/E	7.5	10.0

The PEG ratio is calculated by dividing the P/E by the expected growth rate (g):

$$\text{PEG ratio} = \frac{P/E}{(g \times 100)}$$

Assume that company A and company B report the values in Table 5.17.

Based on this information, company A is more attractive for an investor than company B. By investing $15 in company A, the resulting EPS is $2.0; on the other hand, by investing in company B, the resulting EPS is $1.5. A higher EPS means potentially higher dividends.

According to the Theory of Finance, an investor should not, however, only rely on current information, but must also consider future prospects. Assume that:

- the expected growth rate of company A is 5%;
- the expected growth rate of company B is 15%.

Therefore, the PEG is calculated as follows:

$$\text{PEG}_{\text{Company A}} = \frac{7.5}{(5\% \times 100)} = 1.50$$

$$\text{PEG}_{\text{Company B}} = \frac{10.0}{(15\% \times 100)} = 0.67$$

Company A has a PEG > 1. This means that company A tends to be overvalued, as an investor is asked to pay a more than proportional price compared to future earnings growth. Conversely, company B has a PEG < 1. This means that company B tends to be undervalued, as an investor is asked to pay a "convenient" price compared to future earnings growth.

In calculating the PEG ratio, it is necessary to consider that:

- the estimated growth rate depends on various factors, partly within and partly outside the company; this estimate is more complex in times of greater market volatility, as there may be no correlation between historical results and those expected;
- in calculating the P/E, current, trailing, and forward earnings can be used. Current and trailing earnings are preferable, as they are based on more reliable values. With forward earnings there is a risk of considering the expected growth twice: one in earnings and another one in the growth rate.

In general, the PEG ratio is considered suitable when it comes to valuing high-growth companies, although distorting effects are possible. A start-up with a high growth rate and a still low stock price could be considered undervalued, while a large and stable company may not be judged as attractive due to its low growth.

5.9.3 Price/Book Value

The P/BV multiple measures the value of a business based on the BV of equity per share:

$$\text{Multiple} = \frac{\text{Price}}{\text{Book Value of Equity per Share}} = \frac{P}{BV}$$

In practice, this multiple compares the market value of equity and the BV of equity.

We can also show that the P/BV is a restatement of the constant growth DDM (see Sect. 4.6). Assuming that value is equal to market price, the latter is calculated as follows:

$$P_0 = \frac{D_1}{k_e - g}$$

where:

P_0 = actual price of a share
D_1 = expected dividend in period 1
k_e = cost of equity
g = growth rate

The expected dividend (D_1) shall be expressed as follows:

$$D_1 = D_0 \times (1+g)$$

where D_0 is the dividend of the current year; D_0 may be also expressed as:

$$D_0 = EPS_0 \times (1-RR)$$

where:

EPS_0 = earnings per share in period 0
RR = retention ratio
(1 – RR) = payout ratio

Considering that ROE shall be expressed as follows:

$$ROE = \frac{EPS_0}{\text{Book Value of Equity}_0}$$

We deduce that:

$$EPS_0 = ROE \times BV_0$$

Substituting D_1 in the first formula:

$$P_0 = \frac{EPS_0 \times ROE \times \text{Payout ratio} \times (1+g)}{k_e - g}$$

Dividing both sides by EPS_0:

$$\frac{P_0}{EPS_0} = \frac{P}{E} = \frac{ROE \times \text{Payout ratio} \times (1+g)}{k_e - g}$$

The equation shows that the determinants of the P/E ratio are:

(a) the expected dividend payout ratio: payout ratio × (1+g);
(b) the ROE;
(c) the cost of equity (k_e);
(d) the expected growth rate of dividends (g).

If a company creates value, the market value is higher than its BV; thus, P/BV > 1 must be considered as a positive indication. Since each sector is characterized by its own financial structure, the adequacy of a multiple must be judged by comparing it with comparable firms in the industry. In general, industries that require more capital (for each dollar of profit) usually trade at P/BV ratios much lower than consulting firms. The P/BV ratio is therefore influenced by financial leverage.

Usually, this multiple is used for investment-intensive companies, while it is less significant for companies with low investment levels. For Apple, Amazon, Netflix, for which most of the value is represented by intangible assets, P/BV is not a suitable multiplier.

Companies that apply different accounting standards cannot be valued using this multiple. For example, in Europe both local accounting standards and IFRS are applicable, the latter being mandatory for listed companies, banks, and finance companies. As a result of fair value, the BV of companies that apply the IFRS is generally higher than that of companies that adopt the local accounting standards, usually based on the historical cost method.

In general, if a company uses market-based accounting standards, such as the IFRS, the difference between market value and BV tends to decrease. For this reason, this multiplier is frequently used by banks and insurance companies: since assets and liabilities are expressed at fair value, the difference between price and BV per share is usually quite small.

Financial leverage also affects the P/BV ratio. A company that finances growth through debt has a lower BV than a company that is financed by retaining earnings and by not distributing dividends. In constructing the peer group, a valuer must therefore consider companies that have homogeneous debt-to-equity ratios.

The P/BV multiple can be profitably used to value distressed companies with negative earnings. Obviously, if a company makes losses for several years, the equity is progressively eroded and also the P/BV can turn negative; in this case it loses its meaning. When valuing distressed companies, the value of assets that cannot be sold, such as goodwill or capitalized costs, should be subtracted from BV.

5.9.4 Price/Free Cash Flow to Equity (P/FCFE)

The EV/Free cash flow to equity (FCFE) multiple compares price with its ability to generate cash flow:

$$\text{Multiple} = \frac{\text{Price}}{\text{Free Cash Flow to Equity}}$$

As a performance measure, cash flow:

- is neutral, since it is not influenced by either accounting standards or accounting policies;
- is objective, because it measures value based on data that are certain.

The main limitation of FCFE is that it is subject to a certain degree of volatility over time, as it is influenced by various elements, such as trade receivable turnover, trade payable turnover, inventory turnover, CapEx, interest, dividends, debt repayment or issuance, and so on.

Ultimately, FCFE does not have the same stability as earnings. For this reason, although it is a multiple based on objective data, its application is less widespread than P/E.

5.10 Application of Multiple to the Target Company

Once the peer group has been identified and the multiple (or multiples) have been selected, the EV of the target company can be calculated.

The *first step* is to calculate the main statistics of the peer group; if the group is homogeneous, comparable companies should express relatively homogeneous multiples, although some outliers are inevitable.

Assume that the peer group is made up of US publicly traded companies of the beverage industry (Table 5.18).

The most common statistics a valuer can calculate are the following: minimum value (Min); maximum value (Max); mean; median; standard deviation (St. Dev.). They are reported in Table 5.19; in addition, correlation with the market bap was also calculated.

In the example in Table 5.20, the P/E and the EV/EBITDA have a higher dispersion compared to EV/Sales, as the range of values is wider. This is also confirmed by the standard deviation, which has relatively high values: 22.57 for the P/E; 5.85 for the EV/EBITDA. Conversely, EV/Sales has standard deviation of 2.30.

The dispersion of multiples can be better understood through the quartile distribution (Table 5.20).

The quartile distribution also confirms that the EV/Sales multiple has a more homogeneous distribution.

Furthermore, it is interesting to observe the correlation between each multiple and market cap. This analysis is useful to verify whether there is a correlation between the market cap value and the corresponding value of the

Market-Based Method 171

Table 5.18 Beverage companies multiples ($ mil)

No.	Company	Market cap	P/E	PEG	EV/Sales	EV/EBITDA
1	Anheuser-Busch InBev	$200,199.7	22.7x	18.10	5.87x	16.0x
2	The Coca-Cola Company	$179,419.1	20.7x	25.12	4.74x	17.2x
3	Pepsico	$150,718.3	25.6x	31.19	2.77x	14.2x
4	Diageo	$64,445.6	16.3x	15.87	5.65x	18.1x
5	Constellation Brands	$30,329.9	64.0x	47.88	5.39x	16.1x
6	Monster Beverage Corporation	$26,019.3	24.5x	17.50	8.64x	22.2x
7	Molson Coors Brewing Company	$20,998.9	25.0x	32.60	6.09x	34.6x
8	Dr Pepper Snapple Group	$16,677.7	31.1x	42.15	3.02x	11.8x
9	Brown-Forman Corporation	$16,237.0	6.10x	NA	6.03x	16.7x
10	The WhiteWave Foods Company	$9836.2	92.5x	52.86	2.86x	22.1x
11	National Beverage Corp.	$2382.6	NA	NA	2.93x	16.2x
12	The Boston Beer Company	$2103.7	38.5x	NA	2.25x	11.4x
13	Coca-Cola Bottling Co.	$1653.6	55.5x	NA	0.87x	11.7x
14	Cott Corporation	$1571.6	21.0x	NA	1.23x	10.7x
15	Farmer Bros.	$583.8	NA	NA	1.08x	16.3x
16	Lifeway Foods	$185.3	33.8x	21.10	1.49x	20.7x
17	Jones Soda Co.	$19.0	NA	NA	1.28x	NA

Source: FactSet Research Systems, Bloomberg, Capital IQ. Reported by William Blair Equity Research, Feb 2017

Table 5.19 Multiples statistics

Statistics	P/E	PEG	EV/Sales	EV/EBITDA
Min	6.10x	15.87	0.87x	10.70x
Max	92.5x	52.86	8.64x	34.60x
Mean	34.90x	30.44	3.66x	17.25x
Median	25.30x	28.16	2.93x	16.25x
St. Dev.	22.57	13.32	2.30	5.85
Correlation with market cap	−0.32	−0.39	0.36	−0.05

Table 5.20 Distribution in quartiles

Multiple	Quartile 1	Quartile 2	Quartile 3	Quartile 4	Sparkline
P/E	21.43	25.30	37.33	92.50	
EV/Sales	1.49	2.93	5.65	8.64	
EV/EBITDA	13.60	16.25	18.75	34.60	

multiple. The correlation is positive for EV/Sales only: this means that companies with a higher market cap have a higher EV/Sales ratio; on the other hand, companies with a lower market cap have a more modest EV/Sales ratio.

If the valuer considers that the peer group contains outlier values, he or she can eliminate the outlier comparables. For example, in this case both the minimum value and the maximum value of each multiple could be eliminated. The result is shown in Table 5.21.

As can be seen, the peer group is now more homogeneous, as confirmed by the significant reduction in the standard deviation and by the quartile distribution (Table 5.22).

The *second step* consists in calculating the EV of the target company. The valuer must decide:

- which statistics should be used;
- whether to use one multiple only or several multiples.

In a peer group with a narrow range of values, the mean and median can be used interchangeably. In a peer group with wide ranges of values, such as the one in the example in Table 5.19, using the median is preferable. In general, the weighted average is not recommended, as the allocation of weights may be subjective.

The choice of using one or more multiples depends on how they are able to interpret the value of the firm. In the example in Table 5.19, the P/E multiple has too high a standard deviation to be considered significant. Thus, using the EV/Sales and the EV/EBITDA is preferable.

The former has the most homogeneous values, and indeed, the lowest standard deviation too. However, since the EV/Sales does not take into account the cost structure, also using the EV/EBITDA is appropriate given the characteristics of the industry.

There are numerous potential combinations that depend on the number of elements in the peer group; the quality of the data; the relevance of statistical analyses; the characteristics of the industry; the characteristics of the target company; the sensitivity of the valuer.

The income statement of the target company is shown in Table 5.23.

By applying the median of EV/Sales and EV/EBITDA without outliers (Table 5.22), we obtain the values shown in Table 5.24.

Since the results are homogeneous, the EV of the target company can be calculated using the EV average, which is $2,626,500.

Table 5.21 Multiples statistics without outliers

Statistics	P/E	PEG	EV/Sales	EV/EBITDA
Min	16.30×	17.50	1.08×	11.40×
Max	64.00×	47.88	6.09×	22.20×
Mean	31.56×	29.46	3.51×	16.48×
Median	25.30×	28.16	2.93×	16.25×
St. Dev.	14.61	11.17	1.92	3.53
Correlation with market cap	−0.41	−0.35	0.45	−0.03

Table 5.22 Distribution in quartiles without outliers

Multiple	Quartile 1	Quartile 2	Quartile 3	Quartile 4	Sparkline
P/E	22.28	25.30	34.98	64.00	
EV/Sales	1.87	2.93	5.52	8.64	
EV/EBITDA	14.65	16.25	17.88	22.20	

Table 5.23 Target company's income statement

Income statement	
Sales	$850,000
Operating expenses	($550,000)
Gross margin	**$300,000**
Labor cost	($130,000)
EBITDA	**$170,000**
Amortization	($60,000)
EBIT	**$110,000**
Interest	($10,000)
Earnings before taxes	**$100,000**

Table 5.24 Enterprise value of the target company

	Multiple	EV
EV/sales	2.93×	$2,490,500
EV/EBITDA	16.25×	$2,762,500

Finally, the valuer must perform a sensitivity analysis to verify how the EV changes as the parameters change. In this case, for example, sales and EBITDA margin can be taken as parameters.

Since the EBITDA margin is 20% ($170,000/$850,000), in the matrix we can calculate how the EV changes as the following parameters change (Table 5.25):

Table 5.25 Stress test matrix

		EBITDA Margin		
		15%	20%	25%
Sales	$800,000	$2,147,000	$2,472,000	$2,797,000
	$850,000	$2,281,000	$2,625,500	$2,971,813
	$900,000	$2,415,375	$2,781,000	$3,146,625

- EBITDA margin (15%, 20%, 25%);
- Sales ($800,000; $850,000; $900,000).

The gray boxes show the minimum, average, and maximum values of the sensitivity analysis.

6
The Cost Approach

6.1 The Rationale of the Cost Approach

The rationale behind the cost approach is that a buyer will pay no more for an asset than the cost to obtain an asset of equal utility, whether by purchase or by construction, unless undue time, inconvenience, risk, or other factors are involved.

This valuation approach often serves as a valuation floor since most companies have greater value as a going concern than they would if liquidated. Usually the cost approach complements the information that can be obtained with the income approach or with the market approach; more rarely it is used as a stand-alone valuation method. This method can only be used if the other methods are not applicable or in cases where the value of the firm is mainly linked to specific assets, such as plant or equipment.

Under IVS 105 such approach should be applied under the following circumstances:

(a) "participants would be able to recreate an asset with substantially the same utility as the subject asset, without regulatory or legal restrictions, and the asset could be recreated quickly enough that a participant would not be willing to pay a significant premium for the ability to use the subject asset immediately;
(b) the asset is not directly income-generating and the unique nature of the asset makes using an income approach or market approach unfeasible; and/or

(c) the basis of value being used is fundamentally based on replacement cost, such as replacement value".

The cost approach is like taking a "snapshot" of the value of the firm, by adjusting the book value of assets and liabilities to identify the current value, based on the following formula:

$$\text{Current Value of the firm} = \text{Equity Book Value} + (\text{Current value of Assets} - \text{Book Value of Assets})$$

To understand how the method works, let us consider the balance sheet in Table 6.1. The book value of the firm is reflected by shareholder's equity, which is $400:

The book value is measured according to the accounting standards, which are designed to provide rules for the correct representation of accounting data, but are not suitable for determining the value of a firm. Thus, we have to move away from the rationale of the accounting standards and calculate the current value of assets.

Assuming that:

- Current value of plant = $400;
- Current value of property = $1800;

the value of the firm can be calculated based on the adjustments in Table 6.2.
The current value of the firm is therefore calculated as follows:

$$\text{Current Value of the firm} = \$400 + (\$2200 - \$1500) = \$1100$$

Table 6.1 Book value of the firm

Assets		Liabilities	
Plants	$500	Shareholder's equity	$400
Property	$1000	Operating liabilities	$500
Receivables	$200	Interest-bearing debt	$900
Cash and cash equivalents	$100		
Total assets	$1800	Total	$1800

Table 6.2 Adjustment to book value

	Book value	Adjustment	Current value
Plants	$500	($100)	$400
Property	$1000	$800	$1800
Total	$1500	$700	$2200

The current value of an asset can be calculated according to two methods:

1. Replacement cost method: Replacement cost is the price that an entity would pay to replace an existing asset at current market prices with a similar asset offering equivalent utility;
2. Reproduction cost method: Reproduction cost is the cost of reproducing an asset or property with the same materials and specifications.

6.2 Replacement and Reproduction Cost

Under IVS 105, *replacement cost* is "the cost that is relevant to determining the price that a participant would pay as it is based on replicating the utility of the asset, not the exact physical properties of the asset", adjusted for physical deterioration and/or obsolescence.

For example, a sim-free iPhone 5s of 64Gb had a cost of $849 in 2014. Assuming that the smartphone is depreciated over five years, in 2017 its book value was $170. In 2017, the replacement cost can be calculated based on the iPhone X 64Gb price, equivalent to $999. The two smartphones are not exactly comparable, as the features of iPhone X are well above those of iPhone 5s, but their utility and functionality for an average user are almost similar. As noted in IVS 105, the replacement cost is generally "that of a modern equivalent asset, which is one that provides similar function and equivalent utility to the asset being valued, but which is of a current design and constructed or made using current cost-effective materials and techniques".

Reproduction cost is the expenditure required to reproduce an asset at current prices. The level of reproduction is assumed to be exact, involving the same materials and specifications as were used for the original asset.

Under IVS 105 "Reproduction Cost is appropriate when either the cost of a modern equivalent asset is greater than the cost of recreating a replica of the subject asset, or the utility offered by the subject asset could only be provided by a replica rather than a modern equivalent".

For example, when evaluating a plant, the valuer should estimate all costs to exactly rebuild that asset, using the same material and providing equivalent function.

Reproduction cost is a less objective method than replacement cost, as it requires an estimate based on subjective parameters. Replacement cost is based on the current prices of similar assets; somehow, it is a sort of market value. On the other hand, reproduction cost requires a calculation that takes into account both direct costs (materials and labor) and indirect costs, such as transport costs, installation costs, professional fees (design, permit, architectural, legal, etc.), commissions, overheads, taxes, finance costs (e.g. interest on debt financing), and profit margin/entrepreneurial profit to the creator of the asset.

This calculation requires information on the exact technical specifications of the asset and whether a statement of work has been provided on which the calculations should be based.

In both cost configurations, depreciation must be taken into account. Under IVS 105 depreciation "refers to adjustments made to the estimated cost of creating an asset of equal utility to reflect the impact on value of any obsolescence affecting the subject asset". In other words, depreciation is a loss in the real existing use value of property.

Obsolescence is one of the causes of depreciation. There are three types of obsolescence: functional obsolescence, physical obsolescence, and economic obsolescence.

Functional obsolescence is defined as the loss of value of an asset due to inefficiency or inadequacy of the asset itself. For example, functional obsolescence is a reduction in the usefulness or desirability of an object because of an outdated design. In general, functional obsolescence may be due to:

- an excess of investment, due to innovations and the availability of new materials;
- functional inadequacy due to an excess of operating costs.

Physical obsolescence is defined as the loss of value of a tangible asset attributable to wear and tear. It may depend on use, maintenance, exposure to the atmosphere and the environment, failures caused by vibrations, accidents, and so on. Physical obsolescence can be "curable" or "incurable", depending on the characteristics and useful life of the asset. For example, a ten-year-old personal computer is "incurable", as its useful life would still be modest, even if it were repaired.

Economic obsolescence is defined as the loss of value due to external factors and can be due to various causes, such as the increase in raw material prices not offset by an increase in the finished product prices, decline in demand, increased competition, high inflation, and new rules or regulations.

6.3 Plant and Equipment Valuation

Plant and equipment are durable use goods, used as a production tool or to be rented to third parties; they include:

1. fixed installations: electrical system, heating system, fire protection system, gas distribution system, compressed air distribution system;
2. production machinery, including connections, pipes, and foundations;
3. means of internal transport, such as forklifts, tractors, and in general vehicles not authorized for driving on public roads;
4. laboratory equipment;
5. office furniture and equipment;
6. servers, personal computers, printers, photocopiers;
7. special equipment for specific productions;
8. vehicles.

The cost configurations used are those examined in Sect. 6.2, namely, reproduction cost and replacement cost.

The reproduction cost of plant and equipment is the cost necessary, as at the estimate date, to reproduce an exact replica of the asset, having the same characteristics and made of the same materials. Such reconstruction is only justified if it is the most affordable way to replace the good. If an exact reconstruction is not possible (e.g. because some materials are no longer available) or is not technically valid, due to subsequent innovations, the replacement cost must be used.

Replacement cost is the cost necessary to purchase plant and equipment built using current technologies and materials, in order to replace the existing asset with one that offers the same capacity, performance, and utility. Replacement cost can be calculated in the following ways:

1. detail method;
2. trending method.

The *detail method* consists in summing up the costs of all the components that make up the asset (assemblage costs). Direct costs include costs of materials, labor, transportation, fitting, and so on. Indirect costs include professional fees, legal fees, licenses, safety costs, financial charges, remediation costs, and so on.

Theoretically, this method is accurate, but it is not always applicable. Data for the individual components may not be available and in any case identifying a certain value for each component is not easy. For example, the cost of materials depends on various factors, such as type of supplier (wholesale or retail), discounts applied, quantities purchased, and so on. Moreover, this method requires that all the components necessary to construct an asset be identified and that a statement of work be provided.

The *trending method* consists in applying an adjustment index to the historical cost of the asset to obtain its current value. This method is very empirical, as it is difficult to identify an index that reflects technological improvements.

In general, valuers should consider a number of factors that affect plant and equipment. These factors can be:

1. Asset-related;
2. Environmental-related.

Under IVS 300, the asset-related factors are as follows:

- the asset's technical specification;
- the remaining useful, economic, or effective life, considering both preventive and predictive maintenance;
- the asset's condition, including maintenance history;
- any functional, physical, and technological obsolescence,
- if the asset is not valued in its current location, the costs of decommissioning and removal;
- for machinery and equipment that are used for rental purposes, the lease renewal options and other end-of-lease possibilities;
- any potential loss of a complementary asset;
- assets may be permanently attached to the land and could not be removed without substantial demolition of either the asset or any surrounding structure or building;
- an individual machine may be part of an integrated production line where its functionality is dependent upon other assets.

Under IVS 300, the environmental-related factors are as follows:

- the location in relation to the source of raw material and market for the product;

- the impact of any environmental or other legislation that either restricts utilization or imposes additional operating or decommissioning costs;
- substances and toxic wastes that may be in certain machinery and equipment have a severe impact if not used or disposed of appropriately;
- licenses to operate certain machines in certain countries may be restricted.

7

Intangible Assets Valuation

7.1 The Increasing Role of Intangible Assets

Intangible assets play an increasingly important role in business strategies. Over the past 25 years, many US and European companies have relocated their production operations, while preserving control mainly on research, development, innovation, and brand.

Intangible assets are the main competitive advantage for many firms. This is true not only for companies where intangible assets are evidently pre-eminent, such as pharmaceutical, biotechnology, or web companies. Intangible assets are also important in more traditional sectors, such as fashion, the food industry, toys, and publishing.

Table 7.1 shows the weight of investment in intangible assets as a percentage of value added in some industrialized countries between 2000 and 2013. It is quite evident that these investments have grown over time and are proof of the ever-increasing importance of intangible assets.

Thus, the valuation of intangible assets has become an increasingly relevant topic, both because they significantly influence the value of a firm and because they are frequently negotiated, and, therefore, valued on a stand-alone basis.

In some cases, the value of the firm coincides with the value of its intangible assets. For example, Amazon's value is marginally dependent on tangible assets, although the company recently invested in both logistics and distribution companies, such as Whole Food; Amazon's value is mainly linked to its innovative platform, the design of new services, and the development of new logistics solutions. Despite Amazon moves millions of products worldwide, the nature of its business is essentially intangible. Accordingly, the value of Amazon is linked to this dimension.

Table 7.1 Investments in intangible assets (% officially measured value added)

Countries	2000–2007 (%)	2008–2009 (%)	2010–2013 (%)
Austria	9.6	11.2	12.2
Belgium	11.0	13.0	14.5
Denmark	13.2	15.0	15.3
Finland	15.3	19.5	20.1
France	15.8	16.8	17.8
Germany	12.3	12.6	12.0
Greece	7.4	9.2	9.1
Hungary	8.6	9.6	10.0
Ireland	9.7	14.9	15.7
Italy	8.9	9.5	9.9
Netherlands	11.0	11.3	12.6
Portugal	5.8	7.5	7.7
Spain	5.3	6.4	7.5
Sweden	21.0	22.2	22.4
UK	11.3	11.2	11.5
US	13.3	14.6	15.0

Adapted from: C. Corrado, J. Haskel, C. Jona-Lasinio, M. Iommi. Intangible investment in the EU and US before and since the Great Recession and its contribution to productivity growth, European Investment Bank Working Papers 2016/08

In some cases, it is difficult to distinguish the value of the intangible asset from the value of the firm. For example, the book you are holding in your hands is published by Palgrave Macmillan, a subsidiary of Springer Nature, which is one of the leading publishing groups in the world. The company is engaged in a traditional business, the output of which is made up of tangible assets, such as books, academic journals, monographs. However, Palgrave Macmillan's competitive advantage lies not only in its tangible assets but also in the intangible ones, such as brand, distribution, ability to attract authors and readers, logistics, marketing, and ability to create synergies with the parent company and the other subsidiaries of the group. Thus, the value of Palgrave Macmillan does not just depend on the number of publications it sells, but also on its know-how, which makes it one of the leading players in the publishing industry.

Ferrari is another example. At first glance, Ferrari shows the typical characteristics of a capital-intensive company: it manufactures an undoubtedly tangible product; it operates in a plant where the product is fully assembled; it needs a large workforce. However, a more in-depth examination clearly reveals that the company's competitive advantage lies not only in the outputs but also in the inputs. More specifically, these include design-related know-how, design, brand, technological innovation, registered patents, and participation in Formula 1 races. When buying a Ferrari, buyers are often unable to fully appreciate its technological content and their choice is rather based on status symbol, appearance, the feeling of owning an exclusive asset.

In light of the foregoing, how much of Ferrari's value lies in its tangible assets and how much in its intangible assets? Providing an answer is not easy, as tangible and intangible aspects tend to overlap and the value of the firm is influenced by both.

In some cases, the value of the firm lies outside of it. For example, the value of large law firms or large consulting companies certainly does not lie in their tangible assets, which are often negligible. Their value is essentially related to two areas. The first is inherent in the company and concerns the brand, reputation, and organizational system. The other area lies outside the company and consists of the skills and know-how of the people who work there. If these people were to leave the company, its value would greatly diminish.

For example, Arthur Andersen, one of the best-known consulting firms in the world, broke up in 2001 after being found guilty of failing to control Enron. In 2000, Arthur Andersen had earned revenues for $8.3 billion and employed 80,000 professionals worldwide. The following year, it had virtually disappeared from the market. Its know-how, that is, its true asset, quickly dispersed, moving to Accenture, Protiviti, BearingPoint, as well as to the Big Four (Deloitte, E&Y, KPMG, PricewaterhouseCoopers) and smaller consulting firms.

The value of an intangible asset is often considered as more uncertain than that of a tangible asset, but this is a false belief, especially in the current dematerialized economy.

Take, for example, the clothing industry in Italy. In the last 20 years, apparel manufacturers recorded significant contractions in revenues and profitability, especially due to the relentless relocation to the Far East. On the contrary, the fashion houses that commission the production of those items of clothing achieved significant increases in revenues and cash flow. What is the reason for this different performance?

Since manufacturers carry out an easily replicable activity, they were affected by the competition of firms that could apply lower prices; due to higher fixed costs, Italian producers could not stem the delocalization process, thus losing profit and market shares.

On the other hand, the fashion houses were selling a brand; in other words, they were able to sell their apparel at high prices because buyers were not simply buying a product, but a lifestyle.

This example shows that well-grounded intangible assets can command an average higher return than tangible assets.

It is interesting to note that the accounting standards provide that an intangible asset with an indefinite useful life should not be amortized (International Accounting Standards (IAS) 38 and FASB Topic 350), thereby acknowledging the significant competitive advantage that can be derived from intangible assets.

7.2 Definition and Identification of Intangible Assets

Intangible assets can be defined in various ways. A convincing definition is provided by IVS 210: "An intangible asset is a non-monetary asset that manifests itself by its economic properties. It does not have physical substance but grants rights and/or economic benefits to its owner."

Under the IFRSs and US Generally Accepted Accounting Principles (GAAP), an intangible asset must simultaneously comply with the following three requirements (the definitions are taken from IAS 38):

1. identifiability;
2. control over a resource; and
3. existence of future economic benefits.

The definition requires an intangible asset to be *identifiable* to distinguish it from goodwill. An asset is identifiable if it either:

(a) is separable, that is, is capable of being separated or divided from the entity (firm) and sold, transferred, licensed, rented, or exchanged, either individually or together with a related contract, identifiable asset, or liability, regardless of whether the entity intends to do so; or
(b) arises from contractual or other legal rights, regardless of whether those rights are transferable or separable from the entity or from other rights and obligations.

An entity (firm) *controls* an asset if the entity has the power to obtain the future economic benefits flowing from the underlying resource and to restrict the access of others to those benefits. The capacity of an entity to control the future economic benefits from an intangible asset would normally stem from legal rights that are enforceable in a court of law. In the absence of legal rights, it is more difficult to demonstrate control. However, legal enforceability of a right is not a necessary condition for control because an entity may be able to control the future economic benefits in some other way.

The *future economic benefits* flowing from an intangible asset may include revenue from the sale of products or services, cost savings, or other benefits resulting from the use of the asset by the entity.

Under IVS 210 there are many types of intangible assets, but they are often considered to fall into one or more of the following categories:

(a) **Marketing-related**: Marketing-related intangible assets are used primarily in the marketing or promotion of products or services. Examples include trademarks, trade names, unique trade design/shape/color, and Internet domain names.
(b) **Customer-related**: Customer-related intangible assets include customer lists, backlog, customer contracts, and contractual and non-contractual customer relationships.
(c) **Artistic-related**: Artistic-related intangible assets arise from the right to benefits from artistic works such as plays, books, films, and music, and from non-contractual copyright protection.
(d) **Contract-related**: Contract-related intangible assets represent the value of rights that arise from contractual agreements. Examples include licensing and royalty agreements, service or supply contracts, lease agreements, permits, broadcast rights, servicing contracts, employment contracts, and non-competition agreements.
(e) **Technology-based**: Technology-related intangible assets arise from contractual or non-contractual rights to use patented technology, unpatented technology, databases, formulae, designs, software, processes, or recipes.

In this chapter, we are not dealing with goodwill. Although goodwill is a relevant intangible asset, it is not separable from the business to which it relates; hence it is not autonomously identifiable. The value of goodwill is any residual amount remaining after the value of all identifiable tangible, intangible, and monetary assets less liabilities and potential liabilities have been deducted from the value of the firm. It may be related to various elements, including:

- company-specific synergies arising from a combination of two or more businesses;
- opportunities to expand the business into different markets;
- the benefit to be derived from future customers;
- the benefit of an established network.

7.3 The Valuer's Tasks

The valuation of intangible assets can be more complex than a business valuation, as the object of the valuation has less clear boundaries and requires the ability to correctly define the characteristics of the asset.

For example, a patent cannot be valued without analyzing the legal protections that ensure the exclusive use of its content; a brand can be valued differently depending on whether it is being sold between two independent parties or it is being tested for impairment in accordance with accounting standards.

Therefore, valuers must carefully identify the purpose of the valuation. According to IVS 210, the intangible assets valuation can be performed for a variety of purposes, such as:

(a) **financial reporting:** "valuations of intangible assets are often required in connection with accounting for business combinations, asset acquisitions and sales, and impairment analysis. For instance, under IAS 36 and IAS 38, an entity is required to test an intangible asset with an indefinite useful life for impairment by comparing its recoverable amount with its carrying amount (i) annually, and (ii) whenever there is an indication that the intangible asset may be impaired";

(b) **tax reporting**: "intangible asset valuations are frequently needed for transfer pricing analyses, estate and gift tax planning and reporting, and *ad valorem* taxation analyses. The role of transfer pricing rules is to provide the fair profit allocation, allowing a state to benefit from the productivity and manufacturing carried out in its territory". Unquestionably "things become even more complicated when it is necessary to establish a transfer price for intangible assets, since the price of intangible assets may be included in the price of the goods, or the intangible assets could be the independent objects of contracts";

(c) **litigation**: "intangible assets may be the subject of litigation. A forensic valuation is performed for purposes of either breach of contract claims or tort claims". Even if it is not easy to generalize, IVS 201 provides both examples of breach of contract claims (employment agreements; non-competition agreements; non-solicitation agreements; use licenses and other intellectual property licenses; franchise agreements; intellectual property commercialization or development agreements), and tort claims (interference with business relationship; interference with business opportunity; interference with contractual rights; infringement; disparagement or defamation; fraudulent misrepresentation; condemnation and eminent domain);

(d) **negotiation**: "valuers are often asked to value intangible assets as part of general consulting, collateral lending and transactional support engagements".

When valuing an intangible asset, the valuer must therefore gather the necessary information to:

- identify and circumscribe the intangible asset;
- verify the specific characteristics of the asset in terms of function, type of benefits generated, competitive advantages;
- analyze the set of legal rights, protections, and limitations;
- identify licensing and sublicensing agreements, confidentiality, development, marketing and use rights, and any other obligations;
- get to know the history of the intangible asset;
- estimate the residual economic life and the legal life of the intangible asset;
- appreciate the direct and indirect economic benefits that the intangible asset will produce during its economic life;
- be informed about any disputes (past and current) related to the asset;
- evaluate the potential of the intangible asset in terms of further commercial use;
- identify whether the highest and best use of the intangible asset is its current use;
- identify whether the highest and best use of the intangible asset is stand-alone or as part of a group of assets.

7.4   Valuation Approaches

Under IVS 210 three valuation approaches can be applied to the valuation of intangible assets:

1. Income approach
2. Market approach
3. Cost approach

The *income approach* determines the value of an intangible asset by reference to the present value (PV) of future income, cash flows, or cost savings that could be reasonably expected to be achieved by a market participant owning the asset.

The *market approach* provides an indication of value by comparing the subject asset with identical or similar assets for which price information is available.

The *cost approach* is based on the economic principle that a buyer will pay no more for an asset than the cost to obtain an asset of equal utility, whether by purchase or by construction.

All methods share the purpose of identifying the value of an intangible asset at a given date. Valuers must select the method they deem most appropriate, given the surrounding circumstances, the purposes, and the characteristics of the intangible asset.

7.5 The Income Approach

There are various methods used for valuing intangible assets under the income approach. The most common are:

1. Relief-from-royalty method, (also known as "royalty savings method");
2. Premium profits method (also known as "With and Without");
3. Excess earnings method;
4. Greenfield method.

Each of these methods is examined in the following pages.

7.5.1 Relief-from-Royalty Method

According to IVS 210, under the relief-from-royalty method, "the value of an intangible asset is determined by reference to the value of the hypothetical royalty payments that would be saved through owning the asset, as compared with licensing the intangible asset from a third party. Conceptually, the method may also be viewed as a discounted cash flow method applied to the cash flow that the owner of the intangible asset could receive through licensing the intangible asset to third parties." The formula is as follows:

$$\text{Value of the intangible} = PV(r) \sum_{t=0}^{n} R \times RR(1-t)$$

where:

$PV(r)$ = present value at a specific discount rate (r)
R = revenues
RR = royalty rate
t = tax rate

The application of the method involves several steps.

First, the revenues obtained from the use of the intangible asset must be valued; this metric is adopted because royalties are usually calculated as a percentage of revenues. Alternatively, other metrics may also be used, such as per-unit royalty, if there is evidence that their use is more frequent in any given industry. Projected revenues must take into account the useful life of the asset. For example, if a pharmaceutical patent expires after three years, the projections cannot exceed this time horizon.

Secondly, it is necessary to estimate the hypothetical royalty rate that would be paid if the asset were licensed from a third party. There are two methods for calculating the hypothetical royalty rate.

The first method is based on *market royalty rates* for comparable or similar transactions. In order for this method to be applied, the following conditions must be met: (a) comparable intangible assets are available; (b) which are covered by a license agreement and (c) for which royalty rates are available. There are specific databases that offer this information: in most cases at a charge, but some provide free information.

The most delicate aspect is identifying the comparable assets, as intellectual property is precisely protected for its uniqueness. Therefore, the objective of this process is to identify intangibles that have similar functions and that are used in the same scope of application. Thus, to construct a panel of suitable comparables, valuers are required to perform not only an economic analysis, but also a technical analysis.

The reports provided by specialized providers usually contain the following information:

(a) royalty rates as a percentage of some financial bottom line;
(b) licensee and licensor information;
(c) relationship between the parties to the agreement (related or unrelated);
(d) description of the property licensed or sold, such as IP property, field of use, and so on;
(e) other compensation, such as milestone and upfront payments;
(f) transaction terms, such as agreement date, exclusivity, geographical restrictions;
(g) arm's length or related party status as available;
(h) source of information (Securities and Exchange Commission [SEC] filings, news articles, company news releases);

Sometimes agreements can be renewed or renegotiated. Valuers must ensure that they obtain the most recent version of the agreement.

Furthermore, they must conduct their search on a worldwide basis, as it would be reductive to analyze comparable intellectual properties with respect to a single country or a specific area only. For example, a search limited to US patents may not provide a suitable panel of comparables and may exclude significant intellectual properties. Hence, the database must ensure global coverage; in this regard, professional databases are evidently better equipped in terms of coverage and updating of the data.

Table 7.2 Factors considered in the adjustment of the royalty rate

No.	Factor	Consideration
1	Age, absolute	Long established or newly created trademark
2	Age, relative	Older or newer than competing trademarks
3	Use, consistency	Used consistently on related products or inconsistently on unrelated products
4	Use, specificity	Used on a broad range of products and services versus narrow range
5	Use, geography	Has wide appeal (e.g. can be used internationally) versus narrow or local appeal
6	Potential for expansion	Unrestricted versus restricted ability for use on new and different products
7	Potential for exploitation	Unrestricted versus restricted ability for licensing in new industries and uses
8	Associations	Trademark associated with positive versus negative person, event, or location
9	Connotations	Name has positive versus negative connotations and reputation among consumers
10	Timeliness	Trademark is perceived as modern versus old-fashioned
11	Quality	Trademark is perceived as respectable versus less respectable
12	Profitability, absolute	Profit margins on associated products is higher versus lower than industry average
13	Profitability, relative	Profit margins on associated products is higher versus lower than competitor(s)
14	Expense of promoting	Low versus high cost of advertising and marketing of trademark
15	Means of promoting	Numerous versus few means to promote the trademark
16	Market share, absolute	Associated product has high versus low market share
17	Market share, relative	Associated product has higher versus lower market share than competitor(s)
18	Market potential, absolute	Products are in an expanding versus contracting market
19	Market potential, relative	Market for products expanding faster versus slower than competitor(s)
20	Name recognition	Trademark has high versus low recognition among consumers

Since it may be difficult to identify comparable intellectual properties with a good degree of approximation, valuers may consider adjusting the royalty rate. These adjustments must be made considering various elements. Table 7.2 shows an example of adjustments to a trademark.

A second method is based on a *split of profits* that would hypothetically be paid in an arm's length transaction by a willing licensee to a willing licensor for the rights to use the subject intangible asset. Such method is used in the absence of market royalty rates for identical or similar assets. This method originates from transfer pricing and is to be used as a secondary alternative method to the previous one, as it is based on subjective estimates that can reduce the significance of results.

After estimating the hypothetical royalty rate, the valuer must:

1. apply the selected royalty rate to the projections to calculate the royalty payments avoided by owning the intangible asset;
2. estimate any additional expenses for which a licensee of the asset would be responsible. IVS 210 correctly states that "a royalty rate should be analysed to determine whether it assumes expenses (such as maintenance, marketing and advertising) are the responsibility of the licensor or the licensee. A royalty rate that is 'gross' would consider all responsibilities and expenses associated with ownership of a licensed asset to reside with the licensor, while a royalty that is 'net' would consider some or all responsibilities and expenses associated with the licensed asset to reside with the licensee". Depending on whether the royalty is 'gross' or 'net', according to IVS 201, "the valuation should exclude or include, respectively, a deduction for expenses such as maintenance, marketing or advertising expenses related to the hypothetically licensed asset";
3. determine the appropriate discount rate and PV of the intangible asset.

For example, company XYZ intends to calculate the value of a patent based on the relief-from-royalty method. Table 7.3 shows the details of royalty contracts relating to patents comparable to those of XYZ.

The royalty average and median are, respectively, 1.71% and 1.75%. The median (1.75%) is used to calculate the market royalty rate.

Table 7.3 Comparable transactions royalty rate

Licensor	Licensee	License time (years)	Standard Interpretations Committee (SIC) code	Degree of exclusivity	Royalty Low (%)	Royalty High (%)	Other fee
Licensor 1	Licensee 1	10	XX	Exclusive	0.5	1.5	–
Licensor 2	Licensee 2	10	XX	Exclusive	1.0	2.0	$1 M minimum
Licensor 3	Licensee 3	10	XX	Exclusive	1.5	2.5	–
Licensor 4	Licensee 4	10	XX	Exclusive	1.0	1.5	–
Licensor 5	Licensee 5	10	XX	Exclusive	2.0	3.0	$200 K minimum
Licensor 6	Licensee 6	10	XX	Exclusive	1.5	2.5	–
				Mean	1.25	2.17	**1.71%**
				Median	1.25	2.25	**1.75%**

Table 7.4 Value of the patent

	n + 1	n + 2	n + 3	n + 4
Revenues attributed to the patent	$800,000	$850,000	$880,000	$920,000
× Market-based royalty rate	1.75%	1.75%	1.75%	1.75%
= Pre-tax-avoided patent expenses	$14,000	$14,875	$15,400	$16,100
− Income tax (30%)	$4200	$4463	$4620	$4830
= After-tax-avoided patent expenses	$9,800	$10,413	$10,780	$11,270
Discount factor	9%	9%	9%	9%
PV of tax-avoided patent expenses	$8991	$8764	$8324	$7984
Value of the patent	$34,063			

Assuming remaining useful life = 4 years; tax rate = 30%; discount factor = 9%, the value of the patent is calculated based on expected revenues (Table 7.4).

Since the hypothetical costs and royalty payments are tax deductible, a tax rate is applied in order to determine the after-tax savings associated with ownership of the intangible asset. For certain purposes (such as transfer pricing), the effects of taxes are generally not considered in the model.

If appropriate for the purpose of the valuation the valuer can calculate and add the tax amortization benefit (TAB) for the subject intangible asset. TAB refers to the PV of income tax savings from the tax deduction generated by the amortization of an intangible asset.

Finally, under IVS 210 a valuer should consider the following factors:

- the competitive environment. Specifically, the size of the market, the availability of realistic alternatives, the number of competitors, barriers to entry and presence (or absence) of switching costs;
- the importance of the intangible to the owner;
- the life cycle of the intangible.

7.5.2 Premium Profit Method

The premium profit method (also known as "With and Without" method) indicates the value of an intangible asset by comparing an estimate of the profits or cash flows that would be earned by a business using the asset with those that would be earned by a business that does not use the asset.

The formula is as follows:

$$\text{Value of the intangible} = PV_1(r) \sum_{t=0}^{n} \begin{pmatrix} \text{Revenues} \\ -\text{Expenses} \\ -\text{CapEx} \mid \text{WC} \\ -\text{Taxes} \end{pmatrix}$$

$$- PV_2(r) \sum_{t=0}^{n} \begin{pmatrix} \text{Revenues} \\ -\text{Expenses} \\ -\text{CapEx} \mid \text{WC} \\ -\text{Taxes} \end{pmatrix} + PV_3(r) \text{TAB}$$

where:

$PV_1(r)$ = present value of "With" scenario
$PV_2(r)$ = present value of "Without" scenario
$PV_3(r)$ = present value of TAB

Under IVS 201 the comparison of the two scenarios can be done in two ways:

(a) "calculating the value of the business under each scenario with the difference in the business values being the value of the subject intangible asset, and
(b) calculating, for each future period, the difference between the profits in the two scenarios. The present value of those amounts is then used to reach the value of the subject intangible asset".

While this method may theoretically seem intuitive, in practice it is difficult to identify the expected Nopat or the expected free cash flows "Without" the contribution of an intangible asset.

When the results of a company entirely depend on an intangible asset, as in the fashion business, this method is difficult to apply; in such cases, the brand is usually the main asset. Let us assume that a company annually sells 100,000 T-shirts at a price of $100 each; revenues amount to $10,000,000. Considering that an unbranded T-shirt sells for $15, the valuer should identify the effects on the cost structure and calculate EBIT in the "With" and "Without" scenario. This is practically impossible, because (a) for an unbranded product, selling 100,000 T-shirts a year is unmanageable; (b) the cost structure should be completely redetermined; (c) a different business model should be considered; (d) a different level of investments and financial leverage should be assumed. In other words, a valuer should estimate the profitability of Armani as if it were a small T-shirt manufacturer in the province of Milan rather than a global player.

If the "weight" of the intangible is modest, the premium profit method can be applied. For instance, such method is frequently used in the valuation of non-competition agreements. A non-competition agreement is a contract between an employer and employee; it lays out binding terms and conditions about the employee's ability to work in the same industry and with competing organizations upon employment termination from the current employer.

In applying the Without scenario, the valuer must consider:

(a) the decrease in revenues due to the loss of a part of the competitive advantage provided by the intangible asset;
(b) the decrease in costs associated with the intangible asset, such as advertising costs, R&D, costs for participation in fairs, and so on;
(c) the increase in costs that an intangible asset helps keeps under control. For example, without a patent a firm may be obliged to use a different and more expensive production technology.

Once the results have been estimated for each of the two scenarios, the valuer can calculate the value of the intangible asset:

- through the difference between the annual discounted cash flows (DCFs) in the "With" scenario and in the "Without" scenario;
- through the difference between the value of the firm in the "With" scenario and the value of the firm in the "Without" scenario.

Let us assume that a company intends to evaluate a secondary brand, the contribution of which can be easily identified and measured. The management calculates the expected free cash flow both in the "With brand" scenario and in the "Without brand" scenario (Table 7.5).

In the "Without" scenario, a reduction in EBITDA and change in WC is assumed. CapEx are assumed to remain constant. A discount rate = 9% is estimated.

In Table 7.6, the value of the brand is calculated using the difference between the annual DCFs of the "With" scenario and those of the "Without" scenario.

In Table 7.7 the value of the brand is calculated through the difference between the value of the firm in the "With" scenario and the value of the firm in the "Without" scenario.

Intangible Assets Valuation

Table 7.5 With and Without scenarios

	t + 1	t + 2	t + 3	t + 4
Cash flow statement "WITH"				
EBITDA	$60,000	$65,400	$69,500	$75,300
Tax paid	(−$12,000)	(−$13,734)	(−$14,595)	(−$15,813)
Gross cash flow	**$47,400**	**$51,666**	**$54,905**	**$59,487**
Change in working capital (WC)	$6800	$3200	$7500	$8200
Increase of long-term investment	$5400	$4800	$6900	$5200
Decrease of long-term investment	(−$2500)	0	(−$4300)	0
Free cash flow	**$37,700**	**$43,666**	**$44,805**	**$46,087**
Cash flow statement "WITHOUT"				
EBITDA	$48,000	$52,320	$55,600	$60,240
Tax paid	(−$10,080)	(−$10,987)	(−$11,676)	(−$12,650)
Gross cash flow	**$37,920**	**$41,333**	**$43,924**	**$47,590**
Change in WC	$5200	$3000	$6300	$6500
Increase of long-term investment	$5400	$4800	$6900	$5200
Decrease of long-term investment	(−$2500)	0	(−$4300)	0
Free cash flow	**$29,820**	**$33,533**	**$35,024**	**$35,890**

Table 7.6 Value of the brand by comparing the "With" and "Without" DCF

Value of the brand	t + 1	t + 2	t + 3	t + 4
Free cash flow With	$37,700	$43,666	$44,805	$46,087
Free cash flow Without	$29,820	$33,533	$35,024	$35,890
FCF With − FCF Without	$7880	$10,133	$9781	$10,197
Discount rate	9%	9%	9%	9%
DCF	$6632	$9297	$7553	$7224
$\sum$ DCF = value of the brand	**$30,706**			

Table 7.7 Value of the brand by comparing the value of the firm in the "With" and "Without" scenarios

	t + 1	t + 2	t + 3	t + 4
Value of the firm "WITH"				
FCF	$37,700	$43,666	$44,805	$46,087
Discount rate	9%	9%	9%	9%
DCF	$34,587	$36,753	$34,598	$32,649
$\sum$ DCF With	**$138,587**			
Value of the firm "WITHOUT"				
FCF	$29,820	$33,533	$35,024	$35,890
Discount rate	9%	9%	9%	9%
DCF	$27,358	$28,224	$27,045	$25,425
$\sum$ DCF Without	**$108,052**			

The value of the brand is calculated by subtracting the DCF in the "Without" scenario from the DCF in the "With" scenario:

$$\text{Value of the brand} = \Sigma \text{DCF}^{\text{"With"}} - \Sigma \text{DCF}^{\text{"Without"}}$$
$$= \$138{,}587 - \$108{,}052 = \$30{,}535$$

The result using one or the other calculation is almost identical.

7.5.3 Excess Earnings Method

The excess earnings method estimates the value of an intangible asset as the PV of the cash flows attributable to the subject intangible asset after excluding the proportion of the cash flows that are attributable to other assets required to generate the cash flows ("contributory assets"). According to IVS 210, "it is often used for valuations where there is a requirement for the acquirer to allocate the overall price paid for a business between tangible assets, identifiable intangible assets and goodwill". The formula is as follows:

$$\text{Value of the intangible} = PV_1(r) \sum_{t=0}^{n} \begin{pmatrix} \text{Revenues} \\ -\text{Expenses} \\ -\text{CACs} \\ -\text{Taxes} \end{pmatrix} + PV_2(r) \text{TAB}$$

where:

$PV_1(r)$ = present value at a discount rate (r)
$PV_2(r)$ = present value of TAB
CACs = contributory asset charges

The method can be applied using:

(a) several periods of forecasted cash flows ("multi-period excess earnings method" or "MPEEM"); as most intangible assets have economic lives exceeding one period, the MPEEM is the most commonly used method;
(b) a single period of forecasted cash flows ("single-period excess earnings method")

Theoretically, the method can also be applied by capitalizing a single period of forecasted cash flows, but such method is only appropriate if the intangible asset is operating in a steady state with stable growth.

The MPEEM is commonly used to value the primary income-generating asset of a company or of a business unit (BU). Such method can be applied as follows.

First, the following metrics must be estimated for a sufficient number of years (or for the useful life of the asset):

- revenues driven by the subject intangible asset and related contributory assets;
- expenses required to generate such revenues. Expenses should be adjusted to exclude those related to the creation of new intangible assets that are not required to generate the forecasted revenue and expenses.

Secondly, the contributory assets needed to achieve the forecasted revenue and expenses must be identified. Contributory assets are those that are used in conjunction with the subject intangible asset in the realization of prospective cash flows. Contributory assets include WC, fixed assets, assembled workforce, and identified intangible assets other than the subject intangible asset.

Subsequently, the valuer must determine the appropriate rate of return on each contributory asset considering the risk associated with that asset; in each forecast period, the valuer has to deduct the required returns on contributory assets from the forecast profit to arrive at the excess earnings attributable to only the subject intangible asset.

Finally, using an appropriate discount rate, the valuer has to calculate the PV and, eventually, add the TAB for the subject intangible asset.

Table 7.8 Revenue and expenses related to the contributory assets

		n + 1	n + 2	n + 3	n + 4
Revenues		$1229	$1290	$1355	$1422
Customer erosion	20%	80%	64%	50%	40%
Effective revenues		$983	$819	$683	$569
Cost of goods		$572	$477	$397	$331
General costs		$121	$101	$84	$70
EBITDA		**$290**	**$242**	**$201**	**$168**
Amortization		$95	$74	$60	$48
EBIT		**$195**	**$168**	**$142**	**$120**

Table 7.9 Contributory assets charges (fixed assets and working capital)

		n + 1	n + 2	n + 3	n + 4
Opening fixed assets		$569	$572	$575	$577
CapEx		$130	$130	$130	$130
Amortization	20%	$127	$127	$127	$127
Ending fixed assets		$572	$575	$577	$580
Return on	8%	$46	$46	$46	$46
Revenues		$1229	$1290	$1355	$1422
CAC – fixed assets	3.5%	3.7%	3.6%	3.4%	3.3%
Opening WC		$99	$105	$113	$120
Change		$8	$8	$5	$7
Ending WC		$107	$112	$118	$126
Return on	3.0%	$3	$3	$4	$4
Revenues		$1229	$1290	$1355	$1422
CAC – WC	0.3%	0.3%	0.3%	0.3%	0.3%

Table 7.10 Contributory assets charges (fixed assets and working capital)

		n + 1	n + 2	n + 3	n + 4
EBIT		$195	$168	$142	$120
Taxes	30%	$59	$50	$42	$36
CAC – property, plant & equipment (PP&E)	3.5%	$34	$29	$24	$20
CAC – WC	0.3%	$3	$2	$2	$1
Adjusted Nopat		$100	$86	$73	$62
Discount factor		11%	11%	11%	11%
PV		$90	$70	$54	$41
Value of customers		$255			

Assume, for example, that the management of a company intends to calculate the value of customers. The revenues and expenses related to the contributory assets are estimated (Table 7.8) taking into account an annual 20% customer erosion rate, based on historical information.

Based on fixed assets and WC forecasts, the CAC is calculated, by considering (Table 7.9):

- a "return on" investment rate based on the cost of equity and the risk profile of the asset = 8%, for fixed assets;
- a "return on" investment rate based on short-term borrowing rates = 3%, for WC.

Taking EBIT as the basis and assuming a tax rate = 30%, the adjusted Nopat is calculated, also based on the CACs. The value of customers is then calculated (Table 7.10) assuming a discount rate = 11% and no TAB.

Intangible Assets Valuation   201

Table 7.11 Greenfield method

	n + 1	n + 2	n + 3	n + 4
Sales	$60,000	$66,000	$72,600	$79,860
Cost of goods	($54,000)	($59,400)	($65,340)	($71,874)
R&D	($5700)	($5280)	($5082)	($4792)
EBITDA	**$300**	**$1320**	**$2178**	**$3194**
Change in WC	$500	$1000	$1200	$1400
CapEx	$400	$400	0	0
Free cash flow	**($600)**	**($80)**	**$978**	**$1794**
Discount rate	9%	9%	9%	9%
PV	($550)	($67)	$755	$1271
PV	$1409			

7.5.4 Greenfield method

According to IVS 210, under the Greenfield method, the value of the subject intangible asset is determined using cash flow projections that assume the only asset of the business at the valuation date is the subject intangible. All other tangible and intangible assets must be bought, built, or rented. The formula is as follows:

$$\text{Value of the intangible} = PV_1(r) \sum_{t=0}^{n} \begin{pmatrix} \text{Revenues} \\ -\text{Expenses} \\ -\text{CapEx} \mid \text{WC} \\ -\text{Taxes} \end{pmatrix} + PV_2(r) \text{TAB}$$

where:

$PV_1(r)$ = present value at a discount rate (r)
$PV_2(r)$ = present value of TAB

Particularly, under IVS 210, "the Greenfield Method is conceptually similar to the excess earnings method. However, instead of subtracting contributory asset charges from the cash flow to reflect the contribution of contributory assets, the Greenfield Method assumes that the owner of the subject asset would have to build, buy or rent the contributory assets". IVS 210 underlines that, "when building or buying the contributory assets, the cost of a replacement asset of equivalent utility is used rather than a reproduction cost."

The valuation is based on the expected cash flows deriving from the sole use of the intangible asset.

Table 7.11 shows an example of the Greenfield method as applied to intellectual property. As can be seen, the expected cash flows are negative for the first years.

7.6 The Market Approach

The market approach provides an indication of value by comparing the subject asset with identical or similar assets for which price information is available.

As noted by IVS 210, "transactions involving intangible assets frequently also include other assets"; "the heterogeneous nature of intangible assets and the fact that intangible assets seldom transact separately from other assets means that it is rarely possible to find market evidence of transactions involving identical assets. If there is market evidence at all, it is usually in respect of assets that are similar, but not identical."

In applying this method, it is first necessary to identify the prices or valuation multiples in respect of identical or similar intangible assets. Subsequently, adjustments must be made as required for such transaction values or valuation multiples, to reflect the differentiating characteristics or attributes of the subject asset and the assets involved in the transactions.

Given the difficulty in identifying comparable assets, the market approach is rarely used.

7.7 The Cost Approach

Under IVS 210, "the cost approach is based on the economic principle that a buyer will pay no more for an asset than the cost to obtain an asset of equal utility, whether by purchase or by construction".

The cost approach can only be applied to the valuation of intangible assets when it is possible to reasonably estimate either the reproduction or the replacement cost of the subject asset. In this context:

(a) **Reproduction cost** is the cost that would be incurred in replicating the asset. It would reflect the time, investment, and processes involved in creating the subject asset, at costs prevailing at the valuation date. The difficulty in estimating this cost concerns both the ability to separate the

costs incurred to construct the asset from maintenance costs and the ability to identify the indirect costs based on an appropriate driver;
(b) **Replacement cost** is the cost of creating a modern equivalent asset that offers the same utility or functionality as the subject asset. Due to changes that have occurred in the market (such as consumer tastes and technological changes), the processes involved in creating the subject asset may no longer be appropriate.

The following costs must be considered:

- the direct and indirect costs of replacing the utility of the asset, including labor, materials, and overhead;
- the cost of advertising and promotion;
- legal, licensing, and patent registration fees;
- the impact of tax deductibility for the costs incurred in researching or developing an intangible asset.

The cost approach is mainly used for intangible assets that have no identifiable income streams or other economic benefits, such as self-developed software, acquired third-party software, websites, assembled workforce.

The cost approach is not applicable when the intangible asset is unique, or its creation is now outdated. For example, the cost of reproducing Gucci's brand cannot be calculated, as there are so many variables to be considered that summarizing them in a formula is impossible; furthermore, the sum of the direct and indirect costs mentioned above could not in any way reflect the actual value of the brand.

There is a relationship between reproduction cost and replacement cost, which can be summarized by the following formula:

$$\text{Reproduction Cost} = \text{Excess Capital Costs} - \text{Curable Costs} \\ + \text{Developer's Profit} + \text{Entrepreneurial Incentive} \\ = \text{Replacement Cost}$$

The value of the asset can be calculated by taking into account obsolescence:

$$\text{Value of the Asset} = \text{Replacement Cost} - \text{Economic /Functional Obsolescence}$$

Excess capital costs are costs incurred in the past and which, based on current know-how and current market conditions, should no longer be incurred. For example, due to progress in research, the costs incurred today to develop a computer processor are lower than those of five years ago; the costs incurred to promote a brand through the Web are far lower than those incurred in the 1980s and 1990s of the past century.

Curable costs are the costs incurred by a firm to remedy any damage suffered by the asset due to accidental events or inadequate protection. For example, a defective product can damage the company image and, hence, the brand; to protect the brand and regain consumer confidence, a company may be forced to make specific investments.

The developer's profit is the profit that a third party would reasonably be willing to pay to buy the intangible asset. Reproduction cost must include not only the costs necessary to construct the asset, but also the surplus a company would pay to the seller under normal market conditions. In the transition from the concept of cost to the concept of value, we must also consider the return on capital that a third party would expect to receive as remuneration for the systematic risk of the business.

Conversely, entrepreneurial incentive is a remuneration measure for non-systematic risk, that is, the generic risk an entrepreneur bears to conduct business in the market.

Developer's profit and entrepreneurial incentive must be calculated only if:

- it is reasonable to assume that an entity would be willing to pay a premium to obtain the intangible asset, considering its characteristics;
- the asset was not built internally, but was purchased from third parties;
- the asset has been recently constructed and has not suffered any damage.

If the intangible asset to be valued is recent, the effects of obsolescence need not be considered.

In general, when calculating the effects of obsolescence, the useful life of the intangible asset must be taken into account. An empirical criterion consists in identifying the average market life of similar intangibles. For example, in the clothing sector a mid-range brand has an average life of ten years; if the brand to be valued has been on the market for six years, a residual useful life of four years is statistically likely. This is obviously an empirical analysis to be verified by the valuer, based on the information in his or her possession.

Functional obsolescence is the impairment of the usefulness of a device or equipment due to a design defect, or due to its inability to be upgraded or modified to serve the user's current needs. For example, the need for increasingly large data storage has caused the disappearance of floppy disk drives. Some mobile phone manufacturers did not realize the epochal change caused by the introduction of smartphones; the ensuing technological gap with Apple or Samsung led to the downsizing of some historical brands while new brands became popular in the market.

Economic obsolescence is the reduction in the desirability or economic life of an asset caused by factors such as regulatory changes, technological changes, and excess supply. Economic obsolescence can be measured in terms of loss of profitability over time. The average percentage change in profitability is a good benchmark in this respect. For example, let us assume that the products linked to a certain brand recorded a 5% decline in profitability on average; if the valuer estimates that the residual useful life is four years, economic obsolescence is 20%.

7.7.1 Value of the Workforce

An example of the workforce valuation through the replacement cost is illustrated below. Assuming that the firm has four BUs, Table 7.12 shows the average salary per person.

The statistics on recruitment cost and on unproductive training period—that is, the months necessary to train a person and make him/her suitable for employment—are identified based on an analysis of historical data (Table 7.13).

Table 7.12 Average salary per person

Workforce	Total salary	Number of employees	Average salary per person
	(a)	(b)	(c) = (a)/(b)
BU 1	$200,000	10	$20,000
BU 2	$375,000	15	$25,000
BU 3	$480,000	16	$30,000
BU 4	$216,000	8	$27,000
Total	$1,271,000	49	$102,000

Table 7.13 Statistics on recruitment cost and on unproductive training period

Workforce	Recruitment cost % of salary	Unproductive training period (months)
BU 1	8	2
BU 2	10	1.5
BU 3	9	1
BU 4	12	1.5

Table 7.14 Value of the workforce calculation

Workforce	Average salary per person (c) = (a)/(b)	Recruitment cost % of salary (d)	Recruitment cost (e) = (c) × (d)	Unproductive training period (months) (f)	Training costs (g) = (f) × (c)	Replacement cost per person (h) = (e) + (g)	Total replacement cost (i) = (h) × (b)
BU 1	$20,000	8	$1600	2	$3333	$4933	$49,333
BU 2	$25,000	10	$2500	1.5	$3125	$5625	$84,375
BU 3	$30,000	9	$2700	1	$2500	$5200	$83,200
BU 4	$27,000	12	$3240	1.5	$3375	$6615	$52,920
Total	$102,000					$22,373	$269,828

Using this information, the value of the workforce can be calculated, as per the calculation framework in Table 7.14.

The value of the workforce is $269,828. Valuers can also determine this value using the FTEs (full-time equivalents).

7.7.2 Value of a Computer Software

A logistics company uses three internally developed softwares: one is used to manage the logistics business, one for financial management, and one for reporting. The management wants to calculate the value of the software and estimates both the development effort of a new software (in terms of people/month) and the overall costs. Considering that the average salary of people working in IT is $4000 a month, the calculation of the replacement cost is shown in Table 7.15.

The average hourly cost per employee is $25 (= $4000/20 working days/8 hours per day). Based on a quote, the management knows that the price asked by an external software house is $40/hour. Therefore, the total outsourcing cost, which corresponds to the replacement cost new, is $140,800 (= $40 × 20 working days × 8 hours per day × 16 weeks).

The developer's profit is therefore $25,800 (= $140,800 − $115,000). The entrepreneurial incentive is not calculated (Table 7.16).

Table 7.15 Replacement cost of software

Software	Estimated development effort in person/month	Cost per person (month)	Direct cost	Overall costs	Replacement cost
	(a)	(b)	(c) = (a) × (b)	(d)	(e) = (c) + (d)
Logistics	16	$4000	$64,000	$20,000	$84,000
Financial management	4	$4000	$16,000	$5000	$21,000
Reporting	2	$4000	$8000	$2000	$10,000
Total	22		$88,000	$27,000	$115,000

Table 7.16 Replacement cost new

Softwares	Replacement cost new
Logistics	$84,000
Financial management	$21,000
Reporting	$10,000
Replacement cost	**$115,000**
Developer's profit	$25,800
Replacement cost new	**$140,800**

Table 7.17 Functional obsolescence

Software	Replacement cost	Replacement cost new %	Functional obsolescence
Financial management	$84,000	$24,150	$4830

Table 7.18 Economic obsolescence

Software	Replacement cost	Replacement cost new %	Economic obsolescence
Logistics	$84,000	$96,600	$3299

Table 7.19 Value of software

Softwares	Replacement cost new
Logistics	$84,000
Financial management	$21,000
Reporting	$10,000
Replacement cost	**$115,000**
Developer's profit	$25,800
Replacement cost new	**$140,800**
Functional obsolescence	($4830)
Economic obsolescence	($3299)
Value of softwares	**$132,671**

The IT manager informs that the financial management software is subject to functional obsolescence, estimating it at −20%, based on a comparison with other software available on the market. In Table 7.17, the replacement cost new of the financial management software is calculated, by increasing the original replacement cost by 22%. A −20% reduction is applied to the replacement cost new.

The company's chief financial officer (CFO) informs that due to technological changes, the logistics software failed to properly interface with the customer management software, causing delays in some shipments. This caused a contraction of EBIT from $20.5 million to $19.8 million (−3.41%).

In Table 7.18, the replacement cost new of the logistics software is calculated, by increasing the original replacement cost by 22%. A −3.41% reduction is applied to the replacement cost new.

The value of the software is shown in Table 7.19.

8

Premiums and Discounts in Business Valuation

8.1 Value of the Firm and Value of the Shares

In theory, the value of a share should be calculated by dividing the value of the firm by the number of shares:

$$\text{Value of a Share} = \frac{\text{Value of the Firm}}{\text{Number of Shares}}$$

In practice, the calculation is more complex, as the pro-rata ratio can be used to calculate the theoretical value of one share, but does not work when business interests are involved. Indeed, shares may be subject to a premium or discount, depending upon whether they represent controlling or minority interests.

For example, an individual or entity that holds a controlling interest can actively influence the company's strategies and, therefore, its value. An individual or entity that holds a minority interest has less power and may have to accept decisions taken by the majority.

Thus, in business valuations, a stake may have a different value than the corresponding share of the firm's value. In other words, the value of a 60% stake does not correspond to 60% of the company's value, but it is worth "something more" as it gives its holder the right to control the company; likewise, the value of a 15% stake does not correspond to 15% of the company's value, but it is worth "something less" as this investment does not provide its holder with the power to control the company.

The aforesaid "something more" is called premium; the "something less" is called discount.

Therefore, premiums and discounts are positive or negative adjustments to be applied to the value of the shares in order to take into account the shareholders' business interests.

8.2 Premiums and Discounts

In literature, four basic levels of value (Fig. 8.1) are generally considered:

1. synergistic value;
2. controlling interest value;
3. marketable minority interest value;
4. non-marketable minority interest value.

On this basis, the following types of premiums and discounts can be identified:

1. Control premium (CP) and discount for lack of control (DLOC);
2. Discount for lack of marketability (DLOM).

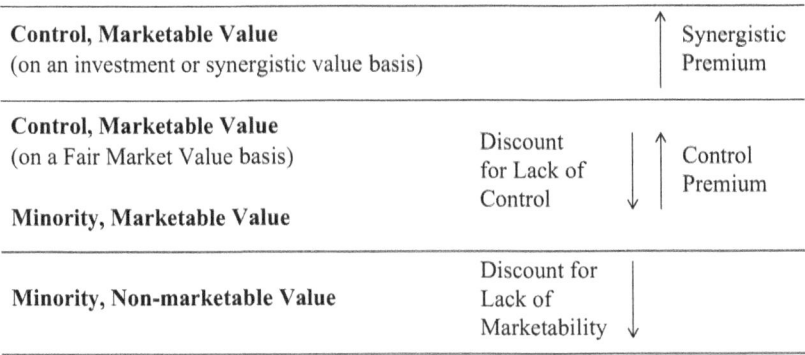

Fig. 8.1 Basics of value. (Source: NACVA, Valuation Discount and Premiums, 2012)

8.3 CP and DLOC

Control premium (CP) is an amount or a percentage by which the pro-rata value of a controlling interest exceeds the pro-rata value of a non-controlling interest to reflect the power of control. *Discount for lack of control (DLOC)* is an amount or percentage deducted from the pro-rata share of value of 100% of an equity interest in a business to reflect the absence of some or all of the powers of control.

Control is the power to direct the management and policies of a business enterprise. According to IFRS 10, "an investor controls an investee when it is exposed, or has rights, to variable returns from its involvement with the investee and has the ability to affect those returns through its power over the investee". According to IFRS 10, control is based on the existence of three elements:

- power over the investee;
- exposure, or rights, to variable returns from its involvement with investee;
- the ability to use its power over the investee to affect the returns.

An investor has power over an investee when the investor has existing rights that give it the current ability to direct the relevant activities, such as:

- selling and purchasing of goods or services;
- managing financial assets during their life (including on default);
- selecting, acquiring, or disposing of assets;
- researching and developing new products or processes;
- determining a funding structure or obtaining funding;
- establishing operating and capital budgets;
- appointing, remunerating, and terminating an investee's key management or service providers.

Under IFRS 10 "power arises from rights. Sometimes assessing power is straightforward, such as when power over an investee is obtained directly and solely from the voting rights granted by equity instruments such as shares, and can be assessed by considering the voting rights from those shareholdings. In other cases, the assessment will be more complex and require more than one factor to be considered, for example when power results from one or more contractual arrangements. (…)". IFRS10 underlines that "if two or more investors each have existing rights that give them the unilateral ability to direct different relevant activities,

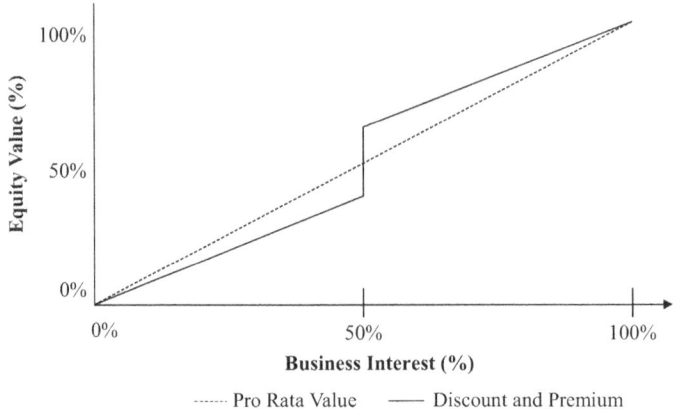

Fig. 8.2 Control premium and discount for lack of control

the investor that has the current ability to direct the activities that most significantly affect the returns of the investee has power over the investee."

Figure 8.2 shows the CP and the DLOC.

As mentioned, the equity value (%) of a minority interest is lower than its pro-rata value; on the contrary, the equity value (%) of a controlling interest is higher than its pro-rata value.

The equity value (%) can be calculated using the following formula:

$$EqV(\%) = EqV_{pr}(\%) \times a$$

where:

EqV(%) = equity value (%)
EqV_{pr}(%) = equity value pro rata (%)
a = coefficient for premium or discount

If the business interest = 50%, the coefficient a = 1.
If the business interest >50%:

$$a = \left[(1 - CP) + \frac{CP}{BI}\right]$$

where:

CP = control premium (%)
BI = business interest (%)

If the business interest <50%:

$$a = 1 - MD$$

where MD = minority discount (%), which can be calculated as follows:

$$MD = 1 - \left(\frac{1}{1+CP}\right)$$

Let us assume that the equity value = $1,000,000 and equity consists of 100,000 shares. The pro-rata value of each share is $10. If an investor is willing to buy 51,000 shares (51%) with a CP = 15%, the equity value (%) is calculated as follows:

$$EqV_{pr}(\%) = \$1,000,000 \times 51\% = \$510,000$$

$$EqV(\%) = \$510,000 \times \left[(1-15\%) + \frac{15\%}{51\%}\right] =$$

$$EqV(\%) = \$510,000 \times 1.14 = \$583,500$$

In practice, to acquire a 51% equity interest with an equity value of $510,000, the investor must pay $583,000; the higher amount of $73,000 is the CP (a = 1.14).

The closer the equity interest is to 51%, the greater the CP, while the CP declines to the average value when the equity interest reaches 100%.

The application of a majority premium is based on the ability to control the company with just a portion of voting rights (51% and up); hence, the entire benefit of control can be obtained without buying the entire capital. Therefore, the value of one share is higher when control is held through majority shareholdings, compared to acquiring 100% of the shares. Clearly, the greater the control obtained by the investor by acquiring a smaller portion of equity, the higher the premium.

This can be verified empirically. With reference to the previous example, under the same conditions, we can calculate how the coefficient "a" changes assuming that the investor purchases 60%, 70%, and 80% of the shares.

$$a_{60\%} = \left[(1-15\%) + \frac{15\%}{60\%}\right] = 1.10$$

$$a_{70\%} = \left[(1-15\%) + \frac{15\%}{70\%}\right] = 1.06$$

$$a_{80\%} = \left[(1-15\%) + \frac{15\%}{80\%}\right] = 1.04$$

The ratio of the "a" coefficient to the number of shares acquired is inversely proportional.

In analyzing the drivers of the value of control, it has been shown in the literature that such drivers are attributable, on the one hand, to the ability to control the company and, secondly, to the possibility of obtaining "special" benefits from the company that may fall outside the corporate purposes.

It thus follows that the ability to allocate CPs is greater the more the governance models enable it, that is, the easier it is for the majority to impose its will on the minority. Majority premiums are therefore:

- higher in countries where the legal system is less oriented to the protection of minorities and where the judicial system does not ensure a prompt response in case of breaches;
- lower for listed companies as the control exercised by the market and the regulators tend to reduce the scope for "private" benefits;
- higher for small private companies, where the majority often coincides with the management.

A business interest valuation is different both from the valuation of a firm and from the evaluation of an individual share. This means that:

(a) the value of a business interest may differ from the sum of the values of the individual shares;
(b) the value of the firm may differ from the sum of the values of the individual business interests.

This is because:

- the benefits generated by the firm are not necessarily divisible on a proportional basis;
- the risks are not necessarily the same for the different categories of shareholders;

Table 8.1 Control premium and controlling interest

Controlling interest (%)	Control premium (%)
50–55	30–40
55–60	25–30
60–70	20–25
70–85	15–20
85–100	0

- the information to which the various categories of shareholders have access are not necessarily equal and symmetrical.

In calculating premiums and discounts, valuers must apply extreme caution. Indeed:

1. care must be used not to confuse them with the risk premium, which, being a variable of the discount rate, is normally an integral part of the calculation of the basic value of the firm;
2. premiums and discounts are largely the result of a discretionary and overall judgment. Therefore, valuers must avoid using premiums and discounts of significant size, especially if they are derived from open source statistics. Specific databases are available, such as the *FactSet Mergerstat/BVR Control Premium Study*, which enable more targeted searches, based on the industry and the size of the business.

Although valuers should check the characteristics of the business on a case-by-case basis, the CP is generally comprised in the ranges specified in Table 8.1.

8.4 Discount for Lack of Marketability

Under IVS 105 DLOM "should be applied when the comparables are deemed to have superior marketability to the subject asset". IVS 105 correctly underlines that "a DLOM reflects the concept that when comparing otherwise identical assets, a readily marketable asset would have a higher value than an asset with a long marketing period or restrictions on the ability to sell the asset. For example, publicly-traded securities can be bought and sold nearly instantaneously while shares in a private company may require a significant amount of time to identify potential buyers and complete a transaction." The formula is as follows:

$$\text{Value of the business interest} = \text{Value of the firm} \times (1 - \text{DLOM})$$

In practice, the DLOM can be significant, since the transfers of unlisted companies are often characterized by difficult negotiation. It may fluctuate in a range between 15% and 30%, depending on the following parameters:

- the nature of the firm's assets: the DLOM may be high when assets are difficult to sell separately;
- the size of the business: the smaller the size, the higher the DLOM;
- the ability to generate cash flow: the greater the ability to generate cash flow, the lower the investment pay-back time and, therefore, the DLOM;
- the number of shareholders: the higher the number of shareholders, the greater the DLOM.

Sometimes, both the DLOM and the DLOC are applicable to a business interest. These two discounts should not be summed up, but must be calculated separately.

For example, a 40% business interest is subject to a DLOC = 20% and a DLOM = 30%. Assuming that the value of the firm = $200,000, the minority interest is calculated as follows:

Value of the Firm = $200,000
Value of the firm "private" = Value of the Firm × (1−DLOM) = $200,000 × (1−30%) = $140,000
Value 40% "pro rata" = $140,000 × 40% = $56,000
Value 40% "minority" = $56,000 × (1−20%) = $44,800

The same result can be obtained by first calculating the DLOC and then the DLOM.

Value of the Firm = $200,000
Value 40% "pro rata" = $200,000 × 40% = $80,000
Value 40% "minority" = $80,000 × (1−20%) = $64,000
Value of the firm "private" = $64,000 × (1−30%) = $44,800

In both cases the value of the business interest is $44,800.

8.5 Other Discounts

The National Association of Certified Valuators and Analysts (NACVA) lists other types of discounts, such as:

- blockage discounts;
- key person discounts;
- restrictive agreement discounts;
- investment company discounts.

Under IVS 200, "*blockage discounts* are sometimes applied when the subject asset represents a large block of shares in a publicly-traded security such that an owner would not be able to quickly sell the block in the public market without negatively influencing the publicly-traded price". IVS 200 points out that a "blockage discounts may be quantified using any reasonable method but typically a model is used that considers the length of time over which a participant could sell the subject shares without negatively impacting the publicly-traded price."

The *key person discount* is applied when the performance of a firm largely depends on the skills of some specific persons (such as CEO, CFO). In such cases, the value of some key persons represents a part of the value of the firm. If such key persons leave the company, the value of the company may decline. The key person discount is rarely applied and especially in small businesses its value is subjective and depends on a wide range of parameters that the valuer must consider.

The *restrictive agreement discounts* apply to buy-sell agreements, restricted stock agreements, and so on, that can limit the shareholder's ability to sell or transfer stocks. According to NACVA, "the impairment increases with the severity of the restriction. Value impairment due to the presence of restrictive agreements is generally incorporated into the overall discount for lack of marketability."

The *investment company discounts*, also called *holding discounts*, are based on an observation of actual situations. Frequently, the sum of the net asset values of the subsidiaries is higher than the value of the listed holding company; indeed, the market tends to accept that only part of the value of the subsidiaries be transferred to the holding company. This discount may range between 20% and 60%.

Index

A

Accounting standards
  IAS 38, intangible assets, 185
  IFRS 10, control and business interests, 211
  revenue recognition, 96
  role of IFRS, 40
Adjusted beta, 92
Altman Z Score Plus, 107
Amazon.com, 35, 128
American Society of Appraisers (ASA), 21
Apple Inc., 27, 79
Arbitrage pricing model (APM), 97
Assets
  current, 42
  non-current, 42
  reclassified assets, 42
  relationship with liabilities, 42
Assumed transaction
  assumed date of transaction, 6
  assumed parties of transaction, 6–7
  definition, 6

B

Bankruptcy
  financial statement analysis, 71–76
Bases of value, 7
  liquidation value, 8
  market value, 7
Beta
  adjusted beta, 93
  arbitrage pricing model (APM), 97
  definition, 90
  levered beta, 93–96
  multibusiness company beta, 96–97
  unlevered beta, 96
  weakness of beta, 97–98
Bond rating
  government bonds, 86
  interest rate, 86
  risk of default, 86
Book value
  cost-based method, 176
  price-to book value, 167
Business assets, 44–45

Business interest
  control premium (CP), 211
  discount for lack of control
    (DLOC), 211
Business life cycle, 51

C
Capital asset pricing model (CAPM)
  adjusted CAPM, 103–104
  beta, 89
  formula, 85
  return on equity (ROE) and
    CAPM, 52
  risk-free rate, 86
  risk premium, 98
Capital expenditures
  amortization, 48, 145
  in manufacturing companies, 65
Cash flow
  cash flow statement, 49
  free cash flow to equity, 81
  free cash flow to firm, 81
  See also Discounted cash flow;
    Expected cash flows; Terminal value
Cash flow statement, 49
Cash ratio, 59
Company specific premium (CSP), 104
Comparable firm
  comparable firm beta, 93
  financial statement analysis, 41
  selection of a peer group, 130
  See also Comparable companies
    method; Comparable transaction
    method
Comparable companies method
  application tool, 137–139
  selection of peer group, 137–139
Comparable transaction method
  application tool, 137–139
  relief-from-royalty method, 190–194
  selection of peer group, 137–139
Competitive advantage

growth rate, 113
of intangible assets, 51, 184
relationship with value, 27
Context analysis
  external elements analysis, 27–29
  internal elements analysis, 25–27
Control
  control method, 10, 17
  control over a resource, 186
  control premium, 211
Controlling interest
  type of transaction, 136
  valuation report, 14
  See also Control premium
Control premium (CP), 211
Cost-based method
  definition, 175
  at a glance, 9–10
  replacement cost, 177–178
  reproduction cost, 177–178
Cost of capital
  asset side and equity side, 80
  relationship with ROE, 52
  relationship with value creation, 33
  weighted average cost of capital
    (WACC), 108
Cost of debt
  formula, 105
  remuneration of lenders, 53
  return on debt (ROD), 107
  weighted average cost of capital
    (WACC), 108
Cost of equity
  beta, 90
  capital asset pricing model
    (CAPM), 85
  risk-free rate, 86
  risk premium, 98
Cost of goods sold, 63
Cost of sales, 63
Country risk premium, *see* Equity risk
  premium
Current assets, 42

Current liabilities, 42
Current ratio, 59
Current value, 176, 177

D

Debt, 2, 17, 30, 33, 34, 45–47, 49, 50, 52–54, 56, 59–61, 65–73, 75, 76, 81, 85, 90, 92, 95, 105, 107–109, 115, 116, 118, 119, 129, 136, 164, 169, 170, 176, 178
   See also Cost of debt; Debt-to equity ratio; Financial structure
Debt-to-capital ratio, 68
Debt-to-equity ratio
   formula, 69
   levered and unlevered beta, 94
Debt-to-sales ratio, 69–70
Default
   equity risk premium (ERP), 98
   financial analysis of distressed firms, 71
   risk of default, 108
   spread, 105
Disclosure
   quality of, 40
   valuation report, 18
Discounted cash flow (DCF)
   asset side (levered) valuation, 81
   discount rate, 85
   equity side (unlevered) valuation, 81
   expected cash flow, 77
   present value, 82
   risk, 84
   terminal value, 110
Discount for lack of control (DLOC), 211
Discount rate
   capital asset pricing model (CAPM), 102
   cost of debt, 104
   cost of equity, 85
   definition, 85
   weighted average cost of capital (WACC), 108

Distressed firms
   financial statement analysis, 71
   profitability, 73–74
Dividend discount model (DDM)
   formula, 120
   payout ratio, 52, 71
   relationship between P/E and DDM, 163
   retention ratio, 121
Dividends
   dividend policies, 70–71
   expected dividends, 101
   payout ratio, 52

E

Earnings before interest, taxes (EBIT)
   calculation, 48
   margin, 54–57
   multiples, 145
   terminal value, 115
Earnings before interest, taxes, depreciation and amortization (EBITDA)
   calculation, 48
   margin, 56
   multiples, 143
Economic obsolescence, 178
Economic value added (EVA), 34
Effective tax rate, 108
Enterprise value
   asset side and equity side approach, 129
   formula, 124
Enterprise value to EBIT (EV/EBIT)
   comparison between EV/EBITDA and EV/EBIT, 148–162
   definition, 145
Enterprise value to EBITDA (EV/EBITDA)
   comparison between EV/EBITDA and EV/EBIT, 148–162
   definition, 143

Enterprise value to free cash flow (EV/FCF), 147
Enterprise value to Sales (EV/Sales), 142–143
Equitable value, *see* Bases of value
Equity
  cost of equity, 85
  debt-to equity ratio, 69
  financial structure, 33
  return on equity (ROE), 51–52
Equity risk premium (ERP)
  definition, 98
  historical averages method, 100
  implied method, 101
  modified historical averages method, 100
Equity-to-capital ratio, 68
Excess earnings method (EEM)
  contributory assets charge, 200
  formula, 198
  multi-period excess earnings method (MPEEM), 198
  tax amortization benefit, 198
Expected cash flows
  factor influencing expected cash flows, 78
  risk, 84
Expected growth, *see* Growth rate

F

Facebook, 3
Financial statement analysis
  analysis of past results, 30–31, 79
  how to set up the analysis, 39–41
  ratio analysis, 50–71
  reclassified balance sheet, 42–47
  reclassified income statement, 47–48
Financial strategy
  debt-to-capital ratio, 68
  debt-to-equity ratio, 69
  debt-to-sales ratio, 69
  in distressed firms, 75–76
  equity-to-capital ratio, 68
  at a glance, 65

Financial structure
  debt-to equity ratio, 69
  financial sources and value creation, 33
  financial structure and investments, 65–66
  financial structure and profitability, 50
  financial structure and risk, 66
Firms
  comparable firms, 132
  distressed firms, 71
  life-cycle, 51
  private firms, 107, 216
Free cash flow to equity (FCFE)
  asset side and equity side valuation, 80
  capital asset pricing model (CAPM), 85
  cash flow statement, 49
Free cash flow to firm (FCFF)
  asset side and equity side valuation, 80–82
  cash flow statement, 49
  weighted average cost of capital (WACC), 108
Functional obsolescence, 178

G

Goodwill, 187
Greenfield method, 201–202
Gross margin, 47
Growth rate
  PEG ratio, 165
  terminal value, 113

H

Historical results
  analysis of past results, 30
  relevance, 17
Holding discount, *see* Investment company discount

Index

I

Income-base method
  definition of, 77
  discounted cash flow, 81
  at a glance, 10
Income statement
  ratio analysis–profitability, 50
  reclassified income statement, 47
Inflation
  expected cash flows, 83
Information
  documentation and choice of valuation method, 32
  segment information, 40
  source of information, 16
Intangible assets
  accounting standards (IAS 38), 185
  categories of, 186–187
  cost approach, 202–205
  definition, 186
  income approach, 190–202
  increasing role in business strategies, 183
  market approach, 202
  purpose of valuation, 188
  as a source of competitive advantage, 36
Integrated valuation approach (IVA)
  choosing parameters in the market-based method, 144
  definition, 23–24
  financial statement analysis as a base of, 39
  identifying the most appropriate value in DCF, 117
  non-financial information, 40
Interest coverage, 70
Interest rate
  equity risk premium (ERP), 99
  financial structure, 51
  return on debt (ROD), 107
  spread, 105

International reporting financial standards (IFRS)
  application of, 40
  control definition, 211
  difference with valuation standards, 18
  discounted cash flow (DCF), 36
  price-to book value (P/BV), 169
  revenue recognition, 143
International Valuation Standard Council (IVSC)
  code of ethical principles for professional valuers, 12–13
  compliance with valuation standards, 19
  at a glance, 20
Inventory turnover
  calculation, 63
  cost of goods sold, 63
  cost of sales, 63
Investment
  investments and financial structure, 65–66
  investment value/worth (*see* Bases of value)
  return on investments (ROI), 53
Investment company discount, 217

K

Key person discount, 217

L

Liabilities
  current liabilities, 42
  non-current liabilities, 43
  reclassified liabilities, 42–43
  relationship with assets, 42
Life cycle
  business life cycle, 44
  end of life cycle, 8
  of intangibles, 194
Liquidation value, *see* Bases of value

Liquidity
　in distressed firms, 74–75
　liquidity management, 57
　operating working capital turnover, 61
　short-term liquidity ratios, 59–61

M

Market-based method
　definition, 123
　at a glance, 10
　See also Multinational firms; Multiples method
Market rent, see Bases of value
Market value, see Market-based method; Multiples
Minority discount, see Discount for lack of control
Multinational firms
　comparables, 29
　multiple method, 126
Multiples
　application of multiple to the target company, 170–174
　asset side multiples, 129
　choice of multiple, 139
　comparable companies method, 130–134
　comparable transaction method, 135–137
　correlation with performance measure, 140
　enterprise value and equity vale, 7
　equity side multiples, 129
　selection of peer groups, 130–139

N

Net debt
　asset side and equity side in DCF method, 81
　asset side and equity side in multiple method, 129
　calculation, 45
Net operating profit after taxes (NOPAT), 34
Net present value, See Present value
Non-current assets, 42
Non-current liabilities, 43

O

Operating expenses, 47
Operating income, see Earnings before interest, taxes (EBIT); Earnings before interest, taxes, depreciation and amortization (EBITDA)
Operating risk
　beta, 93
　industry operating risk, 131
　relationship with profitability, 50
Operating working capital turnover, see Working capital

P

Patents, see Intangible assets
Payout ratio
　dividend discount model, 122
　payout ratio and retention ratio, 52
　price-to book value (P/BV), 167–169
　price-to earnings (P/E), 163–165
PEG ratio, 165–167
Physical obsolescence, 178
Plant and equipment valuation, 179–181
Premium profit method ("with and without" method), 194–198
Present value
　excess earnings method, 198
　formula, 83
　Greenfield method, 201–202
　premium profit method, 194–198
　relief-from-royalty method, 190–194
　time horizon, 82–83

Price
  multiples method, 123
  price and market value, 7
  price and value, 4
  price range, 127
  stock price, 134
Price-to book value (P/BV)
  definition, 167–169
  P/BV and dividend discount model (DDM), 167
Price-to earnings (P/E)
  definition, 163–165
  P/E and dividend discount model (DDM), 163
Price-to free cash flow to equity (P/FCFE)
  definition, 169–170
Private firms
  Altman Z Score Plus, 107
  control premium and discount for lack of control, 216
  discount for lack of marketability, 215–216
  rating, 105
Private-held companies, *see* Private firms
Professional skepticism
  analysis of information, 16
  expected cash flows, 79
  valuation approach, 31
Profitability
  in distressed firms, 73
  at a glance, 50
  profitability and financial structure, 50
  profitability and risk, 50
Profit margin, *see* Earnings before interest, taxes (EBIT); Earnings before interest, taxes, depreciation and amortization (EBITDA)
Purpose of valuation, 32

Q
Quick ratio, 59

R
R&D
  investments in, 26, 30
  time horizon, 51
Ratio analysis
  dividend policies, 70
  financial strategy, 65–71
  at a glance, 50
  liquidity management, 57–64
  profitability, 50
Real estate
  debt-to equity ratio, 69
  valuation standards, 19
  volatility, 78
Reclassified Balance sheet, 42
Reclassified income statement, 47
Regression
  multiples, 140
  raw beta, 92
Relief-from-royalty method
  formula, 190
  market royalty rates, 191
  split of profits, 192
Replacement cost
  cost-based method, 177–178
  intangible assets, 202
Reproduction cost
  cost-based method, 177–178
  intangible assets, 202
Required return on equity (RROE), 101
Restrictive agreement discount, 217
Retention ratio
  calculation, 52–53
  dividend discount model (DDM), 122
  price-to book value (P/BV), 167–169
  price-to earnings (P/E), 163–165
Return on assets (ROA)
  calculation, 53
  differences among ROI, ROA and ROE, 54
  spread between ROI and WACC, 53

Return on debt (ROD), 107
Return on equity (ROE)
    calculation, 51
    differences among ROI, ROA and ROE, 54
    ROE and CAPM, 52
    sustainable growth rate, 70
Return on investment (ROI)
    calculation, 53
    differences among ROI, ROA and ROE, 54
    spread between ROI and WACC, 33, 53
Revenues
    debt-to sales ratio, 69
    in distressed firms, 72
    growth, 31
    revenue recognition, 143
    revenues and inflows, 58
Risk
    beta, 90
    capital asset pricing model (CAPM), 102
    cost of equity, 85
    discount rate, 85
    discounted cash flow (DCF) method, 84
    equity risk premium (ERP), 98–102
    return on quity (ROE), 52
    risk and return, 51
    risk appetite, 65
    risk of default, 105
    systematic and non-systematic risk, 204
Risk-free rate
    cost of equity, 86–90
    geographical relevance, 89–90
    time horizon cost of equity, 86–89
Risk premium, *see* Equity risk premium

S

Sector
    characteristics of the industry, 78
    comparable companies method, 131
    cross-sectional comparison, 41
    industry trend, 28
    sector beta, 93
Shareholder
    dividend discount model (DDM), 120–122
    dividend policies, 70
    dividends, *see* Dividends, payout ratio
    profitability, 50–51
    return on equity (ROE), 51
    Shareholder's business interest, *see* Business interest
Small stock premium (SSP), 104
Standard deviation, 137–139
Standard error, 137
Start-up firms
    organizational structure, 26
    PEG ratio, 165–170
    return on equity (ROE), 90
    volatile performance, 134
Statutory tax rate, 108
Stock
    premium, *see* Small stock premium
    price, 134
    risk, 85
    value, 101
Subsidiary, 11
Sustainable growth rate, 70
Synergistic value, *see* Bases of value

T

Tax rate
    beta, 94
    comparable companies method, 134
Terminal value
    cash flow *vs.* EBIT, 114–115
    discount rate, 112
    formula, 111
    growth rate, 113
    market value, 117
    role of terminal value in DCF, 115
    salvage value, 118
Time series, 41, 112, 148
Total debt coverage, 70
Trade payables turnover, 62

Trade receivables turnover, 62
Turnover ratio
    calculation, 57
    turnover of individual assets, 57
Type of transaction, 136
Types of valuation, 14

V

Valuation
    objective and subjective component of, 8–9
    standardized valuation, 36–37
Valuation report, 14
Valuation standards, 20
Value
    actual value and potential value, 35–36
    bases of value, 7–8
    choosing the valuation approach, 31–32
    creation of, 33–35
    definition, 4–5
    difference between price and value, 4
Value of a computer software, 207–208
Value of a share, 209
Value of the workforce, 205–207
Value per share, 121
Valuer
    difference between a valuer and an auditor, 30
    identification of, 14–15
    requirements, 12

W

Weighted average cost of capital (WACC)
    capital asset pricing model (CAPM), 85
    cost of debt, 105–108
    formula, 109
    spread between ROI and WACC, 33
Whole Food Market, Inc., 128
"With and without" method, *see* Premium profit method
Working capital
    in distressed firms, 75
    operating working capital turnover, 61–64

The manufacturer's authorised representative in the EU is Springer Nature Customer Service Centre GmbH, Europaplatz 3, 69115 Heidelberg, Germany. If you have any concerns regarding our products, please contact ProductSafety@springernature.com

Printed and bound by CPI Group (UK) Ltd, Croydon, CR0 4YY

23/03/2026

02076735-0018